PATH OF EMPIRE

A volume in the series

The United States in the World

Edited by Mark Philip Bradley and Paul A. Kramer

PATH OF EMPIRE

Panama and the California Gold Rush

Aims McGuinness

Cornell University Press
Ithaca and London

First published 2008 by Cornell University Press
First printing, Cornell Paperbacks, 2009

Printed in the United States of America

Library of Congress Cataloging-in-Publication Data

McGuinness, Aims, 1968–
    Path of Empire : Panama and the California Gold Rush / Aims
    McGuinness.
        p.   cm.—(The United States in the world)
    Includes bibliographical references and index.
    ISBN 978-0-8014-4521-7 (cloth : alk. paper)
    ISBN 978-0-8014-7538-2 (pbk : alk. paper)
    1. United States—Foreign relations—Panama.   2. Panama—
Foreign relations—United States.   3. Americans—Panama—
History—19th century.   4. Watermelon Riot, Colón, Panama,
1856.   5. Panama—History—19th century.   6. California—
History—1846–1850.   7. California—Gold discoveries.
I. Title.   II. Series.

    E183.8.P2M36 2008
    327.730728709'034—dc22   2007028868

Cornell University Press strives to use environmentally responsible suppliers and materials to the fullest extent possible in the publishing of its books. Such materials include vegetable-based, low-VOC inks and acid-free papers that are recycled, totally chlorine-free, or partly composed of nonwood fibers. For further information, visit our website at www.cornellpress.cornell.edu.

Cloth printing	10	9	8	7	6	5	4	3	2	1
Paperback printing	10	9	8	7	6	5	4	3	2	1

For my parents
and for Jasmine

Contents

Acknowledgments   ix

Prelude: April 15, 1856   1

Introduction: In the Archive of Loose Leaves   4

Chapter 1. California in Panama   16

Chapter 2. The Panama Railroad and the Conquest
of the Gold Rush   54

Chapter 3. Sovereignty on the Isthmus   84

Chapter 4. "We Are Not in the United States Here"   123

Chapter 5. U.S. Empire and the Boundaries of Latin America   152

Conclusion: Conversations in the Museum of History   184

Coda: With Dust in Our Eyes   200

Notes   205

Bibliography   231

Index   243

Acknowledgments

This book began at the University of Michigan, where Rebecca J. Scott offered inspiration, direction, countless marginal comments, and many cups of tea. For guidance during my years in Ann Arbor, I am also grateful to Sueann Caulfield, Frederick Cooper, Fernando Coronil, Earl Lewis, Julie Skurski, and J. Mills Thornton. Jane Burbank, Matthew Connelly, Sandra Gunning, María Montoya, Martin Pernick, David Scobey, Julius Scott, and Michael Zeuske also provided valuable help as the project evolved. My time at Michigan was enriched by friends including José Amador, Katherine Brophy-Dubois, Adrian Burgos, Laurent Dubois, Frank Guridy, Richard Kim, John McKiernan-González, Kate Masur, April Mayes, Julianne O'Brien-Pedersen, David Pedersen, Lara Putnam, and Kerry Ward. Paul Eiss proved once again to be the ideal roommate and friend.

While at the University of Michigan, I benefited from financial support from the U.S. Department of Education/Jacob Javits Fellowship, the Department of History, Latin American and Caribbean Studies, the Rackham Graduate School, and the Center for Afro-American and African Studies. A Fulbright Scholarship administered by the Council for International Exchange of Scholars enabled my final year of research in Panama and Colombia.

Alfredo Castillero Calvo and Ángeles Ramos Baquero provided sage counsel and warm hospitality throughout my time in Panama City. The wonderful museum they created together, the Museo del Canal Interoceánico, became my classroom for the study of Panama's past, and I treasure the memory of the evenings I spent discussing history on their balcony.

The advice and works of Alfredo Figueroa Navarro influenced this project greatly, and his friendship helped sustain me over the course of many trips to Panama.

Among the others to whom I owe thanks for acts of kindness in Panama are Almyr Alba, José Álvaro, Fernando Aparicio, Celestino Andrés Araúz, Carlos Castro, Rolando Cochez, Jorge Conte Porras, Rémi and Cecilia Carite, Pantaleón García, Joaquín Gil de Real, Nelva Nivia González, Rolando Hernández, Eric Jackson, Stella de Lañas, Marixa Lasso, Sandra Lezcano, Florencio Muñoz, Martín Guillermo Ortiz, Patricia Pizzurno Gelós, Frank Robinson, Peter Sánchez, Fermín Santana, Eduardo Tejeira, and Josefina Zorrita. I also benefited from advice provided by Michael Conniff, John Lindsay-Poland, Thomas Pearcy, Orlando Pérez, Gloria Rudolf, and Peter Szok. I am grateful to Argelia Tello for our informative and enjoyable conversations about Panamanian history over brunch. Belsi Medina proved to be of great assistance to me as she has to many other Fulbrighters in Panama. I offer thanks to Carlos Guevara Mann for his friendship over the years and for sponsoring a talk that I gave as part of the national celebration of Panama's centennial in 2003. Tomás Mendizábal of the Instituto Nacional de Cultura did me the favor of extending an invitation to participate in the official commemoration of the Tajada de Sandía in April 2006.

During my visits to Panama the Torres Moreno family provided me with meals, a place to sleep, and a model of how to treat other human beings. I am deeply indebted to Doña Carmen, Don Alonzo, Cary, Eric, José, and Renán.

In Bogotá I received help from Mauricio Archila, Hayley Froysland, Juan Miguel Gómez, Fernán González, Jaime Jaramillo, Rocio Londoño, Laura Mayorga, Ivan and Marisa Mustain, Juan Camilo Rodríguez Gómez, Maytte Restrepo, Eduardo Sáenz, and Hermés Tovar. The staff of the Fulbright Commission in Bogotá, particularly Consuelo Valdivieso, provided valuable support.

I benefited from advice on matters of Colombian and Latin American history from George Reid Andrews, Charles Bergquist, Ann Farnsworth-Alvear, Michael Jiménez, Catherine Legrand, Michael LaRosa, and Frank

Safford. A lunch over fish tacos with Nancy Appelbaum proved critical for the writing of this book, and I am indebted to her for the support she has offered since I first ventured into the realm of Colombian history. Since James Sanders introduced me to the Archivo General de la Nación in Bogotá, he has been a friend and a constant source of advice—the next *chocolate* is on me.

I am thankful to the many librarians and archivists who offered their help and insights as I worked on this book, including the staffs of the Archivo Nacional de Panamá, the Archivo del Consejo Municipal de Panamá, the Biblioteca Nacional de Panamá, the Biblioteca "Simón Bolívar" of the Universidad de Panamá, the library of the Panama Canal Commission, the Archivo General de la Nación (Bogotá), the Archivo del Ministerio de Relaciones Exteriores (Bogotá), the Biblioteca Nacional de Colombia, the Biblioteca "Luis Angel Arango" (Bogotá), and the Biblioteca del Congreso (Bogotá). In the United States I received assistance from staff members of the U.S. National Archives, the Library of Congress, the Autry Library, the Bancroft Library, the California Historical Society, the Huntington Library, and the University of Michigan's Clements Library, Bentley Library, and Harlan Hatcher Graduate Library. The people of the American Geographical Society Library and the Interlibrary Loan Department at the University of Wisconsin–Milwaukee were also immensely helpful and tolerant of my endless requests.

Fellowships provided by the Huntington Library and the W. H. Keck Foundation enabled me to spend a fruitful six months in the Huntington's collections in San Marino, California. Peter Blodgett and Dan Lewis helped me to think better about the book and generously provided advice on manuscripts and secondary sources. While at the Huntington I also learned from conversations with William Deverell, Benjamin Johnson, Susan Lee Johnson, George Sánchez, and Elliott West.

I thank Stephen Aron—director of the Institute for the Study of the American West at the Autry National Center—for his advice on this project and also for the opportunity to present a paper at the Institute's Western History Workshop. I would also like to express my gratitude to Louise Pubols of the Autry for her insights into history and her friendship during my stay in Los Angeles.

I learned from commentators and audiences at presentations of this work at meetings of the American Historical Association, the Organization of American Historians, and the Latin American Studies Association as well as audiences at Carnegie Mellon University, the Latin American History

Workshop of the University of Chicago, the School for Advanced Re-search in Santa Fe, the Facultad de Humanidades of the Universidad de Panamá, and the Universidad Católica Santa María la Antigua in Panama City. I feel fortunate that Julia Greene has joined the select ranks of "Pana-manianists" in the United States and I thank her for the opportunity to present my work to the Department of History at the University of Col-orado–Boulder. Patricia Limerick of the University of Colorado helped start me down the road of western history many years ago when I met her after playing my bagpipes at the Tattered Cover Bookstore in Denver.

I am grateful to my colleagues in the Department of History at the University of Wisconsin–Milwaukee for creating a stimulating environ-ment for the study of global history. Those who offered help on the book include Margo Anderson, David Buck, Bruce Fetter, Michael Gordon, Vic-tor Greene, Anne Hansen, Reginald Horsman, Douglas Howland, Will Jones, Joseph Rodriguez, Kristin Ruggiero, John Schroeder, Robert Self, Amanda Seligman, Daniel Sherman, and Merry Wiesner-Hanks. I also ap-preciate the assistance I received from members of the departmental staff, including Cynthia Barnes, Anita Cathey, and Louise Whitaker. The Center for Latin American and Caribbean Studies, the Center for International Education, and the College of Letters and Science supported my research generously. A year-long fellowship at UWM's Center for 21st Century Studies provided me with valuable time and intellectual community. I am grateful to Daniel Sherman, director of the center, the center's staff, and other fellows who joined me in 2003–2004.

In Milwaukee I relied on the support of friends including A. Aneesh, Anne Basting, Erica Bornstein, Christina Ewig, Will Jones, Nan Kim-Paik, Brad Lichtenstein, and Peter Paik. Frank P. Zeidler, Milwaukee's most recent socialist mayor, inspired me through the example he set as a citizen and a historian.

I am most appreciative of the superb editing of Alison Kalett at Cornell University Press. I am also grateful to Kimberley Vivier, who did a splendid job of copyediting the book, and to Cameron Cooper for all of her help. Ange Romeo-Hall guided me expertly through the end of the editing pro-cess with forbearance and grace. My thanks also go to Philip Schwartzberg, who went to heroic lengths to make the maps and to Dave Prout, a great in-dexer. Mark Bradley has been a source of support in ways too many to count.

In its final stages the book benefited immensely from suggestions made by Stephen Aron and an anonymous reader for Cornell University Press.

I also appreciate the advice I received on later versions of the manuscript from Jasmine Alinder, Mark Bradley, Laurent Dubois, Paul Eiss, Paul Kramer, and James Sanders. I am very grateful to Rebecca J. Scott for devoting a long weekend in Ann Arbor to working with me on the manuscript.

My parents, Aims and Susan McGuinness, sustained me from the beginning; as parents and as educators, they are my role models. My brother, Alexander McGuinness, led my way to Latin America, and conversations with him continue to teach me. I am also very grateful to Jim and Mary Alinder and to Scott and Mickey Street for their support over the years. Alice McGuinness, my daughter, provided the combustion I needed to bring this endeavor to a close.

Since we met for the third time, a fire has burned in my heart for Jasmine Alinder. My gratitude to her has no bounds.

Prelude

April 15, 1856

On the evening of April 15, 1856, José Manuel Luna was selling fruit from a small stand located near the railroad station in Panama City when he was approached by a group of three or four drunken men from the United States. One of the men seized a slice of watermelon and asked about the price. Luna answered him in English that the fruit cost a *real*, the equivalent of a dime in U.S. currency. The man bit into the watermelon, tossed the fruit to the ground, and then turned his back to Luna without offering anything in return.

When Luna demanded payment, the drunken man taunted him instead with a vulgarity. Luna repeated his demand, this time with a warning. The drunk responded by pulling a pistol from his belt, and then Luna drew a knife. One of the other drunken men attempted to resolve the problem by offering Luna a coin. But the conflict did not end there. A Peruvian named Miguel Habrahan leaped forward from the small crowd that had gathered around the scene and seized the drunken man's pistol. The two wrestled for a moment before Habrahan freed himself and ran off with the pistol into the nearby neighborhood known as "La Ciénaga," or "the Swamp"—a maze of small houses made of cane and thatched with palm fronds. The drunken men pursued him into the heart of the neighborhood. It was then that the real trouble began. Or at least this is how José Manuel Luna later remembered the incident to officials in Panama City.[1]

Soon after the argument between Luna and the drunk, the bell of the parish church began to toll and hundreds of men from Panama City's poor suburbs rushed to La Ciénaga. Fights broke out between some of these men and immigrants from the United States who were bound for California, most of whom had arrived in Panama City only a few hours earlier by train. Many of the immigrants took refuge inside the nearby railroad station.

A large crowd of people from the surrounding suburbs soon gathered outside the station along with members of the police. Angry words were exchanged between members of the crowd and people inside the building. Under circumstances that would be hotly debated afterward, shots were fired and members of the police and the crowd rushed into the station to confront the immigrants who were inside. By the morning of the next day at least seventeen people lay dead. Two were from Panama. Most of the others were U.S. citizens who had arrived in Panama City that very day.

The events of April 15, 1856, are known by Panamanians today as El Incidente de la Tajada de Sandia (The Incident of the Slice of Watermelon), or more concisely, La Tajada de Sandía. To readers from the United States, this may seem like a peculiar name for one of the bloodier moments in the history of U.S. westward migration by sea. But in Panama watermelon does not carry the same connotation of racialized humor that the fruit has in the United States. Nor is the Tajada de Sandía a laughing matter. In national histories of Panama today, the event serves to usher in a long chronicle of contention and conflict with the United States that continues into the present. The significance of the event resembles that of the Boston Tea Party—an act of resistance that emblemizes the contributions of everyday people to the national struggle against the tyranny of empire.[2]

My own study of the Tajada de Sandía began soon after the latest U.S. invasion of Panama, which took place in December 1989. By the time I arrived in Panama City, four and a half years later, the bodies of the invasion's victims had all been buried and most of the rubble had been swept away. But scars left by the invasion were not hard to detect, especially in the poor neighborhoods located near the National Archive of Panama.

The National Archive is housed in a neo-classical building that has been grayed by decades of exposure to the exhaust of passing automobiles and buses. On my first visit to the archive, I walked through its grand entrance and found my way to the director's office, where I presented a letter of introduction. After signing my name in the register of researchers, I found a table in the reading room and set about searching the index to the archive's collection of documents from the nineteenth century.

My goal at the time was to write a history of the United States in nineteenth-century Panama, starting with the California Gold Rush. I had come to Panama City with the goal of including Panamanian voices in the history I hoped to write. As I surveyed the index, however, I felt a sense of disappointment. I found only a few references to documents that related explicitly to conflicts involving the United States.

I filled out a request slip related to one of these documents, one connected to the Tajada de Sandía, and handed it to an archivist. She returned after a half hour and informed me that the document was not where it was supposed to be. Somewhat deflated, I filled out another slip and handed it to the archivist. She went back to the vault and then returned to tell me again that the document I had requested was not there. After this sequence was repeated a few more times, I screwed up my courage to ask if I could at least see where the documents were supposed to be.

Most of the archive's documents from the nineteenth century had been bound into large blue books, or *tomos*. The archivist brought me the book that had once held the first document I had requested. I opened it up. As the archivist had said, the document was not there. When I pressed back the pages, however, I could see the yellowed stubble of the document's remains in the binding of the book. Someone, it seemed, had removed the document with a blade of some kind. I showed the binding to the archivist and she nodded. The National Archive received little support from the government, she explained, and many of its holdings were in poor condition, had been misplaced, or had never been catalogued.

I returned to my rented room that night feeling discouraged. Finding Panamanian voices in the archive was proving more complicated than I had imagined. With a guilty conscience, I reassured myself by recalling that the United States intervened militarily in Panama thirteen times between 1856 and 1903.[3] Surely I could find something in the archive that related explicitly to this history. As it turned out, however, I was wrong. Over the next six weeks I found none of the documents that the index identified as being related to the history of conflicts involving the United States. It seemed as if someone had completed my research before me and had systematically removed the evidence from the archive. But who could have done such a thing, and why? These questions would haunt me until the conclusion of my final research trip to Panama three and a half years later.

Introduction

In the Archive of Loose Leaves

The discovery of gold in California in 1848 kindled hope in many different places. As reports of fabulous riches spread, legions of people abruptly uprooted themselves and set off in search of rosier futures. Hundreds and then thousands of immigrants from seemingly every corner of the world arrived, and a relatively isolated outpost on the Pacific coast was dramatically transformed into a crowded place of frenzied commerce and breathless anticipation.

The sudden convergence in tight quarters of so many people of such different origins produced challenges to hierarchies of class, color, and nationality as well as cherished distinctions between men and women. To some, the rush for riches would bestow unprecedented opportunities for material gain and political power. To others, the rush would bring tragedy and disenfranchisement. Soon enough, however, the excitement engendered by the quest for gold would fade, the crowds would be corralled, and the streets would grow quiet again. A less tumultuous era would follow as an economy that once seemed to offer chances to many came to be dominated by a few. Yet long after the rush had run its course, memories of the golden era of California would live on in stories that continue to be told into the present.

For those who know the history of the California Gold Rush in the United States, the story line just presented may seem all too familiar. But how does the story read differently if we consider that the "outpost" described above could just as easily have been Panama City as San Francisco? The idea that the discovery of gold could contribute to such dramatic changes in a place so far from the goldfields themselves may come as a surprise to readers in the United States. But the gold rush was also an event in the history of Panama. Panamanians refer to the gold rush today as "La Fiebre del Oro" (the gold fever) or more simply as "La California."

How did California, a place now located in the United States, become a period of time in the history of Panama? This book seeks to answer this question using documents found in archives located in Panama, Colombia, and the United States. During the late 1840s and early 1850s, events on the Isthmus of Panama were closely related to developments in California, and they were similar in some respects as well. Yet there were also important differences that may surprise readers more conversant with the history of California during the gold rush. By removing the lens of history from the more familiar territory of California to the isthmus that connects the Americas north and south, we may gain a better understanding of the possibilities that the gold discovery in 1848 helped unleash.

The impact of the gold rush was felt in many places beyond California, but perhaps none was transformed more dramatically than the Isthmus of Panama. Between the end of 1848 and 1856 this slender spit of land was remade into one of the principal conduits for the great maritime migration to the goldfields of California. During those same years Panama saw the building by a U.S. company of the first transcontinental railroad in world history, the final abolition of slavery, the establishment of universal manhood suffrage, the foundation of an autonomous Panamanian state, and the first of what in time would become a long list of military interventions by the United States. A maritime borderland connecting the Atlantic and Pacific worlds, Panama also became a bridge between different regions of the United States—one that was paradoxically subject to the sovereignty of another nation. This other nation was not the Republic of Panama, which became independent from Colombia only in 1903, but rather Colombia's predecessor, the Republic of Nueva Granada, with its capital in Bogotá.

Although most people in the United States today identify Panama with the canal that was completed in 1914, the importance of the isthmus for communication between the east and west coasts of the United States dates back to the late 1840s, more than half a century before. During the gold rush the fastest way to travel between New York City and San Francisco was not over land but over sea via the "Panama Route"—a network of ships whose linchpin was the Isthmus of Panama. Over the isthmus passed a large portion of the people who traveled between the East Coast and California during the gold rush as well as thousands of tons of mail, gold, and silver. The Panama Route would remain the fastest and most comfortable way for immigrants to travel from one coast of the United States to the other until the opening of the second transcontinental railroad in world history across the United States itself in 1869.[1]

Gold-rush demography is difficult to reconstruct, but the best estimates indicate that maritime migration from New York City to California via Panama was greater than overland migration to California over the California Trail between 1848 and 1860. John Haskell Kemble calculated that a minimum of 218,546 people traveled between New York and San Francisco by way of Panama during this period. During the same era, according to John Unruh, approximately 198,000 people migrated to California through Wyoming's South Pass—the principal portal for overland migration to California and other points west. These same calculations indicate that California-bound migration via the Panama Route exceeded overland migration through the South Pass in 1851 and again from 1854 through the rest of the decade. Panama's importance for immigration between the Atlantic and Pacific more generally was undoubtedly greater than the figure presented above, which omits passengers who crossed Panama with origins other than New York City and destinations other than San Francisco. For return immigration from California to the eastern United States, the Panama Route was by far the most popular route during the gold rush, especially after the completion of a railroad across Panama in 1855. Between 1849 and 1859, most of the roughly one fifth of the people who made it to California and then decided to return to the eastern United States made their voyage home by way of Panama.[2]

Until the establishment of the Pony Express and then the overland telegraph in the United States in 1860–61, the Panama Route was the primary, fastest, and most reliable route for the transmission of news and other information between the eastern United States and California. Until 1869, most of the mail sent between the two coasts of the United States and most of the gold and silver that was sent eastward from California also passed over Panama. Steamship lines including the Pacific Mail Steamship Company and the United States Mail Steamship Company won contracts from the U.S. government to ship mail. These firms allied with express companies

TABLE 1.
Immigrants from New York City to San Francisco via Panama and Westward Overland Migration
through the South Pass, 1848–1860

Year	Travelers from New York to San Francisco via Panama[a]	Overland Migration via the South Pass[b]
1848	335	400
1849	6,489	25,000
1850	13,809	44,000
1851	15,464	1,100
1852	24,231	50,000
1853	17,014	20,000
1854	18,445	12,000
1855	15,412	1,500
1856	18,090	8,000
1857	17,637	4,000
1858	24,621	6,000
1859	26,907	17,000
1860	20,092	9,000
Total	218,546	198,000

[a]*Source*: Kemble, *The Panama Route*, 254.
[b]*Source*: Unruh, *The Plains Across*, 119–120.

tied more closely to overland routes, including the Wells Fargo Company, to transport highly valued, time-sensitive commodities across Panama as well, including specie. Kemble estimated the total worth of the treasure sent from California across Panama between 1849 and 1869 to be $710,753,857.62.[3]

There were other ways to reach California by sea from the East Coast in the mid-1800s. During the first year of the rush, when the availability of transportation in Panama and other isthmian crossing points was relatively uncertain, the majority of those who traveled from the eastern United States to California by sea rounded Cape Horn. After 1850, however, the route around the horn was largely abandoned by sea-going passengers destined for California in favor of routes that combined sea travel with overland shortcuts located to the south of the United States. There were other shortcuts of this kind besides Panama, including routes across Mexico, Nicaragua, and other parts of Central America. These competing routes posed challenges to the Panama Route in the early 1850s, particularly the Nicaragua Route. But Panama never lost its dominance to any of these competitors during the gold-rush era, and by 1855, its preeminence among the isthmian routes was virtually uncontested.[4]

In this book I examine two interrelated arenas of struggle that were central to the remaking of Panama into a nexus of the world economy in

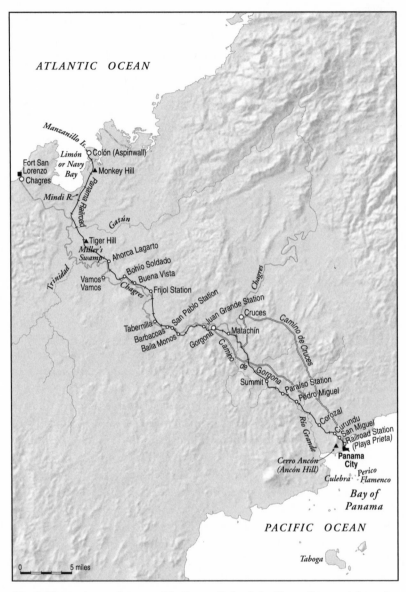

ATLANTIC OCEAN

Manzanillo Is.

Limón or Navy Bay · Colón (Aspinwall)

Fort San Lorenzo · Chagres

▲ Monkey Hill

Mindi R.

Panama Railroad

Gatún

▲ Tiger Hill

Miller's Swamp

Ahorca Lagarto

Bohío Soldado

Buena Vista

Vamos Vamos

Chagres

Frijol Station

Trinidad

Tabernilla

San Pablo Station

Juan Grande Station

Barbacoas

Baila Monos

Gorgona

Matachín

Cruces

Chagres

Camino de Cruces

Camino de Gorgona

Summit

Paraíso Station

Pedro Miguel

Corozal

Río Grande

Curundu

San Miguel

Railroad Station (Playa Prieta)

Panama City

Cerro Ancón (Ancón Hill)

Culebra · Perico · Flamenco

Bay of Panama

PACIFIC OCEAN

Taboga

0 ___ 5 miles

Map 1. The transit zone: the route of the Panama Railroad, the Chagres River, and the roads connecting the Chagres to Panama City, circa 1856. By Philip Schwartzberg.

the late 1840s and early 1850s: communication and sovereignty. Communication, or *comunicación*, was a term that Panamanian writers used regularly in the mid-nineteenth century to refer to the circulation of goods, people, and information from one point on the planet to another. I focus in particular on the highly contested transformation of Panama's transit system from a locally controlled network powered primarily by human beings, mules, currents, and the wind to a more centralized and largely U.S.-owned network of ships and locomotives powered by steam. This transformation took place primarily in a place that Panamanian scholars today refer to as "la zona de tránsito" (the transit zone)—a thin corridor of land that encompassed the transit route across the isthmus and the ports located on either side of that route. Sovereignty, or *soberanía*, has also long been a keyword for Panamanian political theorists and historians. I use the term to indicate the organization and the enactment of power over territory and flows of people, information, and goods through governmental and extra-governmental means. My analysis of sovereignty ranges from the political writings of members of the Panamanian elite to popular struggles over urban space and projects undertaken by the officials of U.S. companies to enforce their own visions of order in the transit zone. Although struggles over sovereignty in Panama during the gold rush were less conclusive than the battle over Panama's system of interoceanic communication, those struggles produced innovations in the exercise of power that would have important implications for the future political organization of Panama and Nueva Granada/Colombia, the subsequent course of U.S. empire in the Americas, and the shaping of the very idea of "Latin America."[5]

The abrupt onset of U.S. immigration to California at the end of 1848 raised a thorny question in Panama: who would benefit from the huge demand for fast transportation across the isthmus to the goldfields? At first, immigrants, gold, and letters from the United States were transported across Panama by local people using mules, canoes, and their own backs. Almost immediately, however, the people who operated this locally controlled network came into conflict with U.S. transportation companies and U.S. immigrants themselves. Prominent members of Panama's mercantile elite saw the gold-rush migration as an opportunity to recapture the economic glory of the colonial period and to establish greater autonomy and perhaps even independence from the national government in Bogotá. Yet at the beginning, those who gained most directly from the rush were relatively poor people of color who lived along the transit route and took advantage of the demand for their labor and other commodities to earn small fortunes from travelers desperate to reach California. As white gold seekers from the United States competed among themselves to buy the services offered by working people in Panama, many reacted violently to what they interpreted as inversions of proper racial hierarchy. But immigrants and some U.S. officials in Panama also sharply criticized U.S. steamship companies for extortionate rates and business practices that in their view placed profit above proper concern for their own countrymen. These conflicts between and within nationalities reflected a deeper instability in Panamanian society—no single group of people from any nation controlled either the communication route across the isthmus or the arena of sovereignty.

The terms of the struggle over communication changed dramatically over the early 1850s with the building of the Panama Railroad, which was inaugurated in 1855. The railroad was constructed by the Panama Railroad Company of New York City. From the beginning of the railroad company's operations, company officials sought to undermine the indigenous transit system, which they saw as a barrier to the successful completion of the line. Faced with the challenge of mobilizing and disciplining the labor of thousands of men from many different places including Nueva Granada, Jamaica, the United States, Ireland, and China, the railroad company turned to a variety of strategies that sought to exert company power over territory that officially formed part of Nueva Granada. These strategies included the creation of a private police force in the transit zone and the construction of a new port city on Panama's Atlantic coast where local government officials exerted minimal power. The city of "Colón" (or "Aspinwall," as company officials insisted on calling it) became arguably the first instance of a U.S.-dominated commercial enclave in Latin American history—a place that remained formally within the bounds of Nueva Granada but was effectively ruled by a foreign-owned company.

As in California during the same period, capitalists from the northeastern United States consolidated control over an economy that only a few years earlier had seemed to offer the possibility of fortunes for anyone with desire and a strong back. The railroad that members of the Panamanian elite had envisioned as the key to Panama's prosperity and political future led instead to an economic depression in Panama, as passengers were whisked across the isthmus with barely a pause to refresh themselves before continuing their journeys by sea.

The transformation of Panama into a transportation nexus with special importance to the United States raised troubling questions about the future of sovereignty in Panama. What was the appropriate form of government for a transit route whose commercial vitality, according to Panamanian boosters, hinged on its immunity to the sovereign claims of any single state? A number of answers were posed to this question in the early 1850s, the most prominent of which was a treatise authored by Justo Arosemena, a Liberal thinker whom Panamanian historians today generally regard as the intellectual progenitor of Panamanian independence. Arosemena proposed the transformation of Panama into an autonomous federal state, one that would remain formally part of Nueva Granada in certain aspects of its governance but independent in others. According to Arosemena's plan, Panama would become the guardian of a transit route that would be fundamentally neutral and open on equal terms to all the world's nations. Arosemena's vision was translated into law in 1855, when the Congress of Nueva Granada voted to establish Panama as the first of what in time would become many federal states within the larger nation.

Other laws passed in Bogotá also had a profound impact on the course of the gold rush in Panama, including the final abolition of slavery in 1852 and the establishment of universal manhood suffrage in 1853. People of color in Panama City and popular groups in rural areas of Panama took advantage of these reforms to claim a larger voice in electoral politics and in the Liberal Party in particular. Popular Liberals organized politically and militarily to defend their interests against not only their adversaries in the opposing Conservative Party but also threats from the United States. The early 1850s saw as well the growing politicization of tensions between people of color and elites in Panama City, including elites in both the Conservative and the Liberal Party. Rumors of caste war or race war suggested the limits to this increase in popular political power, as did conflicts with Anglo-American immigrants in the transit zone. But the most fearsome of the potential threats to black political power and black freedom in Panama was the possibility of invasion by filibusters, the private adventurers who fanned out from the United States in the aftermath of the U.S.-Mexico War with ambitions for further conquest in the hemisphere. The specter of conquest was made more real by the successes of William Walker, the most infamous of the filibusters, who seized control of Nicaragua with a small group of followers and Nicaraguan allies in 1855. Fears of filibuster invasion would play a central role in the violence that took place in Panama City on the night of April 15, 1856—the Tajada de Sandía.

The events of April 15 and the brief U.S. intervention that followed four months later revealed fault lines in Panamanian society that did not fall neatly along national lines. People of color in Panama City faced off against elite Panamanians even as they prepared to protect their city from invaders from the United States. Those same events exposed the complex relationship among filibusters, U.S. commercial empire, U.S. naval power, and the consolidation of Anglo-American power in California. Rather than separate stages or competing processes, the making of the United States as a transcontinental nation and U.S. expansion overseas in Panama were coincident with one another and intertwined.

One of those who linked events in Panama to other faces of U.S. expansion in the late 1840s and early 1850s was Arosemena. His writings before and immediately after the Tajada de Sandía offer an opportunity to rethink a long-standing debate among historians of Latin America about the origins of "América Latina" as an imagined place and an ongoing political project. Following the violence of April 15, Arosemena wrote an essay that sought to rally the Spanish-speaking republics in the Americas against what he perceived as a coordinated assault by the "raza yankee." One of the earliest literary efforts to evoke a specifically "Latin American" unity in the hemisphere, the essay also evinced anxiety about the political power of men of color in Panama. Arosemena's writings and events on the ground during the U.S. intervention of September 1856 present an opportunity to unearth connections between U.S. imperial projects in Panama, the growing power of popular groups in electoral politics in Panama and Nueva Granada more generally, and the history of "Latin America" as a geopolitical concept.

If the gold rush does not immediately conjure up images of Panama in the United States, it is in part because the history of the gold rush has been told primarily as an event in U.S. history by historians in the United States. Over the past three decades, scholars have transformed our understanding of the rush by writing histories of peoples who were long marginalized in traditional Anglo-American accounts of the event, including Native Americans, *californios*, African Americans, women, Mormons, Jews, and immigrants to California from China, Hawaii, Europe, and different points in the Americas. Historians working in this vein have replaced the hackneyed stereotype of the grizzled Anglo forty-niner with a pick in his hand with a more complex and accurate vision of gold rush society in California. Only recently, however, have scholars begun to give sustained attention to the significance of the gold rush of 1848 beyond the shores of California.[6] Recent works have pointed out the importance of the gold rush for women and families left behind by men who headed to California.[7] Others have pointed to the significance of seaports and transit routes in Latin America, including Panama, as scenes of encounters between local peoples and gold rush immigrants in ports and along transit routes.[8] These works have contributed to a longer-standing effort by historians to pursue connections and comparisons between the gold rush in California and later gold rushes in Australia, Canada, Alaska and elsewhere.[9]

"California's gold rush truly has many contexts and thus many histories," as Kenneth N. Owens has reminded us.[10] Much remains to be written about those other histories, especially those that unfolded outside or across the borders of the United States. The exclusive identification of the gold rush or any other event with a single place is worth questioning not only because it impoverishes our understanding of the richness of the past but also because such identification has often served to obscure the darker or more disturbing aspects of events. The identification of events such as the Renaissance, the Enlightenment, and the Industrial Revolution exclusively with Europe has long masked the importance of European colonial ventures for the history of Europe itself. Yet as scholars of colonialism, slavery, and slave emancipation have reminded us, events beyond imperial centers were often intertwined intimately with events in metropoles themselves.[11] Historians of U.S. empire in recent years have also explored connections between what was once regarded strictly as "domestic" history and the history of U.S. imperial projects abroad.[12]

This book is similarly concerned with linkages between events in the United States and Panama. At the same time, I have tried to remain cognizant of a potential problem with such an approach. Although it is laudable to question the strict division between the national history of the United States and the history of U.S. empire overseas, a danger exists when the historical questions that are pursued and the categories of analysis that are employed emerge from the empire alone—even when the aspiration of the historian is explicitly anti-imperialist. Any history that aspires to cross borders must look in multiple directions if it is to be something more than the history of one side of the border writ large.

I do not claim to tell the history of the gold rush "from the Panamanian perspective"—I am from the United States, for one thing, and furthermore, there is no single Panamanian perspective on the past. I have tried, however, to recognize and engage with some of the ways in which Panamanians have told their history: I take seriously the spatial and temporal categories that Panamanian historians have brought to their study of the past, and I attempt to cajole U.S. readers who are not otherwise interested in the history of mid-nineteenth-century Panama to consider how events there were important not just for the United States but for Panamanians in the present as well as the past. Most fundamentally, this approach means thinking of Panama as a place where history happened rather than as a stopover on the way to someplace else. This spatial reorientation entails in turn a change in temporal coordinates. Whereas traditional Anglo-American histories of the gold rush privileged events in California in 1849 as the defining moments of the gold rush, Panamanian historians have highlighted events in Panama in the mid-1850s, including the creation of the Federal State of Panama and the Tajada de Sandía.

In telling the gold rush as an event in the history of Panama, I want to build a bridge between the recent florescence of scholarship on the gold rush in California and a revolution that has taken place in the study of social, cultural, and political history in Panama itself over the past twenty-five years. Led by Alfredo Castillero Calvo, this new wave of historical research has succeeded in calling attention away from the traditional focus on elites toward previously unexplored questions of social, cultural, and economic history. Works by Castillero Calvo, Alfredo Figueroa Navarro, and others have shown the way for historians elsewhere, including those from the United States such as myself.[13] Although historians of Colombia have had relatively little to say about events in Panama in the 1800s, recent developments in the history of popular and regional politics in Colombia have much to offer to an understanding of the isthmus in the gold rush era, particularly recent studies of the Caribbean coast and the region of Cauca.[14]

In making connections across national and regional borders, this book joins in a larger and multifaceted effort to rethink the dominance of the nation in the writing of history, and of the U.S. nation in particular. As a growing number of scholars of U.S. history have argued in recent years, an overly narrow focus on events within the territorial limits of the United States can impoverish understanding not only of other parts of the world but of U.S. history itself. As an antidote to such provincialism, Thomas Bender has called for a more "cosmopolitan" history, one that recognizes that "the United States has always shared history with others."[15]

This book shares the goal of fashioning histories that embody the virtues Bender identifies as cosmopolitan, but it comes to the problem of national history from a different direction, from the fields of Latin American and Caribbean history, where the nation has also enjoyed a long run as a category of analysis and where scholars have also placed national histories under greater scrutiny in recent years.[16]

To recover how peoples and places beyond U.S. borders have figured in U.S. history can help scholars move beyond the national borders that

U.S. historians have often imposed on a global past. But if the goal is a more cosmopolitan history, then U.S. historians will need also to engage with the ways in which events that they have traditionally narrated as U.S. history alone have been told by other peoples as histories of other places.

My thinking about the importance of fostering conversations among histories was shaped importantly by conversations with others in archives, particularly in the National Archive of Panama. Over time, as the archivists there became more familiar with my research through conversations in the reading room, they began to bring me documents they determined might be of interest to me as they encountered them in the archive's vault. In this way the archivists themselves helped to shape the course of my research in important ways and took me down paths I could not initially see.

Some of the documents that archivists brought to me were unbound or loose, either because they had been removed from their original bindings at some earlier time or because they had never been bound at all. These loose documents raised a methodological question: how to cite a record adrift in the archive, with no binding, box, or folder? When I posed this problem to one archivist, he suggested that I cite the location of such documents as the *Archivo de Documentos Sueltos* or the *Archivo de Hojas Sueltas*— terms that may be translated into English as "Archive of Loose Documents" or "Loose Leaves." I use the term *Archivo de Hojas Sueltas* in the notes for this book.[17]

Over time, I came to see the "loose leaf," or unbound document, as an apt metaphor for the gold rush as an event, or at least as I hoped to write it. All bindings in the end are provisional rather than permanent. To regard the gold rush as essentially unbound to any single history, national or not, is to create the possibility of fitting that event into different bindings, and thus the possibility of reading that event in new ways. It is also to open up an opportunity to see more clearly beyond the limits that any single binding imposes on the understanding of the past. Thus the goal of this book: to unbind the gold rush from the confines of U.S. history by telling that event as the history of a small place of global importance in the mid-nineteenth century.

Chapter 1

California in Panama

Not all the dreams kindled by the discovery of gold in January 1848 re-
volved around the gold itself. In Panama what mattered most was the rush
that followed—the massive migration of people to the goldfields from
places as disparate as Hawaii, China, France, Australia, Mexico, Chile, and
Maine. In an era when ships still offered the most reliable and fastest means
of travel between the Atlantic and Pacific coasts of the United States, immigrants setting off for California from the eastern seaboard found in the
crossing of Panama a way to reach San Francisco that was far faster than the
journey around Cape Horn. The surge in demand for transportation across
the isthmus and related services offered an opportunity for Panamanians to
recapture wealth on a scale that had not been seen on the isthmus since the
boom years of the colonial period, when Panama had served Spain as a
gateway to the Pacific coast of the Americas.

Once the gold rush began, however, no agreement followed about how
to take advantage of that opportunity. At first, the gold rush seemed like
a godsend to members of Panama City's merchant elite. At the beginning
of the rush, however, those who appeared to benefit most from the great
demand for speedy transportation were working people of color in the
transit zone. The independence displayed by workers alarmed not only

members of Panama's elite but also white immigrants from the United States, who found themselves unexpectedly dependent upon people whom many immigrants perceived as their racial inferiors. Also maddening to immigrants was what they perceived as the exploitation of their lot by steamship companies from the United States and their agents in Panama City. Rather than a straightforward conflict between nationalities, the struggle over communication in the transit route sometimes pitted people against their fellow citizens in ways that challenged conventional ideas of gender, class, citizenship, and race among Panamanians, people from the United States, and immigrants from elsewhere.

Memories of Former Times

Panama in the mid-nineteenth century was haunted by its former importance as a nodal point in Spain's interoceanic empire. By the time the first Spanish ship appeared off the coast of Panama in 1501, native peoples, fauna, and plants had been taking advantage of the isthmus's possibilities as a land bridge for thousands of years. Before the Spanish conquest Panama's primary importance lay as a nexus between Central and South America. Its value as a bridge between the oceans increased dramatically, however, after the beginning of Spanish settlement in Panama in the early 1500s, and particularly after 1513, when Vasco Núñez de Balboa first glimpsed the body of water that the Spanish would come to know as the "South Sea."[1]

Although Panama produced modest wealth at different points during the colonial period through mining, agriculture, the slave trade, and other activities, its primary importance in the colonial economy derived from its role as a crossroads in trade routes that linked Spain to the Americas and different parts of the Americas to one another and the wider world of the Pacific. The first efforts at Spanish settlement focused on the Atlantic side of the isthmus. These initial experiments were largely abandoned after the founding of Panama City in 1519. Over the next few decades, Panama would serve as a staging ground for further Spanish conquest in Central America, Peru, and other regions of South America. By the middle of the 1500s, Panama had emerged as an important hub in the Spanish fleet system—a shipping network that connected officially designated ports in the Americas on a regular basis to Spain. In this capacity, Panama became the primary conduit for mineral wealth from the Pacific coast of South

America to Spain and the principal point of entry for European goods and enslaved Africans heading in the opposite direction. Two basic strategies were used to connect the two coasts of the isthmus during the colonial period. One involved the transport of people and cargo by mule across the isthmus on roads. The other combined mule transport with transport by boat up and down the Chagres River, which flowed from the interior of the isthmus to its mouth at the port of Chagres, located on the Atlantic coast. A network of roads connected Panama City to the Atlantic coast and to the principal inland ports on the Chagres, Cruces and Gorgona. On Panama's Atlantic coast the port of Nombre de Díos and later the port of Portobelo became the site of trade fairs that gained fame throughout the Atlantic world.[2]

Geography in and of itself was no guarantee of Panama's importance as a place of transit. The flow of people and goods across the isthmus varied with changes in Spanish trading and navigation policy, attacks by Spain's enemies, and the productivity of different areas of the Spanish colonial economy. During the early colonial period, communication across the isthmus was sometimes harried by indigenous peoples as well as maroons— Africans who had escaped slavery and established *palenques*, or independent settlements, in the neighborhood of the transit zone. What began as one of Panama's advantages, its proximity to Spain's political and commercial centers in the Caribbean, became a source of vulnerability as Spain's European enemies extended their reach into the region. Panama became an important site for contraband trade between merchants in Panama and Spain's imperial rivals. Panama's transit route attracted the attention of pirates. The most devastating attack came in 1671, when Henry Morgan, the Welsh buccaneer, carried out a raid that resulted in the destruction of Panama City. Another threat from abroad arose at the turn of the eighteenth century, when a small group of Scots led by William Paterson attempted to start a colony on Panama's Caribbean coast, in the region known as Darién. While the Scots managed to form alliances with indigenous people in the region, the colonization effort soon collapsed under pressures that included disease, internal organizational problems, and Spanish harassment. In 1739 an English attack on Portobelo led by Edward Vernon contributed to a shift in Spanish navigation policy that channeled traffic between Spain and the Pacific coast of South America by way of Cape Horn rather than Panama. The history of the transit route through the rest of the eighteenth and early nineteenth centuries was one of decline marked only occasionally by modest, short-term increases in traffic.[3]

Independence and Union with Gran Colombia

The Spanish American wars of independence in the 1810s briefly revived Panama's importance as a transit point, as the Spanish sought an alternative to the interoceanic route across war-torn Mexico. Panama itself saw little combat during this period other than a failed attack on Portobelo in 1819 by Gregor MacGregor, a Scot in the service of South American patriots. This period of relative prosperity came largely to an end, however, with Spanish defeats in South America. Members of Panama's elite of merchants and landowners declared the independence of the isthmus once the likely fate of the Spanish empire on the American mainland had become clear. Independence was declared first in the provincial town of Villa de los Santos and then in Panama City. Rebels used bribes to convince many of the Spanish troops in Panama City to desert, and no blood was shed for the cause of independence in the capital city of the isthmus. The declaration of independence signed in Panama City on November 21, 1821, announced the adherence of Panama to Simón Bolívar's newly created Republic of Colombia, or Gran Colombia, as historians have come to call it, which included not only the modern-day nation of Colombia but also Venezuela and Ecuador. Panama was now to be ruled not from Spain but from Bogotá.[4]

Although Simón Bolívar never set foot in Panama himself, he gave the isthmus a prominent place in the new political geography he imagined for the Americas. In his "Letter from Jamaica" of 1815, he expressed his hope that the Isthmus of Panama might someday become "the emporium of the world" and even the future site of the world's capital. He invested the isthmus with further significance when he chose Panama City as the site of the Congress of Panama, an attempt in 1826 to craft an international alliance capable of protecting the independence of the states carved out of Spain's mainland empire. Although the congress proved to be a disappointment, Bolívar's identification of Panama as a symbolic bridge among nations would exercise a powerful influence on advocates of political unity among Spanish-speaking polities in the hemisphere, and on Panamanians in particular.[5]

Despite Bolívar's hopes for the isthmus, independence from Spain and rule from Bogotá failed to rescue Panama from penury. Although the government in Bogotá granted a number of privileges to foreign contractors after 1821, no major improvement was made in the infrastructure of the route in the two decades leading up to the discovery of gold in 1848. Even if a contractor had begun serious work, Panamanian merchants would have had to confront a deeper problem: the more general drop in trade between Europe and the Pacific coast of the Americas caused by the wars of independence. The bulk of what little trade took place between Panama and other parts of the world in the decades after independence was with the British island of Jamaica.[6]

Although international commerce in Panama was stimulated by the expansion of British steamship service to both sides of the isthmus in 1842, traffic across the interoceanic route between 1821 and 1848 remained miniscule compared with the boom times of the colonial period. Frustration over this decline fed political discontent in Panama City and contributed to short-lived independence movements against Bogotá in 1826, 1830, 1831, and 1840–41. In 1830 Gran Colombia itself splintered into three independent republics: Ecuador, Venezuela, and Nueva Granada. In this new configuration of political power, Panama remained part of Nueva Granada.[7]

Elite politics in Panama City in the early nineteenth century were driven by the goal of reestablishing the commercial and political importance Panama had enjoyed during its years of prosperity in the colonial period. The name that members of Panama City's mercantile elite gave to the ideal they sought was the same word Bolívar had used in his "Letter from Jamaica": "emporium." This vision of an emporium included both economic and political dimensions. Realizing that Panama lacked the technology and the capital to make major improvements in the route itself, boosters of the transit economy sought to revive the physical infrastructure of the route with the help of foreigners capable of building a canal or a railroad or at least repairing the roads leading across the isthmus, which had eroded seriously by the early nineteenth century. Elite political leaders also expressed support for Panamanian autonomy or outright independence from Bogotá, free trade, and the related concept of "neutrality," or the idea that the transit route should be open to all nations.[8]

None of the revolts against Bogotá in the early nineteenth century involved large-scale military mobilization, and in each case Panama was reintegrated into the national polity with little or no bloodshed. The most sustained effort at separation began in 1840 and ended one year later, when the Panamanian leaders of the rebellion rejoined Nueva Granada voluntarily. Members of Panama City's elite formed the basis of support for these abortive independence movements. The only revolt with significant popular participation was led in 1830 by Gen. José Domingo Espinar, a man of

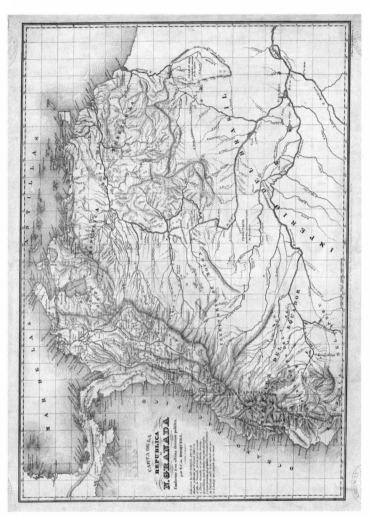

Fig. 1. Tomás Cipriano de Mosquera. "Carta de la República de N. Granada por T. C. de Mosquera." 1852. Courtesy of American Geographical Society Library, University of Wisconsin, Milwaukee.

color from Panama City who had studied medicine and engineering in Peru and distinguished himself as an officer and a close ally of Bolívar during the wars of independence.[9]

The Population of the Isthmus

Sparse census data make it difficult to be precise about the people who inhabited the Isthmus of Panama on the eve of the gold rush. In contrast to censuses taken in the United States in the same period, official records in Nueva Granada did not tabulate the race or color of the country's inhabitants, and the government of Nueva Granada controlled only portions of the isthmus. The official census of 1851 indicated that the entire population of Panama (excluding indigenous peoples) was 138,108. Of those, 52,322 resided in the province of Panama itself, which included Panama City and the transit route.[10]

The basic contours of Panama's social geography in the mid-nineteenth century were shaped early in the colonial period. The transit zone was the most densely populated region of the isthmus and also the place where the power of the provincial government was strongest. The zone was inhabited almost exclusively by individuals of African or Spanish descent and people of mixed origins. The term "negros" or "blacks" became politically charged in Panama and elsewhere in Nueva Granada after independence because of its identification with slavery, an institution that revolutionary governments had officially repudiated. In Panama, "gente de color" or "people of color" was a less controversial term in republican discourse, one that embraced all people who were perceived to descend at least partially from Africans, including people of mixed European and African descent, or *mulatos*. Although less common in Panama by the mid-1800s, the term "pardo" was also used to describe free blacks and mulattos in Panama and elsewhere in Nueva Granada. In contrast to Mexico and some other parts of the Spanish-speaking Americas, the term "mestizo" was rarely used in Panama in the mid-1800s to describe people of mixed indigenous and European descent. Instead, the term "*castas*" (castes) was used to describe people of mixed descent more generally, including *gente de color*.[11]

Gente de color formed the majority of the transit zone's population. The regions located to the east of the transit zone, where the provincial government of Panama maintained a minimal presence, were populated mainly by people of African origins descended from maroons who had escaped from slavery during the colonial period and indigenous peoples. Indigenous people and *gente de color* also predominated in the region along the Atlantic located to the west of the transit zone, where the provincial government was also nearly nonexistent. The presence of governing institutions controlled by Spanish-speaking people was far stronger along the Pacific coast west of Panama City, which was dotted with small towns inhabited mainly by castas. A small settlement of English-speaking immigrants from the British Caribbean was located on the western Atlantic coast at Bocas del Toro, which was almost entirely cut off from the rest of Panama.

Virtually nothing has been written by contemporary historians about indigenous peoples in nineteenth-century Panama, in part because of a scarcity of archival records in Panama itself. By the mid-1500s, the combination of new diseases introduced by European ships and the traumas of conquest had led to the near destruction of Panama's indigenous population. Other indigenous groups began to migrate to Panama by the late 1500s from what is now Colombia and Central America. Although other indigenous peoples also inhabited regions of Panama outside the transit zone by the mid-1800s, historians have written most about the Kunas. The Kunas came to Panama after the Spanish conquest from what is now Colombia. In the mid-1800s, their numbers were concentrated to the east of the transit zone, including portions of the Caribbean coast located to the east of Limón Bay. Kunas sometimes traded in turtle shell and other goods with ship captains from the United States and the Caribbean. But relations with Spanish-speaking inhabitants of the isthmus were relatively slight and generally hostile, including relations between Kunas and *gente de color*. When Kunas traded with others, they sought to do so on terms that clearly gave them the upper hand. The relatively isolated coastal area located to the east of the transit zone was much better suited to interactions of this kind than the transit zone, where the presence of provincial officials was relatively strong and indigenous peoples would have found themselves vastly outnumbered by immigrants and castas. Little evidence exists of an indigenous presence along the transit route during the gold rush.[12]

When the gold rush began, slavery was still a legal institution in Nueva Granada, and the slave population of Panama was probably around 500. The number of slaves in Panama had been decreasing since before the end of the colonial period as a consequence of the region's economic decline. Legislation passed by the national congress of Colombia in 1821 granted freedom to children of enslaved mothers. Some slaves were liberated by their masters. Others won their own freedom through self-purchase or had

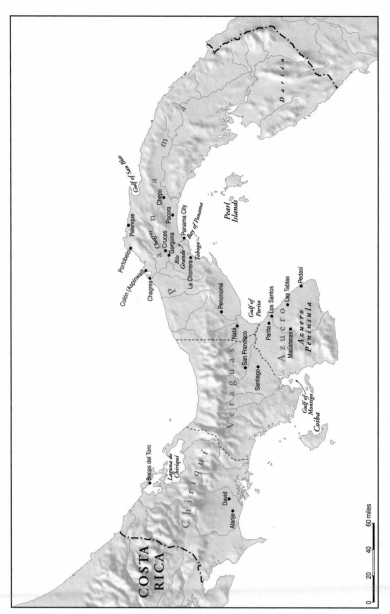

Map 2. The Federal State of Panama, circa 1856. By Philip Schwartzberg.

their liberty purchased for them by free people or government commissions funded by taxes on the estates of slaveholders. Despite the institution's decline in Panama, however, slavery remained a charged issue on the isthmus, as the arrival of thousands of white men from the United States would soon make abundantly clear.[13]

Panama City: San Felipe and the Arrabal

The largest city on the isthmus by far was Panama City, whose population was approximately 4,000 at the beginning of the gold rush. After Henry Morgan's destruction of the original Panama City in 1671, Spanish colonial authorities relocated the settlement to a nearby peninsula that could be defended more easily from attack. The new city of Panama was divided by fortifications into two zones. The area inside the city walls was known as San Felipe, or the "Intramuros." The area outside the walls or "Extramuros" was known as Santa Ana or more commonly the "Arrabal"—a word that can be translated as "the outskirts" or, more negatively, as "the slums." The principal point of exit and entry between the Intramuros and the Arrabal was a fortified gate known as the Puerta de Tierra. The most important political, religious, and commercial buildings as well as the houses of the city's elite families were concentrated on the peninsula. The *cabildo* or town hall, the cathedral, and other buildings in San Felipe were constructed mainly of stone or masonry, many with tiled roofs and balconies characteristic of the living spaces of the wealthy elsewhere in colonial Spanish America. Most of the buildings of the Arrabal were constructed of wood or cane with a few exceptions, including the parish church of Santa Ana. The sharp social distinctions between San Felipe and the Arrabal dated back to the city's refoundation in the late seventeenth century. A small cadre of elite, white families dominated San Felipe. Numbering less than a thousand in 1848, the inhabitants of this part of the city included merchants, landowners with urban and rural properties, clergy, high-ranking government officials, servants, and a small number of domestic slaves. The Arrabal, in contrast, was populated almost entirely by *gente de color*, including artisans and working people who earned livings through activities such as fishing, washing, agriculture, and the business of transport on water and over land.[14]

The most extensive account of social distinctions in Panama from the gold-rush period came in 1851 from the pen of Gen. Espinar, leader of the 1830 independence revolt. After a period of exile, Espinar returned to

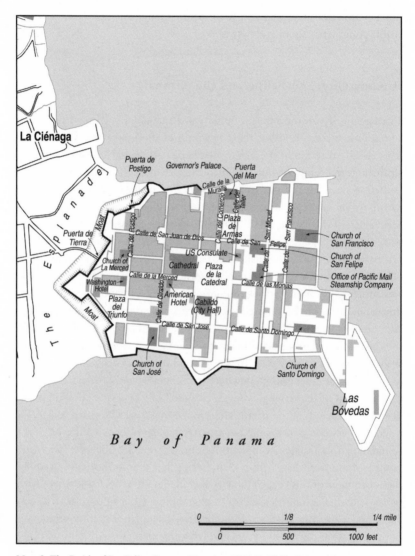

La Ciénaga

Puerta de
Postigo

Governor's Palace

Puerta
del Mar

Calle de la
Muralla

Calle del
Taller

Calle del Comercio

Calle del Postigo

Puerta de
Tierra

Calle de San Juan de Dios

Plaza
de
Armas

San Miguel

Calle de San

Calle de San Francisco

Church of
San Francisco

US Consulate

Calle de San

Felipe

Church of
San Felipe

Church of
La Merced

Cathedral

Plaza
de la
Catedral

Calle de

Office of Pacific Mail
Steamship Company

Washington
Hotel

Calle de la Merced

Calle de las Monjas

Calle de Giraldo

American
Hotel

Cabildo
(City Hall)

Plaza
del
Triunfo

Moat

Calle de San José

Calle de Santo Domingo

The Esplanade

Moat

Church of
San José

Church of
Santo Domingo

Las
Bóvedas

Bay of Panama

0   1/8   1/4 mile

0   500   1000 feet

Map 3. The Parish of San Felipe, Panama City, circa 1856. By Philip Schwartzberg.

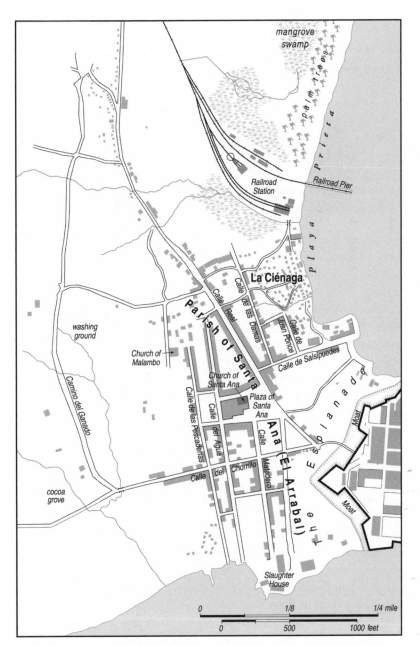

Map 4. The Parish of Santa Ana, El Arrabal, Panama City, circa 1856. By Philip Schwartzberg.

Fig. 2. J. Cameron. "The Grand Cathedral." 1852. Courtesy of the Bancroft Library.

Panama for a brief sojourn shortly after the beginning of the gold rush. Though his views were by no means universally shared by Panamanians, they represent the perspective of an influential man who traced some of his own ancestry to Africans. He presented a picture of Panama during the colonial period as a patriarchal society in which people were divided by colonial law and social practice into three strata or ranks along lines similar to caste regimes elsewhere in Spanish colonial America. These strata were distinguished by both their economic activity and their origins. The loftiest of these ranks was "that of the families of the *conquistadores*, their dependences, and the Spaniards who immigrated to Panama as employees of the royal treasury, military officers for the local garrison, and merchants and rich proprietors." In the middle rank were those "families who were closer to the European race, who occupied subaltern offices in the treasury, municipal government, and other posts, European artisans and other Europeans involved in the trades." The third and lowest rank was also the most populous, that of "creole artisans, European domestic servants, former slaves, and other members of mixed origins in whom the African race predominated." Espinar described these people as "castas" or "el pueblo." He made no mention of indigenous people and slaves and no explicit mention of women, thereby excluding them at least implicitly from a patriarchal definition of society that was delimited by both race and gender. Espinar explained that independence from Spain had led to the decline of this more rigid, colonial system of castes and the relations of deference that had formerly divided the three strata of society into a hierarchy dominated by white men. In place of the colonial caste regime, a more "democratic system" had emerged, one that had led to what he described as a process of "fusion, however slow and imperfect."[15]

The Panama Route on the Eve of the Gold Rush

The colonial social order described by Espinar would come under further stress during the gold rush. The United States began to take a greater interest in Panama with the annexation of Oregon and the beginning of the U.S.-Mexico War in 1846. Although overland migration routes connected California and Oregon to the eastern United States, their importance for commercial and military traffic was small compared with the maritime route that led around Cape Horn, which offered greater speed and security for large cargos and was not impeded by the snow and ice that made overland routes impassable during the winter. The voyage between San Francisco and New York City by sea was almost 14,000 miles, and so the idea of establishing an overland shortcut linking shipping routes in the Atlantic and Pacific had considerable appeal.

In the late 1840s Panama enjoyed a number of advantages over other possible routes across Mexico and Central America. Routes across Mexico (including routes across northern and central Mexico and the Isthmus of Tehuantepec) were located closer to U.S. ports. But even the shortest of these routes, at the Isthmus of Tehuantepec, was significantly longer than other routes across Central America and Panama, and Tehuantepec also required crossing mountainous terrain. Furthermore, Mexico was enemy territory after the start of the U.S.-Mexico War. Crossings in Central America, including the route across Nicaragua, were complicated by the presence on the Atlantic coast of "Mosquitia," a British protectorate ruled officially by an indigenous Moskito king and defended by the British navy, whose officials were fully cognizant of the strategic importance of Central America as a link between the oceans.[16]

In 1846 diplomats from the United States and Nueva Granada signed the "Bidlack-Mallarino Treaty," which established the United States as the guarantor of free and uninterrupted transportation across the isthmus. The United States further agreed to guarantee the sovereignty of Nueva Granada over Panama. In return, Nueva Granada granted U.S. passengers

Fig. 3. J. H. Colton. "Map of the United States." 1849. Courtesy of American Geographical Society Library, University of Wisconsin, Milwaukee.

and cargo unrestricted access to the transit route on terms identical to those enjoyed by citizens of Nueva Granada. For Nueva Granada, the value of the treaty lay principally in the use of the United States as a buffer against the British, whose protectorate of Mosquitia tread on the territorial claims of Nueva Granada in the region.[17]

In 1847, with the U.S.-Mexico War already under way, the U.S. government assigned contracts to private citizens for the delivery of the mail between the east and west coasts of the United States by way of Panama. After a brief period of negotiation, the Pacific Mail Steamship Company of New York City purchased the contract for the Pacific portion of the journey. The U.S. Mail Steamship Company, also of New York City, acquired the contract for the Atlantic leg. Both companies were new creations, although their owners and investors were already important leaders in the steamship industry. The principal figure behind the Pacific Mail was William Henry Aspinwall, while the U.S. Mail was controlled primarily by George Law. Although these two companies were private entities, they received official support from the U.S. government, which provided an annual subsidy for the transportation of the mail and also reserved the right to convert the companies' vessels into warships if military necessity demanded it.[18]

Shortly after acquiring the bid for the Pacific portion of the transit, Aspinwall joined other investors from New York City to form a separate entity to build a railroad across Panama, the Panama Railroad Company. Preparations began even before the news of gold arrived in New York City, and the company was formally incorporated in New York state in April 1849. Among the company's investors was John L. Stephens, a former U.S. envoy to Central America who had won a considerable reputation in the 1840s as the author of vividly written travel accounts, including the two-volume *Incidents of Travel in Central America and the Yucatán*, which introduced U.S. readers to the marvels of the ancient Mayan cities of Mesoamerica.[19]

The Gold Rush across Panama Begins

According to George Totten, chief engineer of the Panama Railroad Company, no more than a dozen passengers crossed Panama in any given month between 1846 and December 1848.[20] This state of relative isolation changed dramatically soon after the news of gold reached the east coast of the United States at the end of 1848. Information about the discovery arrived in Washington, D.C., by ship. Richard Mason, the U.S. military governor of

California, sent two army officers with the news and samples of the gold from Monterey to President James Polk in Washington, D.C. One officer crossed Mexico while the other traveled to Paita, on the coast of Peru, before proceeding to Panama City, crossing the isthmus with his secret, and then continuing by ship. The officer who crossed Mexico arrived first.[21]

The zigzagging route of the army messengers reflected the discordance between the geography of U.S. sovereignty and the geography of communication between the East and the newly annexed Pacific coast. The Mexican province of Alta California had already been conquered militarily by the United States, but California was far closer in terms of transit time to Valparaíso, in Chile, than it was to Washington, D.C. No single piece of information had greater import for the domestic economy of the United States in the decade of the 1840s than the news of gold in California. Yet to convey that information in the fastest manner possible, the two officers entrusted with the news were forced to cross the territory of foreign nations, one of which had only a few months before been at war with the United States. By the time Polk learned of the gold, hundreds of Chileans had already set sail for California, where they would join a diverse assortment of gold seekers who preceded them, including native peoples, *californios*, and resident foreigners in California, among them white men from the United States, European immigrants, and native Hawaiians.

President Polk confirmed the existence of gold in California in his state-of-the-union address on December 5, 1848. In the days that followed, men and women along the eastern seaboard read hyperbolic newspaper accounts or listened as others read to them about fortunes to be scooped out of rivers or picked up off the ground in California. At the beginning of the gold rush, travelers on the East Coast who sought to travel to California had essentially three options: an overland voyage across the United States, a sea voyage around Cape Horn, or a sea voyage to Panama or some other point in Mexico or Central America followed by an overland crossing and a second sea voyage to San Francisco. Under ideal conditions, the ocean voyage around the Horn could easily require four to five months. Under the best conditions, settlers could travel between the Missouri River and California in about four months. In contrast, the voyage between New York City and San Francisco via Panama could be completed in as little as six weeks if the conditions were right. At a time when snow and ice made overland immigration to California impossible, sufferers of gold fever in the East had little choice but to board a ship, which in turn required a considerable initial outlay of cash for the purchase of tickets and for food, shelter, and other

necessaries for the voyage. Because ships on the Pacific coast of the Americas were in considerably shorter supply than ships on the Atlantic side, any
attempt to cross Mexico, Central America, or Panama entailed the additional risk of becoming marooned in a foreign country for weeks and perhaps even months while waiting for a passage to California.[22]

The first of the Pacific Mail's steamships, the *California*, departed New
York City in early October, and its crew and small contingent of passengers
would not learn of the gold in California until they reached Valparaíso. The
U.S. Mail's first steamship on the New York to Chagres line, the *Falcon*, departed New York City shortly before Polk's speech. The news of gold
caught up with the ship only after it entered the port in New Orleans. As
the crew prepared the steamship's departure for Havana, the *Falcon*'s next
port of call, men from the Crescent City rushed hastily aboard with whatever implements they imagined might be useful for striking it rich. A week
and a half later, on December 27, 1848, the *Falcon* arrived in Chagres after
an otherwise uneventful voyage.[23]

How to Cross the Isthmus

Like other immigrants who crossed Panama in late 1848 and early 1849, the
Falcon's passengers passed through several stages as they made their way to
the Pacific coast, each of which was controlled and operated by a distinct
group of workers, many of whom were also proprietors of the means of
transport, including mules and dugout canoes known as *bongos*. The waters
in the harbors at Chagres and Panama City were too shallow to permit
oceangoing ships to draw close to shore, and so arriving ships were forced to
anchor as far as a mile off the coast. Local boatmen provided transportation
from ship to shore using bongos or small sailboats. People arriving at the
port of Chagres continued up the Chagres River in bongos to the town of
Gatún or, if water levels permitted, to the town of Cruces. Passengers either
walked the rest of the way to Panama City through the forest or, more commonly, negotiated with still other local men for transportation by mule.
Travelers also had the option of hiring porters, or "cargadores," who carried
cargo and sometimes passengers on their backs using harnesses.[24]

Transportation across Panama at the beginning of the gold rush was still
highly decentralized, controlled by small operators with at most a few mules
or bongos. Depending on the availability of transport, weather conditions, and
other factors, the entire voyage could take as little as three days or as many as

ten or more. No through tickets across Panama could be purchased. Instead, passengers negotiated transport with local people at every stage of the journey, beginning with their transport from their ship to the port of Chagres.

When the passengers from the *Falcon* began to trickle in to Panama City at the end of December 1848, they found themselves without a ship to carry them north. The *California* was still making its way up the coast of South America. Obliged to save a certain number of tickets to sell in Panama, the captain of the ship had refused to permit new passengers aboard in Valparaíso, despite the appeals of Chileans who were eager to reach San Francisco. But when the ship reached Callao, in Peru, the captain learned that the Pacific Mail's agent at that port had sold tickets to dozens of Peruvians who had heard news of the gold. This time, the captain of the *California* relented and the Peruvian passengers were permitted to board.[25]

In the days following the arrival in Chagres of the *Falcon*, many other ships from the United States arrived off of Panama's Atlantic coast, bearing with them hundreds more men. By the time the *California* was finally sighted off the coast of Panama City, on January 17, 1849, more than a thousand desperate gold seekers had crossed the isthmus to Panama City, all with the same hope of finding a passage by sea to San Francisco. U.S. citizens in Panama City expressed outrage when they learned of the Peruvians who had boarded at Callao. In "indignation meetings" organized in the central plaza of Panama City, immigrants signed petitions that denounced the Pacific Mail Steamship Company and demanded that the company's agent in Panama City expel the Peruvians who had taken places that the gold seekers regarded as belonging rightfully to themselves.[26]

These indignation meetings were among the first of what would become many protests by passengers in the early 1850s against the prices charged by shipping companies as well as conditions on the ships themselves. Among the protagonists in the controversy surrounding the Peruvians was Brigadier General Persifor Smith of the U.S. Army. Smith had arrived aboard the *Falcon* and was on his way to take command of the army in the territory of California. He instructed the U.S. consul in Panama City to circulate a letter among all U.S. consuls in South America warning that on his arrival in California, he would prosecute any foreigners he found in the goldfields as "trespassers on the public lands":

As nothing can be more unreasonable or unjust, than the conduct pursued by persons not citizens of the United States, who are flocking from all parts to search for and carry off gold belonging to the United States in

California; and as such conduct is in direct violation of law, it will become my duty, immediately on my arrival there, to put these laws in force, to prevent their infraction in future, by punishing with the penalties prescribed by law, on those who offend.[27]

Although the objective of Smith's proclamation was to exclude foreigners from California, the protests that inspired that decree were directed toward a U.S.-owned steamship company, the Pacific Mail, which had refused to dislodge its paying customers. The "law" that Smith invoked as a justification for barring foreigners from the goldfields was a chimera, but his proclamation became a forebear to efforts in California to bar foreign miners from the goldfields through legal innovations such as the taxes on foreign miners passed by the legislature after California became a state in 1850.[28]

Despite the protests of enraged U.S. citizens, the Peruvian passengers refused to set foot onshore in Panama City, and the company's agent refused to concede to the demands made by U.S. citizens to expel them. Tensions did not begin to relax until the captain of the *California* agreed to compel the Peruvians to relocate from steerage to the ship's upper deck, and additional accommodations were made so the ship could take on a larger number of passengers. The *California* finally departed Panama City on February 1. On the ship's arrival in San Francisco, nearly all the crew members deserted immediately, including the man who was acting as captain at the time.[29]

Labor and the Making of the Gold Rush

The presence of hundreds of anxious travelers, many of them with substantial savings on their persons, provided a surge of opportunities to make money in occupations that ranged from poling immigrants upriver to selling food and shelter. Unlike some other places on the Pacific coast of the Americas in countries such as Chile, Peru, and Mexico, relatively few Panamanians appear to have been tempted to leave for California, given the rush that was already under way at home. Even as most immigrants to California from the United States sought to leave Panama as quickly as possible, Panama became a destination in and of itself for immigrants from elsewhere, including other parts of Panama and Nueva Granada, Jamaica, South America, and Central America. Some sense of the multiple origins of these immigrants can be gained from judicial records, which required witnesses to state their place of origin. In a trial conducted in 1855 on the island of Taboga, off the coast of Panama City, seven of the thirteen witnesses came from some place other than Taboga or Panama City, including one from Costa Rica, one from Chagres, and five from the rural areas located to the west of Panama City including the towns of Villa de los Santos, Las Tablas, Natá, Capira, and La Chorrera.[30] Those who joined the working population of the transit zone were principally people of color and castas more generally. Recent arrivals from places beyond the isthmus included people of African descent from Jamaica and immigrants from other parts of Central and South America. Estimates for migration to Panama from Jamaica during the 1850s range from 1,500 to as many as 7,000.[31]

The crews of bongos on the Chagres River usually consisted of two or three men: a *patrón*, or boss, who was also usually the owner, and two or three laborers who signed on for finite periods of time to work as oarsmen. In some cases these workers were "peones"—individuals who received an advance payment from a patrón in return for a promise to work until the debt was paid off. Muleteers worked independently, or a man with several animals might organize a small train. Muleteers led trains of animals laden with passengers and cargo between the Chagres River and Panama City as did porters.

Although it was men who did the work of transporting people and cargo, women's labor was essential to a transit system that required passengers to spend a minimum of three days in Panama and often far longer. Women sold food, drink, and lodging along the route and also washed and sewed clothes for money. In Panama City and elsewhere along the transit route, women sold a potent brandy made from sugarcane known as *aguardiente*. Women also sold sexual services, and prostitution flourished in Panama City during the early years of the gold rush. Writing in 1853, one Panamanian man complained that Panama City had become a "school for prostitutes."[32]

Mary Seacole, an immigrant to Panama from Jamaica, followed her brother to Panama sometime in the early 1850s. Born a free woman of color in Kingston in 1805, she kept a hotel and an eating establishment on Panama's transit route and also worked as a healer, using remedies she had learned from her mother in Kingston to treat both local people and travelers for cholera and fevers. Her autobiography, *The Wonderful Adventures of Mrs Seacole in Many Lands*, gives a rich if occasionally embroidered account of the economic activities of fellow West Indians both in the transit zone and in the mining of gold in Veraguas.[33] Mary Jane Megquier, an immigrant from Maine who arrived in Panama in 1849, was happy to discover women's labor very much in demand in Panama City, as she would later find to be the case in California itself.[34]

Male U.S. immigrants in Panama and elsewhere in Latin America in the early 1850s often indulged in fantasies that portrayed local women as lascivious and sexually available. Local men, meanwhile, were often derided by immigrants as lacking in the requisite characteristics of manhood. Fantasies about the male conquest of local women and territorial conquest by the United States frequently became intertwined in the minds of travelers and advocates of U.S. expansion in the hemisphere more broadly. As had been the case with U.S. soldiers during the U.S.-Mexico War, travelers from the United States in Panama often took special note of washerwomen, who sometimes worked without clothes from the waist up. A gold seeker from Alabama named William Penn Abrams noted in his diary on April 4, 1849, "Have seen many women washing in a creek nearby in the model artist attire."[35]

Elite property owners in Panama City rented out their own homes and other buildings that they owned to gold seekers, but with only a few exceptions they had few direct links to the business of transporting people and cargo from one coast to the other. The most dramatic economic gains made at the beginning of the rush were made not by elite merchants but rather by working people involved in everyday occupations, such as tavern keepers, boatmen, and water carriers. The relatively low cost of entering the service economy, combined with abrupt and dramatically heightened demand for services, meant that there was room for many small, independent operators and entrepreneurs in the service economy during the early years of the gold rush.[36]

Some members of Panama's elite were alarmed by the growing economic independence of common people in Panama in both rural areas and along the transit route. Even before the gold rush the economic basis of the Arrabal was importantly distinct from that of San Felipe. The wealth of Panama City's elite was derived principally from landholding and international commerce. In contrast, the livelihood of the Arrabaleños stemmed largely from activities such as fishing, small-scale agriculture, transport, and the provision of services directly to travelers, services that were not mediated or controlled by members of the city's elite. Opportunities to earn cash directly from U.S. immigrants further weakened any dependence of the free poor on elite patrons and employers, as the increased demand for labor led to a rise in wages paid to laborers inside and outside of the transit zone.

In the western region of Chiriquí, for example, a large landholder named James Agnew, who had immigrated earlier in the nineteenth century from the United States, found himself obliged to switch from coffee cultivation to the raising of cattle in the early 1850s as a consequence of the heightened cost of labor caused by the gold rush.[37]

Elites interpreted efforts by working people to take advantage of the increased demand for labor as signs of laziness or worse. Justo Arosemena complained that the local working population had been drawn away from what he perceived as more suitable occupations in agriculture and industry—occupations that placed working people directly under the authority of elites—by the easy fortunes that could be made by boatmen and muleteers, who dealt in cash transactions directly with immigrants. The new opportunities available to working people had contributed in part to what Arosemena perceived as "bad habits," including "semi-idleness and wastefulness."[38] Writing in 1851, the owner of a sugar plantation located in Chepo, east of Panama City, complained that he could no longer find men willing to work for the wages he paid. The decline of slavery had left him bereft of any alternative besides wage labor, and local men could earn more as porters along the transit zone than he could afford to pay them. The result, according to the *hacendado*, was an alarming rise in what he described as "vagabondage"—a complaint that is more accurately interpreted as frustration over the increased mobility and economic options for the isthmus's landless poor.[39]

U.S. Perceptions of Panama

The independence exhibited by working people in the transit zone was also a matter of concern for gold seekers. The majority of immigrants in the early years of the rush were white men from the northeastern United States. Because of the initial investment in tickets that was required for the sea voyage, many of these immigrants were relatively well-to-do or members of the northeastern United States's incipient middle class.[40] Travelers often arrived in Panama from the United States with preconceived ideas about Spanish-speaking people in the Americas and people of African descent derived from prior experiences in the United States, including the consumption of popular cultural forms such blackface minstrelsy, sensational fiction, and the histories of William H. Prescott. Among the characters that inhabited their imaginations were the aristocratic but effeminate and ineffectual *don*, the bashful and enticingly exotic *señorita*, the nefarious and scheming *padre* or priest, and the dim-witted but harmlessly amusing "darky."[41]

In the early years of the gold rush, contemporaries from both the United States and Nueva Granada believed that Panama itself might become, like California, a destination for immigrants from the United States. In the immediate aftermath of the U.S.-Mexico War, ardent expansionists in the United States argued for the annexation of the entirety of Mexico, and some even imagined that the United States might also annex additional territory as well. Panama's strategic importance for the United States made it an obvious candidate for such expansionist speculation. The creation of significant populations of people from the United States along the transit route and in the ports at either end, particularly in Panama City, fed these speculations. Settlers from the United States, Great Britain, France, and elsewhere established their own eating houses, hotels, and other service-oriented businesses in Panama City with names such as the American Hotel as well as English-language newspapers, which in the early 1850s included the *Panama Echo*, the *Panama Star*, and the *Panama Herald*. The *Panama Echo* was of short duration, but the latter two persisted and in 1854 were consolidated into the *Panama Star and Herald*, which is still published today in Panama City as *La Estrella de Panamá*.[42]

Shortages of ships on the Pacific side of the isthmus continued well into 1853. Emigrants could find themselves stranded for weeks and even months awaiting passage north. Some among them saw this delay as an opportunity to earn money from their fellow stranded compatriots, while others worked to sustain themselves when their savings ran low or disappeared altogether. James McMurphy, for example, was stuck in Panama City for more than eight weeks in early 1849 as he awaited a space aboard a ship for San Francisco. He spent his time exploring Panama City, where he considered working for a survey of the Panama Railroad before thinking better of it. He reported to his father on April 8, 1849, that there were some three thousand people from the United States in Panama City, all of them desperate for a passage to California. After failing again and again to obtain a ticket, he and his companions pooled their money to purchase a small brig and then sold tickets to fellow gold seekers. He stated hopefully to his father that he expected to make a profit of five hundred dollars on his stay in Panama.[43]

For those with sufficient savings, the sojourn in Panama City provided an opportunity to survey a foreign land at close range. Some took the time to explore the unfamiliar surroundings, including the bounteous vegetation and unusual fruits. McMurphy, for instance, was apparently an admirer of Panamanian watermelon, for he enclosed five watermelon seeds in a letter to his father with instructions to plant them upon receipt. Others turned to gambling, drinking, and other forms of leisure. Observing and recounting Panamanian customs such as cockfighting was also a favorite pastime.[44] Protestants from the United States sometimes took special interest in observing Catholic religious practices. Religious processions, the celebration of Mass, and other ceremonies could inspire a sense of wonder and awe or produce sharp condemnations. McMurphy was present in Panama during Holy Week and complained that the many different processions and celebrations made it impossible for him to sleep. To his father he wrote, "One would think that all the infernals was let loose & that saten was holding a jubalee." Conflicts between immigrants and Panamanians took place when intoxicated men from the United States entered religious buildings in Panama City wearing hats or treated worshippers disrespectfully in other ways.[45]

In March 1849 John H. Forster, a surveyor originally from Pennsylvania, compared himself and his fellow countrymen from the United States to the conquistadors he had read about in William H. Prescott's popular histories of the Spanish conquest of Mexico and Peru, invoking a common trope for U.S. expansionist writers in the late 1840s. Forster's sense of the inevitability of such conquest may have been heightened by the fact that he was journeying across Panama to join in the survey of the new border created between the United States and Mexico by the conquests of the U.S.-Mexico War. As he meditated on the sight of hundreds of immigrants encamped outside Panama City, he reflected on what he viewed as the likely result of the invasion of Panama and other parts of the Americas by his fellow Anglo Saxons from the United States. "Judging from the past," he wrote, "we can have little doubt of the result. The weak, nerveless, standstill people now occupying those regions of beauty and wealth *must* eventually succumb to the more enterprising and energetic clans of the North."[46]

As Brian Roberts has remarked, white immigrants from the United States were both repelled by and attracted to what they imagined they saw in the people they encountered along the transit route. Immigrants from the northeastern United States came from a place that was undergoing its own kind of revolution—one in which the market was expanding its grasp on everyday life, industrialism was on the rise, and fires of Christian revivalism were burning. White U.S. immigrants appear to have projected upon people they encountered along the transit route their own misgivings and hopes about a seemingly more materialistic world.[47]

Many immigrants relished ascribing what they perceived as the sloth-fulness of Panama's population to the richness of the local vegetation, a common trope in European and Anglo American travel writing about tropical regions in the nineteenth century. As a young Nantucketer, Charles Winslow, approached Chagres in April 1849, he felt qualified to pronounce on the laziness of Panama's native population before he had even disembarked. Observing the surrounding countryside from the deck of the *Crescent City*, he wrote, "The country is so rugged & the inhabitants so indolent that the whole of this vast track of the isthmus is wholly neg-lected."[48] Immigrants were frequently awed by the natural wonders they encountered as they crossed the isthmus. Forster traveled up the Chagres in March 1849. He wrote in his diary of seeing a monkey, a catamount, a cougar, and "hideous snakes," as well as parrots, parakeets, buzzards, vul-tures, turkeys, cranes, and many other birds, along with "myriads of insects." Such sights could inspire marksmen as well, and many travelers arrived in Panama heavily armed in preparation for what they imagined to be the dangers of the frontier.[49]

Often travelers were moved to reflect in melancholy and self-congratulatory terms on what they interpreted as the sharp contrast be-tween Panama's former glory during the colonial period and the seeming rudeness of Panamanians in their own time. All about them, travelers found evidence of what they perceived as decay and decadence. When passengers disembarked at Chagres, they could look up and see, perched on a promontory above the harbor, the ruined fortress of San Lorenzo. At the foot of the fortress the town of Chagres itself consisted of perhaps fifty huts or small houses made of cane with thatched roofs of palm fronds. The roads that led from Chagres to Panama City had been so severely eroded by the rains that at some points they resembled deep ravines; at other places they seemed to disappear altogether in the rain forest. As immigrants approached Panama City, they passed first through the poorest section of the city, the Arrabal, with its maze of thatched cane houses. The fortifications sur-rounding the interior city of San Felipe were tumbling down, and inside the city walls many of the grand buildings constructed of stone during the colonial period were in serious disrepair. Forster described his approach to San Felipe through the Arrabal in dramatic terms: "My entrance into the city of Panama was an event which I shall not soon forget. . . . Suddenly and unexpectedly I found myself in the midst of desolate ruins. High toppling walls, crumbling battlements, moss-covered turrets, broken arches, ancient crosses . . . met my gaze and for a moment I fancied myself threading the ruins of some decayed city of the Old World." For Forster, the ruinous state of the city was yet more evidence of need for energetic northmen such as himself to regenerate Panama's greatness. Speaking of Panama in the feminine, he wrote, "A new spirit has awakened the dormant energy of her people: and her grass-grown streets, so long the abode of silence are crowded with a busy populace. She is indebted to the conquest of California the discovery of gold and the great Exodus of our people for her regeneration. Her position naturally is a splendid one, and there is little doubt that her future will be progressive and that she will attain a position equal to that which she had lost."[50]

Conflicting Visions of Social Difference

White men from the United States frequently experienced difficulty understanding social distinctions among the population of the transit route and were disconcerted by what they perceived as a lack of a clear correspondence between color and status. While many recognized that color mattered in Panamanian society, they were often unsure how it mattered. Theodore Johnson, a physician who crossed Panama in 1849 who was among the first to publish an account of the voyage to California, noted what he regarded as the tendency of "creoles," or people who were at least partially white, to dominate "Negroes" and "Indians," but the correspondence between color and status was not as neat as he would have liked.[51] An anonymous writer in the *Panama Herald* described the "character of the Granadian" as "an intermixture of the Castilian with African and Indian blood, participating largely in the indolent propensities of the one, and uniting them with the degenerating influences of the others." Such a combination was "totally unfit, in its present condition, to be formed into a character of masculine activity and comprehensive energy. . . . It must be changed back to its primal condition—retransposed into its original constitutional elements, or otherwise it must be separated into classes as clearly defined as those which divide the aboriginal, the African, and the Anglo-Saxon races of the United States, before it can be purified of its impurities and rendered capable of being remodeled."[52] Even the whiteness of the Panamanian elite appeared suspect to many white observers from the United States. Writing in 1855, a white journalist from the United States named Robert Tomes acknowledged that in Panama City there were "a few families which boast themselves of pure Castilian blood; but I hardly think they could pass muster before the discerning eye of a shrewd Mississippi dealer in the Negro variety of mankind."[53]

As this latter quotation acknowledged implicitly, regional differences in the construction of race existed in the United States in the mid-1800s. White men who immigrated across Panama during the gold rush did not constitute a monolith, and important distinctions existed among them, including differences in regional origin, class, party, and religion. Nevertheless, the experience of passing through such a profoundly foreign place seems to have led many immigrants from the United States to minimize the differences that existed among themselves. The increased sense of national unity produced by the shared experience of traveling through a different country could lead to alliances across racial divides that might have been less likely in the United States. In 1851, *The Panama Herald* related the story of a "mulatto" from Baltimore named William B. Hance who had immigrated to Panama at the beginning of the gold rush, opened a hotel, married a Panamanian woman, and earned a great deal of money before he was accused of murdering his brother-in-law. Hance was placed in jail in Panama City but was liberated by fellow immigrants from the United States. The fact that the editor of the newspaper did not bother to specify the race of Hance's liberators suggests that they were white.[54] Another article preached against "Disunionists" in the United States, asking them to imagine how disheartened men in the United States now in Panama would feel if they were to learn that their country had been broken in two over the question of slavery.[55]

Accounts written by U.S. immigrants emphasized class rather than region as the key determinant of an immigrant's attitudes toward people in Panama, particularly toward people of color. Forster chided his fellow citizens in a way that betrayed his own sense of superiority over members of the local population: "The Americans seem to have taken full possession of the city—moving acting & directed as if they are the rightful lords of the soil. I am sometimes mortified at the audacity and cool assumption exhibited by my countrymen. I am ashamed of them, of their want of politeness toward the natives of their gross rudeness and domineering manners. They look upon the natives as an inferior race and treat them accordingly, forgetting what is due to a foreign people by whom they are most hospitably received. They forget also to exercise that magnanimity which the truly great always show to inferiors. In this they show inordinate *vanity* and

Fig. 4. Charles Nahl. "Incident on the Chagres River." 1867. Courtesy of the Bancroft Library.

contemptible impudence. Again, I say, I am ashamed of some of my countrymen here. I should like to see them properly *licked* into good manners and decency."[56]

Racial difference as imagined by a white man from the United States could be starkly different from the vision enunciated by Espinar, who saw variations in color as a fading legacy of the colonial period rather than a reflection of innate difference. Certainly color was relevant in Panamanian society. Marriages, for instance, tended to take place among people classified in similar racial terms in parochial records in Panama City. As we will see in the next chapter, some members of the white elite openly questioned the fitness of black men for the full rights of citizenship. Yet color alone did not necessarily prevent a person such as Espinar himself from attaining a position of high status. Whereas Robert Tomes saw a stark difference between whites and anyone who exhibited physical characteristics that could be interpreted as African in origin, color in Panama was defined along a continuum that ranged from *blancos* on one end and *negros* on the other, with *gente de color* and castas more generally falling toward the middle.

Artists from beyond Panama portrayed the interracial milieu of the transit route as a place where no clear hierarchy existed among the races, with

Fig. 5. J. Brandard from a sketch by Frank Marryat. "Crossing the Isthmus." Frank Marryat, *Mountains and Molehills, or Recollections of a Burnt Journal* (New York: Harper and Brothers, 1855). Courtesy of American Geographical Society Library, University of Wisconsin, Milwaukee.

chaos as the result. A painting by Charles Christian Nahl of the Chagres River shows three Panamanian boatmen struggling through rapids in a bongo loaded with passengers from the United states. All three boatmen are clearly portrayed as darker in complexion than their passengers. One of the boatmen is shown falling out of the canoe while the travelers look on with alarm from beneath a canopy located at the stern. Close by, a wrecked bongo warns of the dangers of the river. An image drawn by Frank Marryat portrays the transit route as a scene of total disorder in which what Marryat perceived as proper social hierarchy has been turned on its head. Mules bound about and pitch off their riders. While two men wearing only loincloths carry white passengers on their backs, a distinguished-looking white man with a bald pate sits on his behind, looking bewildered. A black man clad in loincloth overlooks the scene.

Elite Panamanians sometimes remarked with disapproval on the behavior of U.S. whites toward people of color in Panama and the United States. Frederick Ansoatigue, a merchant in Panama City, attributed a "bad feeling expressed by some of the colored population against Americans" due to "the conduct of dissolute persons crossing the Isthmus."[57] Arosemena criticized the exclusion of men of color from political rights in the

United States "for no other reason than the race to which they belong or of which they carry a slight tint."[58] In Arosemena's case, this criticism did not amount to a full proclamation of racial equality, let alone a disavowal of the importance of distinctions among people on the basis of color. But even elite Panamanians who were capable of writing negatively about blacks in their private letters were generally loath to make explicitly derogatory statements about blacks in print or official records for fear of appearing to betray the ideals of transracial republicanism that had emerged during the wars of independence, when black soldiers such as Espinar had proved crucial for rebel victories.[59]

The Habit of Going at Full Speed

At the beginning of the gold rush, immigrants who crossed the isthmus had no choice but to negotiate with different groups of people for transport, food, and shelter at every stage of the journey. These points of negotiation along the transit route were frequently sites of conflict involving travelers and workers in the transit economy. Transactions that white travelers might otherwise have perceived as shrewd seemed treacherous and humiliating when they regarded the other party in the negotiation as racially inferior to themselves. According to Theodore Johnson, the boatmen with whom he and his party had contracted to take them to Cruces backed out of the agreement after they found a better price from other customers. In response, Johnson's compatriots drew bowie knives and revolvers and waved them about, threatening to whip the boatmen and calling for the annexation of the Isthmus of Panama by the United States.[60]

Frank Marryat described porters in Panama as "Indians" who had "lined their pockets with American eagles" and had assumed "American independence."[61] The "Indians" whom Marryat described were almost certainly castas. Nevertheless, his observation pointed to traits in workers along the transit route that white immigrants from the United States often found disconcerting, if not infuriating. Although California had been officially part of the United States for less than a year, many of these gold seekers spoke and acted as if access to the goldfields were a birthright. In Panama this sense of entitlement often led travelers to act as if Panama were already a land that had been conquered by the United States. The same spirit of independence that U.S. whites treasured in themselves now seemed like a direct threat to their entitlement to the spoils of California.

James Tyson, who traveled across Panama twice in 1849, asked emphatically, "Who that has bargained with these slothful and dilatory people, ever knew them to adhere to a contract?"[62] Panamanians' efforts to take advantage of their position in the market were rendered as the negative characteristics of a "mongrel race." Though European and U.S. racial theory in the mid-nineteenth century often portrayed the peoples of tropical climates as inherently lazy and uninterested in improving their material circumstances, the problem in Panama as perceived by whites from the United States was sometimes just the opposite: boatmen, mule drivers, and porters were *too* enterprising.

Gold rush immigrants who sought in Panama some kind of escape from the market revolution found themselves confronted by people who embodied the very characteristics they imagined themselves to be fleeing. As soon as passengers set foot on the beach in Chagres, they found themselves competing with one another to purchase the services of boatmen who charged what most regarded to be extortionate prices. That these boatmen were also men of color was a source of further outrage. Bayard Taylor, the noted travel writer from the United States, described the scene he encountered in early 1849 as white travelers and boatmen negotiated transport upriver. While Taylor's compatriots ran about the beach, "shouting, gesticulating, and getting feverishly impatient at the deliberate natives," the boatmen remained "provokingly cool and unconcerned." As Taylor wrote of the boatmen, "They had not seen six months of emigration without learning something of the American habit of going at full speed."[63]

The tense negotiations on the beach that Taylor portrayed as a clash of "habits" may be better understood as different relationships to time and work. Taylor and others from the United States were anxious to cross the isthmus and leave Panama as soon as possible. They had read many reports of the easy riches to be found in the goldfields of California and were eager to try their luck before all the opportunities were claimed by others.

Reports of danger and particularly of disease led extra urgency to travelers' efforts to leave Panama as quickly as possible. The terms "Chagres Fever" and "Panama Fever" were used to describe any manner of fever-inducing ailment that felled immigrants during their time in Panama City. Outbreaks of cholera took place in Panama in 1848 and 1849. Although boosters of the Panama Route claimed that the tales of rampant disease were exaggerated, the hospital for foreigners established in Panama City by expatriate residents and steamship companies early in the gold rush rarely lacked for patients.[64]

Anxious immigrants found themselves enraged by boatmen and mule drivers, who received the same pay regardless of how quickly they transported their passengers and cargo across the isthmus. They were paid by the journey, not according to the clock or the schedules of the steamship companies. If demand for transport across Panama had been constant, boatmen and mule drivers would have had more incentive to move quickly, so as to be able to transport more cargo and passengers. But at the beginning of the rush, demand surged and then waned with the arrival of each boatload of immigrants. When demand was at its height, it almost inevitably outweighed supply. When boatmen finished a given journey, there were not necessarily customers waiting for them, and so the incentive for speed was minimal. Little harm came to a mule driver if he chose to leave an hour later than his charges wished or to boatmen if they paused for a coffee at a house on the riverbank. Indeed, transit workers appear to have viewed these acts not as deviations from duty but as prerogatives. Sarah Brooks, who crossed Panama in 1852, wrote of the boatmen, "They [the boatmen] were an ugly set, and were constantly inventing excuses for tying up at every hut that promised a drink or a snooze."[65] Forster described his frustration at waking up and finding that the muleteer he had hired to transport him to Panama City was still asleep. Forster woke the muleteer by jabbing him several times with his boot. Once they were under way, Forster insisted on traveling faster and faster, to which the mule driver responded by denouncing "*los Americanos*" as devils.[66]

The work of boatmen had a rhythm that was governed by the bongo's owner and captain, the patrón. It was a rhythm that was marked not by the clock but by the singing or chanting of the boatmen themselves. Johnson, who made the journey up the Chagres in February 1849, described the singing as "a wild, nasal chant, a sort of Spanish improvisatore." He asked the patrón about the meaning of the lyrics and rendered the answer as "de good canoe, de good casa [house], and de good mohare [woman]."[67]

White men from the United States sometimes took delight in ridiculing working people in racial terms. Johnson recounted how he and his companions had made fun of the patrón of their bongo, whom Johnson described as a racially mixed creole. After the patrón entered the water to move the bongo beyond a low point in the river, Johnson and his traveling companions prevented him from climbing back into the bongo and then joked among themselves that the scare had whitened the patrón's skin. As with minstrel shows in the United States, this racist "fun" carried with it the potential for more overt acts of violence against people of color, especially when white travelers found themselves subordinated to or placed on an equal plane with people whom they saw as inferior to themselves.

Even white people from the United States who were accustomed to living in close proximity to people of African descent were often unnerved by the experience of finding themselves placed under the command or authority of people whom they regarded as racially inferior. The fact that boatmen often worked with little or no clothing heightened this anxiety. Forster commented humorously but also with some uneasiness as he described his journey up the Chagres River with two naked men whom he characterized as "negroes." In his pencil sketch of the scene in his diary, he felt obliged to place loincloths on the boatmen which they had not in fact worn.[68]

Concepts of Honor in the Transit Zone

White women from the United States were a tiny minority among immigrants in 1849 and the early 1850s. Those few who made the crossing found themselves the recipients of exaggerated and sometimes unwanted attention from male immigrants and men from Panama. Mary Jane Megquier arrived in Panama at the beginning of 1849 as the only "lady" among the some two hundred passengers aboard the steamship *Northerner*. She expressed gratitude to the captain of the ship for being gallant enough to cede his private quarters to her. After she arrived in Chagres and began her journey upriver, however, she became annoyed by the attentions of local people. She complained that she could not sleep during her first night on the Chagres River because of the constant visits by Panamanians, for whom "a white lady was such a rare sight."[69]

When women from the United States were present, the dynamics of interaction between white men from the United States and men of color from Panama could change in important ways. Forster made his journey upriver as a lone man, and so the vision of scantily dressed men was merely an oddity to him. But when white womenfolk from the United States were subjected to such sights, U.S. men came to see the bodies of black men as potential threats to female virtue.

The relatively small number of white women from the United States who crossed Panama resulted in an increased sense of vulnerability that was felt not only by the women but also by the white men who accompanied them, whose own sense of male honor hinged on their ability to defend the women and children they perceived as their charges. When white women came into contact with men of color in ways that violated strictures against interaction between white women and black men in the United States, the result could be violence. Sarah Brooks described the tumult that occurred after the boatmen on her bongo discarded their clothing to work more efficiently. While the women retreated beneath their umbrellas, their male companions moved quickly to demand that the boatmen replace their garments. She described the horror she felt later in the journey when a black man carried her from the beach in Panama City to a boat that was to ferry her to her ship in the Bay of Panama: "All at once, without a word of warning, I was grabbed from behind. One black arm was around my waist, another under my knees, and I was lifted up and carried straight out into the water. I wanted to scream."[70]

White travelers from the United States were sometimes tempted to think of black transit workers as slaves and to treat them as such by giving peremptory orders and resorting to physical violence in their attempts to impose their will. According to Mary Seacole, boatmen and muleteers "were reviled, shot, and stabbed by these free and independent filibusters, who would fain whop all creation abroad as they do their slaves at home."[71] Seacole's comparison of insolent immigrants to filibusters was apt—immigrants who abused people of color in the manner they were accustomed to doing back in the United States were asserting sovereignty over people in Panama that was analogous to filibusters' ambitions to conquer other lands.

Local working people in Panama's transit zone did not simply sit passively as white immigrants from the United States projected gendered and racialized fantasies of empire upon them. Understanding of male honor also informed the ways in which working men interacted with immigrants. Taylor reported the thoughts expressed by the chief boatman of his canoe on the subject of relations between U.S. travelers and local transit workers as follows: "If the Americans are good, we are good; if they abuse us, we are bad. We are black, but *muchos caballeros* (very much of gentlemen)."[72] Regardless of their color, boatmen and muleteers were free men, and they frequently acted to squelch any attempt by immigrants to treat them as if they were otherwise. Sarah Brooks stated that after her male companions ordered the boatmen they had employed to don more clothing, "a stormy scene ensued"—an indication that the boatmen did not simply accede to passengers' commands.[73] As Seacole recognized, working men were very ready to defend themselves against white men from the United States with their knives.[74]

Yet workers along the transit zone did not simply reject or despise all that came from the United States. Just as some white men from the United States found aspects of Panamanian society that were admirable or attractive, workers along the transit zone also appear to have admired or at least taken interest in some of what immigrants from the United States brought with them besides their money. Bayard Taylor noted that some of the boatmen had picked up popular songs from the United States from their passengers and sang them in broken English, including minstrel songs such as "Oh Susanna!"[75]

The exchange of money for goods and services between immigrants and men from Panama was often a point of tension. Theodore Johnson claimed that a "native" had cheated him over the sale of a deer that the Panamanian had shot. After agreeing to sell the deer to Johnson, the native man sold the deer at a higher price to another buyer. In response, Johnson's "Yankee friend" tried to stop the sale by drawing a bowie knife. When the Panamanian drew his own knife, the man from the United States replaced his own weapon, struck the Panamanian to the ground, and seized the deer. While Johnson offered this account as evidence of cheating by Panamanian men, the Panamanian man's drawing of his own knife can be read as an assertion of dignity and a right to fair dealing, or at least as an unwillingness to conform to a immigrants' notion of what a deer was worth.[76]

Although white men from the United States sometimes appeared to forget that they were on foreign soil, working people in Panama remained very much aware that the immigrants were guests in the country and subject to local laws. According to an article in the *Panama Herald*, a U.S. immigrant who owned a shop in Panama City came into conflict with an employee, a "native negro," upon presenting him with payment for his services. As recounted in the *Herald*, which took the side of the immigrant, the employee became "exasperated on receiving his pay, and drawing his long knife, threatened to take [his boss's] life." After the boss knocked the employee down with a chair, the employee went to see the local *alcalde*— an official whose position combined functions of a mayor and a sheriff. Much to the displeasure of the *Herald*, the alcalde proceeded to jail the boss.[77] The fact that slavery was still a legal institution in Panama at the beginning of the rush added an extra dimension to these conflicts. In her autobiography Mary Seacole told of a dramatic and successful effort by Panamanians to liberate an enslaved woman and her child from her white mistress while in transit across Panama, though she may have invented or embellished the story for dramatic effect.[78] Seacole would go on to serve as a nurse in the Crimean War, earning official recognition from Queen Victoria, and her autobiography evinces a powerful capacity for invention. But her portrayal of Panamanian opposition to slavery was by no means a misrepresentation. For critics of the United States writing in Spanish-language newspapers, slavery served as a metaphor for what arrogant U.S. citizens sought to impose on Panama and as a real institution that might be strengthened in Panama if U.S. whites were permitted to hold sway over the isthmus. The *Revisor de la Política y Literatura Americana* predicted in 1850 that if Panama fell prey to the United States, not only would Panama's property-owning class be reduced to poverty but Panama's *gente de color* would be subjected to "the ultimate degradation," meaning enslavement.[79]

Conclusion

National rivalries influenced conflicts in Panama during the early years of the gold rush, but nationality itself was not always a reliable guide for understanding struggles over the communication route and sovereignty in the transit zone. The early indignation meetings that had prompted Gen. Persifor Smith's declaration that foreign miners would be banned from California were directed not only against Peruvian competitors for space on the boats and in the goldfields but also against the Pacific Mail Steamship Company, which frustrated would-be forty-niners accused of putting the pursuit of profit above the interests of fellow citizens. Both immigrants and shipping companies had been drawn to Panama by the promise of reducing the time required to connect the east coast of the United States to the West Coast. But whereas the passengers hoped to find their fortune in California, the shipping companies sought riches from the savings of travelers. The increased economic independence of working people led to consternation not just to travelers from the United States but also Panamanian elites who found themselves competing with immigrants for the labor of people of lower social status than themselves.

Struggles over "La California" took place in Panama, but they were of a piece with struggles in California itself over who could rightly share in the spoils of conquest. If the gold discovery seemed to many Anglo Americans a blessing from God, events at the beginning of the gold rush indicated that Anglo Americans would not necessarily be the chief beneficiaries of that blessing. There were others who also sought to benefit from the gold discovery—indigenous women, *californios*, African Americans, and immigrants from both sides of the Pacific and the Atlantic.[80] A similar dynamic arose in Panama during the same period. It was members of Panama City's mercantile elite who had hankered most for the rebirth of the transit route. But at the beginning of the rush many of the people who benefited most dramatically from the immigration were working people of color, a significant portion of whom were newcomers to the transit zone.

As in the goldfields themselves at the beginning of the gold rush, no single group in the transit zone enjoyed anything close to what could be described as hegemonic control. Yet Panama was also different from California in important ways in that its political apparatus remained intact and unconquered. Unlike California, which the United States now claimed as its own territory, Nueva Granada was still sovereign over the isthmus. This sovereignty would soon be sorely tested, however, and significantly undermined, by a conquest of a different kind already under way on the Atlantic side of the isthmus.

Chapter 2

The Panama Railroad and the Conquest of the Gold Rush

The keystone in elite Panamanian boosters' aspirations to transform Panama into an emporium was the construction of a canal or a railroad. Lacking the capital required for such a massive undertaking, members of Panama City's merchant and land-owning class looked abroad for assistance and were disappointed repeatedly in the decades after independence from Spain in 1821. When the Panama Railroad Company finally broke ground on the line at the beginning of 1850, the boosters imagined that their prayers would soon be answered. Against tremendous odds, the railroad company managed to inaugurate regular train service five years later, in January 1855. Rather than bring the kind of prosperity envisioned by Panamanian elites, however, the dawn of the railroad era produced very different results: economic depression and the creation of a company-controlled domain on the Caribbean coast that represented one of the first U.S.-dominated enclaves in Latin American history.

The Problem of Labor

Although the Panama Railroad has long been considered one of the great works of engineering of the mid-nineteenth century, the greatest challenge that faced the company was the problem of labor: recruiting, disciplining, and keeping alive a force sufficient for the construction of a railway under extraordinarily adverse conditions.[1] As company officials soon discovered, the gold rush immigration complicated the labor problem considerably by increasing demand for workers and driving up prices more generally in Panama. After a brief initial trip to Panama before the beginning of the gold rush in 1848, John L. Stephens returned to Panama in January 1849 and was shocked by the transformation that had taken place during his absence. Of Panama City he wrote, "The change in this place is most extraordinary. The principal street is occupied almost exclusively by Americans, and prices have gone up to California rates." The unexpected rush of immigrants to California in Panama placed the company in a frustrating position. On one hand, the dramatic growth in traffic increased the potential for profits far beyond the original dreams of the company's founders. On the other hand, the tremendous increase in demand for labor, food, supplies, and other goods made their efforts to capture those potential profits much more expensive than Stephens and the company's other officials had anticipated. As Stephens wrote, "There seems to be a new rush this way, all [of] which indicates the necessity of our road but at the same time increases the difficulty of making it."[2]

To build the railroad, company officials would have to bend the rush to their own purposes. To succeed in this task, however, they would first have to wrest control of Panama's transit system from the boatmen, muleteers, washerwomen, and others in Panama who also saw the potential to profit from the great migration to the gold fields of California. The first battle in this great struggle commenced on the Chagres River nearly as soon as the rush itself began. In mid-January 1849, the shipping company of Howland and Aspinwall, a family concern of William H. Aspinwall, introduced a small steamer named the *Orus* into the lower reaches of the Chagres River. The *Orus* could carry as many as one hundred fifty passengers at a time, as opposed to the five or six customary for the bongos. But the steamer's deeper draft prevented it from reaching the upriver ports of Gorgona and Cruces. During Panama's dry season, between January and April, the ship could not even enter the mouth of the river at times. Over the next two years several other steamers were introduced into the river, including the *General Herrán*, the *Gorgona*, the *Rafael Rivas*, and the *William Aspinwall*. Like the *Orus*, however, they all experienced severe difficulty navigating the river owing to snags and variations in water level.[3]

Nevertheless, the appearance of steamships had a significant effect on the organization of transportation on the river. Though human-powered bongos and other boats continued to possess a monopoly over transit between Gorgona and Cruces, they were forced to cede much of the traffic below Gorgona to the larger foreign-owned ships. Even in stretches of the river where steamboats could not penetrate, boatmen from Panama began to face competition by the end of 1849 from immigrants from Jamaica and the United States who also sought to earn money by rowing, paddling, and poling passengers up and down the river in boats that they either constructed themselves or imported by ship from elsewhere. Some Panamanian boatmen found themselves working as employees of the steamers, allowing themselves to be towed in their bongos behind the steamships until the larger vessels could no longer proceed. At that point they would transport passengers and cargo for the remainder of the journey. As a consequence of this increased competition, the cost of river transportation to Cruces fell to as little as four dollars by the summer of 1850, compared with ten dollars only one year before.[4]

Charles Winslow described the combination of transport by steamer and bongo in a letter dated April 26, 1849. The *Orus* conveyed him and his companions upriver with approximately thirty bongos in tow. At the river town of Dos Hermanos the passengers changed to bongos for the remaining eighteen miles to Cruces. Each of the travelers paid a single price of $8.50 for the journey, which included the transport of one trunk, a valise, and a smaller bag.[5] According to Winslow, the steamer experience proved nearly as startling for the boatmen as for the passengers: "It was a really beautiful sight to see such a multitude of canoes rushing through the water & ploughing it up. . . . Some natives were holding on to keep from falling out, others to keep in company with the rest, some were bailing, some were standing with astonishment at this new & strange sight & all were shouting in unintelligible jargon."[6]

The use of steam power proved more successful on the other side of the isthmus, in the Bay of Panama. In 1850 the Pacific Mail introduced the *Taboga*, a small steamer or *vaporcito* that ferried passengers between a beach known as Playa Prieta, on the outskirts of Panama City, and larger ships in the Bay of Panama. As with steamers in the Chagres, the larger draft of the *Taboga* made it less versatile than the smaller sea-going bongos and sailboats. When the tide was low, the small steamer simply sat in the mud next to the pier. But when the tide was high, the *Taboga* could transport as many as one hundred people at a time at speeds considerably faster than its human and wind-powered counterparts.[7]

Increased competition for passengers on the Chagres sometimes led to conflicts between boatmen from Panama and newly arrived boatmen from the United States and Jamaica. The town of Chagres lay at the foot of the fortress of San Lorenzo, which stood on a promontory above the harbor. By 1851, U.S. settlers had created a separate settlement across the river with wood-framed buildings that included hotels and other businesses that served immigrants. This settlement also became the base of operations for boatmen from the United States who competed against Panamanian boatmen across the river for cargo and passengers.[8]

The bloodiest of these battles took place at the mouth of the Chagres River in October 1851. After boatmen from the United States attempted to establish exclusive control over the transport of passengers between ocean-going ships and the shore, they came into conflict with boatmen from across the river. Stephen Chapin Davis, a New Englander, was on his way back home from California in October 1851 when he witnessed the violence between the boatmen. According to his account, the conflict began when "a [Panamanian] negro came up in his boat alongside the newly painted boat of a white man [from the United States], rubbing and chafing it badly, which somewhat enraged the owner." The two men came to blows, after which the black man drew a cutlass. According to Davis, the cutlass served as a signal and "immediately all the black boatman (som[e] 150 in number) did the same and jumped out onto the levee at this white man, who ran, and they after him." During the battle that followed, residents of both sides of the river attacked one another using guns and knives. According to Davis, men from the Panamanian village of Chagres climbed up to the fortress of San Lorenzo and bombarded the U.S. town across the river with a cannon until they came under fire from "a Rocky Mountain hunter" with a sure shot. Several men died on both sides of the river, and the bloodshed continued until a captain of a U.S. ship threatened to fire his own cannons at the Panamanian town. A formal peace was established by Panamanian officials and the U.S. consul in Chagres, who signed an agreement mandating that all law-abiding boatmen were permitted to conduct their business freely in the port.[9]

Construction of the Railroad Begins

Col. G. W. Hughes of the U.S. Topographical Corps arrived in Panama City at the beginning of 1849 to survey and locate the railway's line. The contract between the company and the government of Nueva Granada stipulated Panama City as the Pacific terminus of the line but left open the location of the Atlantic terminus until the completion of the survey. Although the ports of Chagres and Portobelo were the most obvious candidates for a railroad terminal on the Atlantic coast, they suffered from serious disadvantages, including the existence of surrounding mountains that would render the construction of a railroad extremely difficult. Hughes selected a different line with a smaller vertical rise that began in the less populated location of Limón Bay, located to the east of Chagres.[10]

Under the leadership of George Totten, who took over as chief engineer in 1850, the company hoped to use the Chagres River to transport men and supplies to the initial construction site of the railway, located near the river port of Gorgona. Yet the tremendous volume of traffic and the consequently high prices for transport on the river made it prohibitively expensive for the company to hire a sufficient number of bongos and muleteers. Panamanians were largely uninterested in the dangerous wage labor offered by the company. Work on the railroad would have taken them far away from their homes, and laborers for the company worked in gangs supervised by foremen, with only one day of rest per week. In contrast, a man who worked as a porter, boatman, or muleteer had more latitude in deciding when and how he worked and could sell his labor only when he needed or wanted the money. As Totten wrote in February 1850, "It is impossible to procure labourers on the Isthmus for the work on the Rl. Rd. Not only are wages so exorbitant as to make the work very costly, but the labourers will not work steadily, nor do they wish to do any other work than that of transporting the baggage of the emigrants, by which they gain in a few days sufficient [money] to maintain themselves for a month."[11]

In early 1850 the company placed the steamer *General Herrán* on the Chagres River with the hope of driving the boatmen out of business and, ideally, into the company's service as wage laborers.[12] The company also took measures to undermine local control of overland transportation. In May 1850 William Aspinwall proposed a partnership between the company and Hurtado i Hermanos, a Panamanian-owned "express company" that contracted with steamship and other transportation companies to take baggage and passengers from one side of Panama to the other. With this alliance he hoped to loosen the grip of muleteers along the transit route by rechanneling traffic along the future route of the railway.[13] With the same goal in mind, in June 1850 he proposed an alliance of the Panama Railroad Company with the Pacific Mail and the Royal Mail Steamship companies in order to shift the Atlantic terminus of Panama's transit route from the port of Chagres—a stronghold of the boatmen—to Limón Bay.[14]

At the start of the construction the provincial government of Panama provided convict labor to the company, but the supply of convicts proved unreliable. The company also attempted briefly to exploit the labor of slaves. One of the company's primary contractors in Panama City was Tomás Cipriano de Mosquera, the former president of Nueva Granada, who brought to Panama several slaves from his estates in Cauca Valley, in southwestern Nueva Granada, after completing his presidential term in 1848. Mosquera's slaves briefly worked in the port of Panama City, unloading supplies from company ships. But the directors of the company rejected any further use of slavery, possibly because of fear of the political repercussions in New York, where the company was incorporated.[15]

As plantation owners had done in the 1830s and 1840s in the context of slave emancipation in the British West Indies, the company responded to local workers' antipathy to working under the company's direct control by turning to the importation of indentured and free workers from abroad.[16] The first of these imported workers were free men of African descent from Cartagena, on the Atlantic coast of Nueva Granada.[17] Despite the arrival of the first contingents of these workers in 1850, however, the company made little progress during its first year. In a humiliating turn of events, the company found itself depending on the very boatmen it had hoped to drive out of business for the transportation of its supplies and workers upriver to Gatún. To make matters worse, the proximity of the river trade to the construction site of the railroad made defection a constant temptation for the company's laborers. By May 1850, Totten decided he had no other option but to move the base of the company's works to Manzanillo Island in Limón Bay, far away from the transit zone, where oceangoing ships could deliver supplies directly to a company wharf and workers would find it more difficult to escape the company's grasp.[18] The first victory in the battle between the Panama Railroad Company and workers in the local transit economy had been won by the boatmen of the Chagres.

Through the rest of 1850 and into 1851 the company line progressed from Limón Bay with a view of reaching the Chagres River and choking off the river traffic. The bulk of the company workforce consisted of laborers, who carried out the heaviest, least-skilled work on the railroad. For these workers, Totten clearly preferred the category of men he called "natives," by which he meant workers from Nueva Granada, including Panama and Cartagena. The reason for this preference lay primarily in his perception

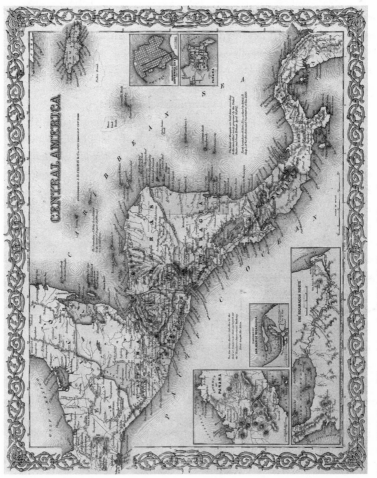

Fig. 6. G. W. Colton, "Central America," 1856. Collection of the author.

that in the Panamanian climate such men would work more efficiently and fall ill at a slower rate than foreigners. Writing in April 1849, before he had officially entered the company's employ, he stressed "the necessity of using all the native laborers that can be obtained, in preference to foreigners, who I do not think can stand the climate."[19]

As he had learned at Gorgona, however, the recruitment of "natives" in Panama itself was nearly impossible, due to their preference for casual labor in the river and overland transport trade. Recruiting from Cartagena proved less difficult but was still far from easy. During his first recruitment trip to Cartagena, Totten found few men willing to commit to six-month contracts with the company in Panama, even when the company provided transport. During a second recruiting trip to Cartagena conducted in July 1850, Totten found that many men were reluctant to disengage themselves from agricultural work. He reported that potential workers had been scared away by "stories about climate, indians & c." As he wrote, "It may be supposed that these men [from Cartagena] could have been brought here by merely sending for them; but that is not the case. My presence was necessary among them. I visited the villages—called them together—talked with them." Only by communicating directly with the men was he capable of "breaking down all the stories—and they were many—which were circulated against us."[20]

The railroad's progress was also impeded by Panama's rainy season, which extends from May through December. Without suitable quarters on Manzanillo Island, company officials and laborers were forced at first to sleep aboard an old ship that was anchored nearby.[21] As rain buffeted Limón Bay in August 1850, Totten reported to the company in New York that the railroad's progress had been paralyzed by desertions: "We have only about 40 men on the Island at present. The rest, having deserted, are running about here without having it in our power to take them."[22] Most of the deserters were men from the city of Cartagena, and Totten declared, "I shall avoid bringing any more of them. The people from the villages . . . are those we want, and they will remain with us."[23] The incentives for desertion were great, as he acknowledged in the same letter. Working conditions on the island were extremely harsh, and many of the company had fallen sick. Totten wrote, "We meet a great deal of water in every direction. Sometimes we pass successive days working over our boot tops. Not only ourselves but the men also fall sick from the exposure. Mr. Baldwin and myself have been obliged to relieve each other in the field operations— each one continuing until he falls sick, and the other then taking his place." Work on land was also hard, as Totten recalled in a letter in which he described clearing vegetation on Manzanillo Island in 1852: "Thick tangled underbrush, impenetrable except with the axe or machete—through which 1000 or 1200 feet made a good days work."[24]

Mental stress took a toll on employees of the company. Totten reported in August that an employee named Mr. Michel was "suffering from a nervous attack, which he attributes to the anxiety he suffered, and the difficulties he encountered, in undertaking to secure the deserters here this week." For those healthy enough to work, the labor regime was nearly unrelenting. Totten reported on August 25 that during the previous twenty-two days the majority of the men had worked "20 and two-thirds to twenty-one and one third days."[25]

With little power to retain laborers who were determined to desert, the company was forced again and again to import more men from other places, including the United States and Jamaica. Totten was skittish about hiring Jamaicans on the railroad works, because of what he perceived as their unsuitable racial characteristics as well as his fear that they would come into conflict with other workers. Using the language of slavery, Totten wrote to Stephens that "the Jamaica labourers require driving or tasking." To keep them from deserting, he proposed that a part of their wages should be withheld until the terms of their contracts had expired. Remuneration for workers from Jamaica was to be higher than that for workers from Cartagena, which Totten saw as a potential source of discord, and he doubted that Irish immigrants whom the company had imported from the United States would tolerate laboring side by side with the new arrivals.[26]

When the first workers from Jamaica finally arrived, on December 4, 1850, Totten expressed disappointment and fear. In his opinion, they did not seem physically fit for hard labor, and many if not all were ex-convicts recently released from prison, which caused Totten to doubt their character.[27] Nevertheless, the company continued to import workers from Jamaica. On December 22, 1850, Totten reported that fifty-two more men had arrived from the island, "a little better lot than the former, but not the kind of labourers we require. I shall send home [some] of these people by the *Crescent City*, of whom some have never worked at all, and others very little."[28]

Workers' Politics

Despite Totten's fears of Jamaican workers, it was white laborers from the United States who initially posed the greatest challenge to the company's regime in Limón Bay. Conflict between the company and white workers from the United States began soon after the arrival in December 1850 of two contingents of men who had contracted to work for one hundred days in exchange for a passage to California. The men had been recruited by two labor contractors employed by the company named Baker and Truesdale. The infusion of these workers brought the number of white workers—in whose ranks Totten included Irishmen—to four hundred. Dismayed by the living and working conditions, 150 of the new arrivals almost immediately conducted a brief strike against the company. In response to workers' demands, Totten traveled to Chagres, where in his words, "I . . . bought up all the blankets and mosquitoe netting I could find."[29] On December 23, the men again struck in response to what they deemed unacceptable conditions. Peter Peirce, a company official based in Limón Bay, wrote to Totten, "I am sorry to inform you that most of the white men on the island have this morning refused to go to work on account of bad coffe and bad bread. I am sorry to say they [do not behave as] well bred men would act under existing circumstances." Among the men's demands was better protection from mosquitoes.[30] On the same day, John Borland reported to Totten on the leadership of the strikers, whom he identified as two of the more skilled workers, including a "Mr. Gridly," whom Totten identified as "a rodman of the red republican school."[31]

Although Totten argued that the men imported from the United States had exhibited "a spirit of disorganization and disinclination to labour" from their arrival in Panama, the fundamental problem lay in differences concerning how the work should be organized. He reported that, contrary to his wishes, the men "were divided into squads, each of which appointed its own captain or foreman." The men also insisted on determining the organization of the work day themselves. According to Totten, one of workers' leaders, a "Dr. Henry," justified his independence and that of his men from Totten's orders by reference to their contract. Totten, on the other hand, insisted that the terms of the contract required the men to take their orders directly from the company, or as he put it, "to work in any capacity to which they may from time to time be respectively appointed under the instructions of the agents or engineer." Despite Totten's efforts to exert his authority, however, he could do nothing when Dr. Henry's men refused to accept orders from the foreman Totten had appointed to direct their work. Totten was similarly helpless when a group of carpenters under Henry refused attempts to separate them from the rest of their companions. In such a circumstance, Totten could do little but grumble and import more men.[32]

By February 1851 Totten reported that desertions had been reduced thanks in part to a proclamation by the governor of Panama, who ordered the arrest and imprisonment of men who broke their contracts with the company. A company official found a number of deserters from the United States in Panama City and successfully prevailed upon the provincial governor to arrest them—a hint of future arrangements between the company and local officials. Totten wrote, "We are . . . indebted to the Governor & authorities at Panama, for their promptness in arresting the deserters, and for the disposition & determination which they exhibit to assist the company."[33]

At the end of January 1851 Totten reported 680 men in the company's employ at points near the Chagres River: 250 U.S. men under contractor Truesdale at Gatún, 130 U.S. men under Dr. Henry at Palenquilla, 150 natives under a contractor named Martines at San Pablo, and 150 more native men under Martines at Gorgona.[34] As the preparation of the line between Manzanillo Island and the Chagres River continued into the dry season, Totten's primary concern remained the recruitment of labor. He continued to construct a corps of workers composed of native men, or what he described as "a strong native force, not only for the wet season, but because they are in every respect the most effective common laborers we have." Shipments of native workers continued to arrive periodically from Cartagena, but the recruitment of natives from the Isthmus of Panama was still thwarted by the possibility of higher pay elsewhere in the transit economy.[35] And though strikes of U.S. workers had ended by the beginning of 1851, Totten was now experiencing problems with the men from Jamaica, who refused to obey the orders of their foreman, a white man from Jamaica whom they threatened to denounce to the authorities there once they returned from Panama.[36]

The Problem of Disease

In late 1850 a doctor employed by the company had suggested that one of its buildings on Manzanillo Island be converted into a hospital. Totten responded favorably to the idea, not because he had great hopes of improving the health of his laborers but rather because he thought a hospital would make it easier for the company to concentrate the sick in one place, keeping them under observation and thus reducing the number of men who feigned illness in order to avoid work. As Totten wrote, "With regard to the building requested by Dr. Gage for a hospital I believe it would contribute to the economy of the work, if hospital regulations be strictly carried out. The well would be more easily distinguished from the sick. There would be fewer imaginary ills among the labourers. The working rolls would always be larger than without it, and when no longer required for this purpose, the building could be appropriated to some other." The hospital did not appear so urgent to him, however, that he felt immediate action should be taken, and he decided to wait until the company had more buildings, "as we are now crowded for room."[37]

Sickness was again ravaging the workforce at the end of February 1851. The rapid decline of white workers from the United States only confirmed Totten's preference for native labor. As he wrote, "Disease has taken hold of the men sooner than I anticipated. I never did suppose that white labor would stand this climate any length of time; but did think they would be able to stand it three or four months at least. In this I am thrown back in my calculations. The last three weeks have diminished our force more than 100 men."[38]

Totten finally relented and ordered the construction of a hospital on Manzanillo Island. He reported in August of 1851 that the building was nearly complete. In the same letter, he stated that "the white force is diminishing as fast as those composing it become incapable of duty. I am sorry to say that this includes also our tracklayers, not one of whom can we spare." He concluded morosely, "This country does not admit of fixed ideas. One is obliged to adapt himself to circumstances. Sickness is constantly breaking in upon one's intentions, and thwarting all his best endeavors."[39]

John A. Liddell, a physician who worked in the company hospital in 1851, reported on the health of the white workers in the *New York Journal of Medicine*. During a four-month period the company admitted 382 sick employees. The most common malady was a disease described by Liddell as "climate fever" or "remittent fever," which was more popularly known as "Panama Fever." Other illnesses included acute dysentery and congestive fever. Liddell concluded that the most work the company could expect from white workers was one month. He estimated that by the second month of the workers' time in Panama, half would be either on the company's sick list or significantly weakened by illness. "Before three months have passed away," he wrote, "a large proportion will either have died or been sent out of the country as unfit for further labor." Every two weeks, he reported, the company sent approximately two hundred infirm white workers back to the United States by ship.[40] Sickness remained a constant problem for the company, especially during Panama's rainy season. Even during the dry season, however, the workforce was sometimes seriously weakened by disease. On January 31, 1853, for example, Totten reported, "About one half of our present force is constantly on the sick list."[41]

Liddell's report and Totten's correspondence suggest that the company's principal approach to disease was not treatment so much as the removal of sick men from the work as soon as possible and their replacement with a constant flow of fresh, healthy workers. Totten's primary motivation for sending sick men back home lay not in a fear that they might communicate disease to other men or a concern for the sick men's well-being but rather a desire to reduce the company's costs, as the care of incapacitated men was expensive. Thus in February 1851, when the company met some resistance from ship captains who balked at transporting sick men aboard their ships, Totten considered it worth the cost of chartering a ship expressly for that purpose. As he wrote, "Considering that we are relieved from their care and attendance for two or three weeks, it is probably after all the most economical arrangement we could make."[42] Native workers were also shipped home—typically to Cartagena—when Totten deemed them "unfit for labor."[43] A similar desire to reduce medical costs in Panama also led Totten to exhort company officials in the United States to screen out unhealthy men before they boarded ships for Panama. As he wrote on February 24, 1851, "In sending men, the company should carefully guard against any who are diseased [with] lung complaints, diseased livers or spleens & syphilis. The latter complaint should come under the same rule as sailors—*receive no pay.*" Syphilitics, according to Totten, had recently caused the company doctors "great annoyance, & were only a constant expense to the company. Some of them died, & [the] rest were sent home."[44]

The First Passengers

Despite continuing struggles to assemble a sufficient concentration of laborers, by the third quarter of 1851 track had been laid on the seven miles of road between Manzanillo Island and Gatún station, and the future line of the railway had been planned as far as Barbacoas, where the railroad was to cross the Chagres River. Meanwhile, work was simultaneously begun on the Pacific side of the route. On October 1, 1851, the first locomotive hauled a line of working cars from Limón Bay to Gatún.[45]

Two months later Totten reported that the company planned to send its first paying passengers over the partially constructed railway. The steamship *Georgia*, bound from the United States, had attempted to land its passengers at Chagres, only to be thwarted by high surf. Threatened by stormy weather, the ship took refuge in Limón Bay. Rather than return to Chagres, passengers on board the *Georgia* made arrangements to travel by train to Gatún, from which place they might continue up the Chagres in bongos.[46] Soon thereafter the *Georgia*'s passengers were followed by those of another steamer from the United States, the *Philadelphia*. On February 9, 1852, Totten wrote that the company planned to transport the passengers of two more steamers—the *Ohio* and the *Cherokee*—past Gatún to the station of Ahorca Lagarto, and he reported optimistically, "This is the beginning of an income which I hope will raise the spirits of our company."[47]

After the news arrived in the United States about the transit of the passengers of the *Georgia* and other steamers on the railway, the price of company stock improved. As Fessenden Nott Otis wrote in his classic history of the company,

> At about this time the affairs of the Company in New York looked very dark and unpromising. The first subscription of one million dollars of stock was expended, and the shares had gone down to a low figure. . . . But on the return of the Georgia to New York, carrying news that the California passengers had landed at Navy [Limón] Bay instead of Chagres, and had traveled over a portion of the Panama Railway, its friends were inspired with renewed hope, the value of its stock was enhanced, and the steadfast upholders of the work were relieved from the doubts and anxieties that had well-nigh overwhelmed them.[48]

By July 1852 the company was transporting passengers 23 miles along the partially constructed line, as far as the station at Barbacoas, at a charge of eight dollars per traveler.[49] On July 3, 1852, the company conveyed a contingent of U.S. troops and some of their family members along the completed portion of the line, a process that required two trips. Among those in the party was future U.S. president Ulysses S. Grant. The passage of the troops over the remainder of the isthmus by mule proved disastrous, however, with many of the party falling sick and dying.[50] Despite this misfortune, Totten remained optimistic about the prospects of the company, reporting by the end of July 1852 that thanks to the partially constructed railway, it was now possible to travel from Manzanillo Island to Cruces or

Gorgona in a single day, as opposed to the two or three days that had been typically required to reach either town by boat from the port of Chagres.[51]

With the completion of the railroad from the Atlantic port of Colón to Gatún, on the Chagres River, a key objective of Aspinwall's plan to undermine the boatmen and supplant the port of Chagres with the company-controlled port of Colón had been realized. Meanwhile, his scheme for consolidating the remaining mule traffic began to bear fruit thanks to an alliance with Mosquera, who was now working with Hurtado i Hermanos. Writing in March 1851, Mosquera reported to Stephens that the express company had purchased all the mules belonging to Zachrisson, Nelson and Co., their chief competitor in the overland express business, and announced that "we are now alone in our business of transport."[52] Mosquera was overly optimistic but his perception of the general trend was accurate. Two years later Hurtado i Hermanos established another partnership with the Pacific Mail for the transportation of the steamship line's passengers and luggage from the end of the railway's still incomplete line to Panama City. This move channeled the overland business of all passengers on the major steamship line between Panama and San Francisco into the hands of a single company.[53]

The Nicaragua Route

Steamship companies such as the U.S. Mail and Pacific Mail had a vested interest in improving the quality and speed of overland transport across the isthmus, especially after the opening of a competing transit route across Nicaragua. Cornelius Vanderbilt, the transit baron of New York City, began exploring the possibility of siphoning off traffic from Panama to Nicaragua in 1849. The chief obstacle to this enterprise was Great Britain, which opposed any U.S. monopoly over interoceanic transit in Nicaragua. In 1850 the Nicaraguan government's award of an exclusive contract to a Vanderbilt-controlled company for the construction of a canal nearly led to conflict between the United States and Great Britain. The Clayton-Bulwer Treaty of 1850 eased tension between the two countries by denying either one the exclusive right to build an interoceanic canal in Nicaragua or anywhere else in Central America.[54] Freed at least temporarily from the threat of British intervention, Vanderbilt's route across Nicaragua began to operate in earnest in 1851. The first stage in the journey from the Atlantic to the Pacific involved transport up the San Juan River from the port of San Juan del Norte on the Atlantic coast, followed by a trip by steamer across Lake Nicaragua and a final journey by land to the Pacific port of San Juan del Sur.[55] Once Vanderbilt and his associates established a regular system of transit from one coast to another, the Nicaragua Route proved to be the Panama Route's most serious competitor. Nicaragua came closest to overtaking the Panama Route in 1853, when approximately 10,000 travelers crossed Nicaragua on their way to San Francisco, compared with approximately 15,000 by way of Panama.[56]

As competitors in the overland transport business declined in number, mule trains increased in size. The few remaining small-time operators found it increasingly hard to compete against large transport companies that replenished their livestock with animals imported from outside Panama. Writing in August 1853, Totten reported that the mule train used to conduct the U.S. mail across Panama consisted of at least one hundred animals. In the same letter, he indicated that there were only three competitive bids from express companies for the mail contract with the Pacific Mail: Hurtado i Hermanos, Joy and Co., and a firm owned by Ran Runnels.[57]

The Appropriately Named Minor Story

Although the company made progress in undermining the indigenous transit system, it ran into a significant obstacle in the form of an ineffectual contractor named Minor Story, an entrepreneur from the United States whose previous jobs as a contractor included work on the Portland and Montreal Railroad. Toward the end of 1852, Story took command of the bulk of the company's construction activities, including the building of a critical bridge across the Chagres River.[58] Totten continued as chief engineer but directed his attention to work closer to Panama City, the acquisition of land for a Pacific terminus, and the repair of the road between Cruces and Panama City. In December 1852, Totten estimated that Story would need at least six thousand men to complete the work for which he had contracted but suspected that Story's force would remain closer to one thousand unless a dramatic increase resulted from more recruiting.[59] Eleven days later he declared, "It does not appear to me that Mr. Story has an adequate idea of the amount of work before him. He should have a force of 4000 *daily laborers*, which will require a force of 6000 men on the work, and recruits by every steamer to keep up the supply."[60] The labor shortages persisted, and Totten's correspondence from the period was filled with pleas for more workers.[61] By the beginning of June 1853 the construction process was in serious danger of stalling. The workforce had been reduced to five hundred men.[62] Minimal progress had been made during the dry season, and now that the rainy season had begun, the bridge over the Chagres remained unfinished, with little prospect of completion in the near future. The contracts of the majority of Story's "white force" had nearly expired, and Totten had scant hope that Story would be able to recruit more native workers, who objected to Story's treatment of their countrymen.[63]

Finally, in August 1853, the company bowed to pressure from Totten: Story was fired, and Totten resumed control of the works.[64] Immediately after regaining command of the company's daily operations, Totten made preparations for a huge increase in imported labor. As Otis wrote, the company's "working force was increased as rapidly as possible, drawing laborers from almost every quarter of the globe. Irishmen were imported from Ireland, Coolies from Hindostan, Chinamen from China. English, French, Germans, and Austrians, amounting in all to more than seven thousand men, were thus gathered in, appropriately as it were, to construct this highway for all nations."[65] Totten sent to Jamaica a representative named Mr. Closson, whom he instructed to procure as many as 150 "coolies," by which he probably meant workers who had been brought to Jamaica from India. He also entered into a contract for 500 laborers from El Salvador, and a labor contractor from Nueva Granada agreed to provide 1,000 to 1,500 workers from elsewhere in Nueva Granada. In addition, Totten expressed hopes of acquiring 300 to 500 men from Chiriquí and Veraguas. Finally, he reported that "700 coolies" had been "ordered from China," and attempts were being made for the importation of men directly from Ireland.[66]

Indentured Workers from China

By the beginning of the dry season, in late December 1853, Totten had managed to increase the labor force considerably through the importation of new recruits from outside Panama. Writing on December 22, 1853, Totten reported to David Hoadley, the company president, as follows: "The actual number of men on the work, deducting those who leave by this steamer, is, white men 649, Jamaican & coolies 160, Natives 1301," bringing the total to 2,110.[67]

In early 1854, the company purchased the contracts of some one thousand indentured laborers from China from British merchants. The experiment soon proved disastrous. Many of the workers succumbed quickly to disease, while others committed suicide.[68] An official British mission sent to investigate the status of indentured workers from China in Panama reported that the approximately 1,040 men who had been transported from Shantou, in Guangdong Province, to the isthmus for work on the railroad had suffered greatly from the climate, fevers, and mistreatment, including abuse from Chinese headmen employed by the company as supervisors. Some of the workers had apparently been misled into believing that they were being shipped not to Panama but to California. Half died within a few months after their arrival. Among these deaths were thirty to forty suicides. Although Otis attributed the high mortality among Chinese workers to the Chinese men's "previous habits and modes of life" and a "melancholic, suicidal tendency," the British mission's report indicates that exploitation, disease, and the deception of labor recruiters played greater roles in the workers' demise.[69]

The company decided quickly to wash its hands of the remaining workers. Of the survivors, a little more than thirty continued to California. Others remained in Panama or relocated to Jamaica to work as agricultural laborers. On September 9, 1854, Hoadley wrote to a firm in Havana called Messrs. R. Morrison & Co., inquiring whether the remainder of the company's contract for the indentured Chinese men, which amounted to more than four years, might be sold to the owners of plantations in Cuba. Hoadley did not explain why the company sought to rid itself of the contract, stating only that the "Chinese Coolies have not been found to answer our expectations in all respects," although he alluded to their poor health. Hoadley's inquiry asked Morrison and Co. "to inform me by first steamer whether our contracts with the Coolies can be disposed of in Havanna—if so, at what price—what would be the character of the treatment they would receive, and whether it would answer to send them to your island in *bad health*."[70]

Labor, Popular Political Power, and Sovereignty

The dynamics of negotiation among company officials, workers, and local officials changed with the establishment of universal manhood suffrage in Nueva Granada as a whole by the newly ratified Constitution of 1853.

Previous property-based limitations on suffrage were abolished, and all provincial governorships were now filled not by presidential appointment but rather popular election by the citizens of a given province, which included every married male and every male who was at least 21 years of age. The presence of provincial officials at Limón Bay was negligible, but as the railroad's works neared Panama City, Panamanian officials began to take an active role in negotiations between the company and laborers from Nueva Granada. When the officials took the side of workers against the company, Totten responded by attempting to go over their heads, registering complaints with the provincial governor and calling on Hoadley to make appeals to the national government of Nueva Granada through its representatives in the United States. In a letter of December 22, 1853, Totten reported that he planned to travel to Panama City to make a direct appeal to the governor of Panama. He was pessimistic about the outcome of this interview, however, because he believed that the governor's capacity to overrule the actions of his own subordinates had been weakened by the fact that his new office was now an elective one.[71]

As Totten prepared for an influx of workers in October 1853, conflicts between the company and Panamanian officials threatened to stall work on the line.[72] In Gatún the superintendent of the railroad station, Mr. Arnold, became embroiled in an argument with a man Totten called a "disorderly drunken person—native," and injured the man in the process. The injured party registered a complaint against Arnold with the local alcalde, who placed Arnold in the stocks and released him only after Totten arrived in Gatún with a district judge to denounce the imprisonment. Meanwhile, the superintendent of the railroad station at the town of Matachín, Mr. I. King, entered into a dispute with the alcalde of Gorgona after King tore down a number of buildings that had been erected near the station with the official's permission. King's justification for the demolition had been that the buildings—which Totten described as "huts of palm leaf and of little value"—had been constructed "with the evident intention of selling spirituous liquors to the workmen, and for other evil purposes—gambling, & c.—contrary to the rules of the work."[73] Most serious of all was the temporary imprisonment of one of the company's superintendents by the *juez*, or judge, of Cruces at the behest of the company's native workers. Mr. Gillett, the superintendent, had been in charge of a group of native laborers who had been detached from the railroad works to make improvements on the road between Cruces and Panama City. According to Totten, the company had entered into an agreement with the laborers specifying that each man was to be paid a total of $1.20 per day. Eighty cents of the $1.20 would be paid on a daily basis, and the remaining forty cents would be paid in a lump sum once work on the road was completed. Withholding a portion of the workers' daily wage offered the company some security at a time when it could recruit workers only on a casual or day-to-day basis. As Totten explained, "The object of this arrangement was, to keep the men under control, and to ensure their return to the Rail Road work."[74]

Conflicts involving company policy, local government, and the increased political power of newly enfranchised citizens raised deeper questions about sovereignty. Totten dearly wished for the support of a government with the capacity to enforce laws that redounded to the company's benefit, but he saw little hope of consistent backing from local government officials in Panama, especially after the 1853 constitution. He proposed a solution to this problem that he admitted was questionable from a legal standpoint but seemed optimal from his perspective as chief engineer of the company. He did not object to local officials' "taking cognizance of misdemeanors committed by the servants of the company personally; on the contrary, I only wish they would be more active in such cases." But when those "petty officers" contradicted the "rules and regulations of the company or the execution of an order given by the authorised agent of the company, especially in every thing relating to its management, I hold that the petty officials, *alcaldes* and c. have no such jurisdiction as they have exercised." In taking this position, he admitted, he was "not certain" whether he was "legally correct." These reservations, however, did not prevent him from sending a letter with his ideas to the provincial governor.[75]

Vigilantism in Colón/Aspinwall and the "Isthmus Guard"

The cornerstone of the first brick building on Manzanillo Island was laid in February 1852. In 1850, the provincial government of Panama had established the name of the incipient island settlement as "Colón," after the discoverer whom English-speakers know as Christopher Columbus. Nevertheless, at a ceremony marking the laying of the cornerstone of the first permanent building on the island, a prominent diplomat from Nueva Granada with close ties to the company suggested that the place be named "Aspinwall," after William H. Aspinwall, the driving force of the Panama Railroad Company and the Pacific Mail. As John L. Stephens confided privately in his correspondence, the name was his idea but he had decided it would be more seemly if the suggestion came ostensibly from an official of Nueva Granada. U.S. citizens and other English-speakers continued to refer to the place as Aspinwall, and the controversy over the name of the place would continue into the late nineteenth century.[76]

The power exercised by the company in Colón was considerable. By the end of 1852 the company's offices were located there, as well as wharves, warehouses, a blacksmith's shop, and other buildings essential to the railroad's operation. In contrast to city and town plans elsewhere in Panama, which radiated outward from a central plaza dominated by a church (or, in the case of Panama City, a cathedral), Colón was platted with a grid like those of the frontier towns created by Anglo-American settlers in the United States in the same era. The port grew rapidly, and by 1854 Colón had reached a population of approximately three thousand people and had about three hundred buildings.[77]

In 1852, an anonymous advocate for the company published a view on the sovereignty question in the *Panama Herald* that resembled that of Totten and was perhaps written by him. The writer asserted that the contract between Nueva Granada and the company granted officials "the total and exclusive right to make their own municipal laws and regulations for the city of Aspinwall" as well as the right to establish both its own police force and courts independently of Nueva Granada. He acknowledged that some might object to what he conceded was a "novel way of erecting independent laws under the sanction of a foreign government, and within the jurisdiction of its own laws." But he insisted that such an arrangement would serve the company and Nueva Granada alike.[78]

Despite these assertions, the actual contract between the company and Nueva Granada stated explicitly that the railroad and the transit route were to remain under the sovereignty of Nueva Granada, and it gave the company no right to establish its own laws, much less enforce them. Differences between company and provincial officials over sovereignty soon became a source of tension. Provincial officials in Colón were frequently greeted with disdain and sometimes violent resistance from U.S. and other foreign residents of Colón, including company officials and tenants who rented company land.[79]

On March 20, 1854, U.S. and other foreign residents in Colón organized a "vigilance committee" that claimed to supersede provincial judicial power. The organizers argued that the provincial government's failure to provide adequate police projection gave them both the moral right and the obligation to establish order themselves. Among the committee members' first steps was to seize control of the provincial jail in Colón, where they came into conflict not only with the prisoners inside but also the Panamanian policemen who stood guard. Hoadley, the company president, pledged publicly to support the committee so long as its existence was necessary.[80] The U.S. editor of the *Panama Star* dismissed concerns that the committee represented a sign that Panama would soon follow the path of Texas, which had been annexed in 1845 by the United States after an initial period of immigration from the United States. He cited what he perceived as the changed tenor of debate over annexation in the United States since 1848 and argued that conflicts over the expansion of slavery within the United States itself had made further territorial aggrandizement impracticable. A more feasible and economical approach was to leave Panama to Nueva Granada so long as international access to the transit route, or "neutrality," was maintained: "A free State, south of her [the United States's] slave-holding States, would never be permitted by the southern interest, and the establishment of slavery again on the Isthmus would not be submitted to by the north. The Isthmus, as a State of the Union, would be a perpetual thorn in her side—a bone of contention, and a source of trouble, causing more responsibility to the federal government than the present obligation that guarantees its independence and neutrality."[81]

Even as the vigilance committee continued its activities in Colón, a related experiment in sovereignty along the lines sketched out by Totten was getting under way in early 1854. The private police force known as the "Isthmus Guard" was commanded by Ran Runnels, a U.S. immigrant to Panama from Texas who had contracted with the company to improve roads along the transit route and who also ran an express company in Panama City. From the beginning of its operations on the isthmus, the company had employed men to round up and discipline workers who deserted or otherwise defied company authority. Despite these efforts, the route across Panama gained considerable fame outside Panama as a place of crime. Banditry on the isthmus even became the subject of a sensational novel about a fictional band of criminals known as the "Derienni."[82] Frequent robberies along the route represented a problem for the railroad and steamship companies not only because of the menace posed to their own property but also because Panama's reputation as a dangerous place threatened to drive potential customers away to Nicaragua or other competing routes.[83] The Panama Route received more bad press in 1854 when exploratory expeditions organized by Great Britain, France, and the United States failed to find an adequate canal route across Darién. Parties involved in the exploration suffered greatly as a result of a series of mishaps that included the exhaustion of food supplies and conflict with indigenous people.[84]

The guard under Runnels's command received its funding from the railroad company and steamship companies who shared a stake in the success of the Panama Route. On July 21, 1854, the provincial governor, José María Urrutia Añino, officially authorized Runnels, Totten, and a select number of local merchants including Gabriel Neira and Carlos Zachrisson, a Swedish immigrant, to work together with local police in the apprehension of criminals along the transit route.[85] On July 30, 1854, Runnels set off from Panama City with twenty men from Nueva Granada under his command to round up and punish people whom the guard identified as miscreants along the transit route. Members of the guard proceeded to capture a number of men accused of crimes including robbery and murder.[86] According to Horace Bell, whom the reader will meet again in Chapter 4, Runnels's success stemmed in part from his hiring of "some black negroes and some Spanish mestizos" as well as white men from the United States who infiltrated criminal gangs along the transit route. As Bell wrote, Runnels "sent his men out as secret agents, the negroes to work among the blacks who were suspected of alliance with the robbers, the Americans associating with the English-speaking riffraff and the mestizos with the native element." On at least one occasion and probably more, the guard hanged its victims from the fortifications of Panama City.[87]

Panamanian judicial records also indicate that the Isthmus Guard was the fruit of a transnational collaboration rather than a unilateral imposition by the company or a project to establish permanent U.S. sovereignty over Panama. In a case involving a man named Peter Hendry, who was accused of theft, Runnels testified to a Panamanian judge on February 23, 1855, that he had captured Hendry at the order of the provincial governor. One of the members of Runnels's guard, a man named Juan Bautista Trujillo, related that he had come to Panama from the province of Neiva and stated that he had worked under Runnels in the apprehension of Hendry along with two other men named Fruto de León and José Manuel Ramos.[88]

The Isthmus Guard ceased its activities in March 1855, after the completion of the railroad, and the vigilance committee in Colón seems to have been disassembled at roughly the same time.[89] Hoadley's correspondence indicates that the guard's short lifespan stemmed from the cost of maintaining the force and Hoadley's sense that its services were no longer needed. In a letter to Edward Flint of the Pacific Mail Steamship Company in December 1854, Hoadley wrote that he had authorized two thousand dollars per month for November and December for the operations of the guard. The need for the organization no longer existed, in Hoadley's opinion, and furthermore, he regarded the financial burden placed on the company for its maintenance to be unfair, given that other major commercial enterprises in Panama had failed to contribute financially to the guard yet benefited from its services. As he wrote to Flint, "If my views of the facts leaning on this subject are correct, this Company has paid altogether more than its just proportion, to sustain a guard from which your Company, the United States Mail Steamship Company, & the underwriters have alike reaped the benefit."[90]

Experiments in vigilantism in Panama resembled the organization of vigilante parties in California in the same era in terms of strategy and self-justification. Whereas vigilantes in California sought to establish control over territory that the United States had already claimed, however, vigilantes in Panama operated with the goal of carving out spaces within the sovereignty of another nation. In contrast to filibusters from the United States who sought to liquidate the sovereignty of other countries altogether, company officials preferred other means, including efforts to sway government officials behind the scenes and temporary measures that could be discontinued after they served their purposes.[91]

Bygone Days of California

Despite continuing problems with labor, the railway made rapid progress after Totten's resumption of control of the works. The bridge across the Chagres was finally completed on November 26, 1853. A locomotive was placed at Panama City in January 1854. A large force of laborers was assembled in Panama City under a superintendent named Mr. Young, and the road was extended from Playa Prieta over the plains surrounding Panama City, through coastal swamps, and then up the valley of the Río Grande. By April 1854, the size of the workforce had grown to some five thousand men and the company expected to increase that number by an additional thousand. Nine months later the two lines of the railway finally met. On January 28, 1855, a locomotive passed over the entire line from Colón to Panama City, and on January 29, paying passengers made the passage over the completed line for the first time.[92]

With the opening of the entire line of the railroad, a passenger could pay twenty-five dollars to a U.S.-owned company and travel from one coast to the other in less than four hours, provided the train did not experience mechanical difficulties along the way.[93] Companies such as the U.S. Mail and Pacific Mail could guarantee passengers arriving in Panama that a steamer would be waiting on the other side of the isthmus to whisk them away to California or wherever else they were destined. The increased coordination of steamship lines meant that a traveler could conceivably walk right off a ship, board a train, and then directly board another ship. With these improvements Panama secured its dominance over the Nicaragua Route, whose use fell off sharply after civil war broke out in 1855. The Nicaragua Route would not begin to recover until the late 1850s, and it would never again threaten the dominance of Panama in the nineteenth century.[94]

The railroad's opening was celebrated officially on February 16, 1855, when a locomotive trailing nine passenger cars and a single baggage car steamed with great fanfare between Colón and Panama City. On board were several prominent passengers, including the U.S. minister to Nueva Granada. As the train left the station at Gatún, it passed beneath an arch of flowers marked with the motto, "The problem is solved, success ever attends an enterprising people."[95]

Success was not the lot of other enterprising people on the isthmus, however, who found their livelihoods ruined or seriously disrupted by the railroad's completion. As the railroad made its conflicted way across the isthmus, it captured more and more of the international traffic that crossed Panama, with the result that an increasing number of boatmen, muleteers, and porters were driven out of their trades. Travelers' demand for food, lodging, sex, washing, and entertainment plummeted as they spent less time on the isthmus. Coins that had previously filled the pockets of workers in the transit and service economies were now channeled into the coffers of the Panama Railroad Company and its allies among the overland and steamship companies.

Writing in 1855, Justo Arosemena reflected that before the gold rush, Panama's transit economy had been so depressed that one prominent jurist had joked that if anyone wanted to visit Panama he should do so right away, for soon there would be nothing left to see. The subsequent rush of migration had given new life to that transit economy. But in Arosemena's view, Panamanians had done too little to convert their new riches into productive industries such as agriculture. On the contrary, agriculture had declined as a result of the gold rush, as workers abandoned the fields in favor of the quick acquisition of cash through labor in river and overland transit, where they could work when and how they pleased. Equally disturbing in Arosemena's view was the decline in artisanal production in Panama, as objects formerly made locally were driven out of the market by cheaper, imported goods that were snapped up by the country's cash-rich inhabitants.[96]

Gen. Espinar, writing four years earlier, had similarly noticed a decline in the local production of goods as men abandoned more traditional occupations to try their luck in the transit zone while foreigners threatened to replace them in the workshops, or *talleres*, of Panama City. Soon, Espinar predicted, the only artisanal production left in Panama would be cigar-making, and he thought even that trade would be rendered obsolete by machines. Hardship in the transit zone was augmented by the increasing demobilization of laborers from the Panama Railroad as the line neared completion. The small palm-thatched houses of cane that had been hastily constructed in the Arrabal to house immigrants who had flocked to the transit zone were now abandoned as their residents returned to rural regions.[97]

Something of the dismay experienced by working people in the transit zone after the building of the railroad may have been communicated by Tomás Martín Feuillet, an elite Panamanian poet, in a poem written in 1856 entitled "How Much?" In the poem, two black women in Panama City complain about the depressed state of Panama's economy and attribute their misfortune to people from the United States. Feuillet's mannered language sought to imitate the accents of Panama City's black population. One of the women exclaims that the land has been ruined since the arrival of "gringos" and that everything has become "American." Everyone seeks to speak English, according to the character, who expresses the desire for the earth to swallow up "those Yankees," whom she claims are worse than any plague or war.[98]

Writing in protest of a tax levied on bakeries in Panama City in 1855, a baker named Pío Luna referred wistfully to "those bygone days of California," when money flowed freely.[99] Robert Tomes similarly noted the changed aspect of Panama when he traveled to the isthmus in 1855 to write an account about the opening of the railroad. Tomes was in a good position to remark on changes in Panama since the onset of the gold rush, for in 1850 he had journeyed across the isthmus by bongo and mule. On his return to Panama, he disembarked in Colón rather than the port of Chagres, where his previous journey had begun. In 1850, Tomes had stepped ashore at a beach filled with "natives" demanding what he had regarded as exorbitant fees for transport upriver. Five years later, Tomes found himself walking down a gangway leading directly from his ship to a wharf owned and operated by the Panama Railroad Company.[100]

Tomes noted other differences as he made his way across the isthmus by train. Recalling his previous journey to Panama City by bongo and mule with a combination of bemused nostalgia and relief that he would never have to make such a trip again, he noted that the once-bustling river port of Cruces was now deserted, rendered "obsolete" by the railroad. A similar fate had befallen the town of Culebra, which had been transformed into a railroad station bearing the English name Summit. The only signs of the town's previous prosperity were a dilapidated groggery and a few "dark women" who attempted to sell oranges, pineapples, and bananas to train passengers. Even for as fervent an advocate of U.S. commercial expansion as Tomes, these were sad sights. Tomes compared the town of Summit to a rag torn from the skirts of the United States in the course of the nation's "helter skelter progress through the wilderness." During Tomes's first visit to Panama City, the streets had been thronged with foreign travelers, sometimes as many as two thousand when ships to California were scarce. Now he guessed that the resident expatriate population of Europeans and North Americans was no more than one hundred, including foreign consuls, merchants, and officers of the railroad and steamship companies. All these changes he attributed to improvements in the "regularity and rapidity of communication between the Atlantic and Pacific by means of the fleets of steamers and the Railroad." By diminishing the time that emigrants to California spent in Panama, these improvements left the inhabitants of Panama with "but little benefit from the transit."[101]

Conclusion

The world ushered in by the construction of the railroad was a far cry from the commercial paradise envisioned by Arosemena and other elite boosters of Panama City's transit economy at the beginning of the gold rush. Rather than a booming commerce, the railroad brought depression to Panama City, even as the gold and the number of passengers crossing Panama grew. Rather than a place of trade, Panama became increasingly a mere point of transit that goods and people passed over on their way to markets located elsewhere, in New Orleans, New York City, or Liverpool. Meanwhile, the proceeds derived from transporting passengers and cargo across the isthmus were diverted outside the isthmus as well, to New York City and, indirectly, to

Nueva Granada, which received an annual subsidy of three per cent of the Railroad Company's declared dividends upon the completion of the road.[102]

As significant as the technological change was the transformation of political order in the Americas. Panama's commercial importance in the colonial period had derived not simply from its status as an intersection in trade routes but also from Spanish imperial trade policies, which established the fairs on Panama's Caribbean coast as one of the few places in the Americas where licit trade could be conducted between Spain and the Americas. By the mid-nineteenth century, in contrast, no overarching empire in the Americas could aspire to impose its will on the vast network of trade that Panama now helped tie together. Merchants had a freer hand in determining where and when they would conduct their trade. The mere fact that products crossed the isthmus did not mean that Panama was necessarily a good place to do business.

Other factors beyond Panamanians' control figured in the making of a great emporium in the mid-nineteenth century. Cities such as Chicago or San Francisco drew their importance in part from the fact that they were confluences. They sat at the juncture of multiple trade routes, and their urban populations constituted important markets in and of themselves. In contrast, the population of Panama was relatively small, and the isthmus primarily served as a junction in a trunk line leading from New York City to San Francisco rather than as a confluence of routes leading to many different places.[103]

The hardships experienced by muleteers, boatmen, bakers, and tavern keepers in Panama paralleled in some ways the changes in mining in the goldfields of California itself. At the beginning of the gold rush, in both Panama and California, people with relatively little capital could earn cash quickly—in Panama by selling services to travelers, in California by placer mining and other techniques that did not require a large investment in technology. By 1856, in both Panama and California, the opportunities for small operators had diminished, as they found themselves increasingly marginalized by companies and corporations with financial ties to cities on the eastern seaboard of the United States. In the northern mining region of California, where gold was first discovered, the relatively easy pickings of the early gold-rush years had been largely picked by 1856, and placer mining had given way to more capital-intensive forms of extraction such as quartz and hydraulic mining. Mining of this kind required expensive equipment and involved a substantial initial investment. Many of the individuals or small groups of prospectors of 1848 and 1849 had retreated from the northern mines or relocated to places where gold could still be found close to the earth's surface, as in the southern mines. In neither place were these transformations linear in nature, and exceptions to industrialism persisted. But as the "days of gold" waned in California, so too did the "days of California" in Panama become a thing of the past, as the railroad company and steamship companies regularized, industrialized, and intensified ties between the two places.[104]

Boosters of the railroad in Panama had not foreseen the price that Panamanians and the nation of Nueva Granada would pay in terms of sovereignty. Whereas commerce and political autonomy had been closely linked in Panamanian political thought throughout the early nineteenth century, the building of the railroad had produced places on the isthmus in which the railroad company's officers effectively ruled, with little oversight by local political officials and sometimes in direct contravention of their orders. The Isthmus Guard was the most egregious and obvious of these incursions into local sovereignty. More enduring was the port city of Colón, which company officials did not even deign to call by its legislated name.

In Colón, the Panama Railroad Company created the first of many "enclaves" that would be made by U.S. companies on Latin American soil. Catherine LeGrand defines such enclaves as "economic zones created by foreign direct investment where capital, technology, management, and sometimes labor are introduced from the outside." As recent scholarship has reminded us, such "enclaves" depended on and were related in important ways to economic activities and social dynamics beyond areas under the direct control of the companies themselves. In the case of the Panama Railroad Company, Colón represented only one terminus of a rail line that led also to Panama City, where the company wielded far less power.[105]

Historians of Latin America have tended to regard enclaves as products of the late nineteenth and early twentieth centuries. The most infamous of these enclaves were those created by the United Fruit Company in Central America, Panama, and South America. But the classic strategies of the enclave identified by LeGrand were pioneered by the Panama Railroad Company in Panama half a century before, in the early 1850s. These same strategies were integral to the making of the United States as a transcontinental republic, as the Railroad Company became a vitally important link in the United States's own internal network of communication.

The Panama Route came to be dominated by capitalists from the United States, and the number of people who crossed Panama increased along with the value of the gold and silver shipped across its territory. Paradoxically, the railroad's growing importance for the United States corresponded with a slippage of Panama from the consciousness of people in the United States. Far fewer travel accounts were written about Panama between 1855 and 1860 than between 1849 and 1855, despite the tremendous increase in the number of people who crossed the isthmus. This decline reflected in part the decrease in time that travelers spent in Panama. No doubt it was also due in part to the greater familiarity of Anglo-Americans with the voyage to California, which was no longer a novelty by 1856. Moreover, travel by train lacked the adventure of traveling up the Chagres River in a bongo or on the back of a mule. When Charles Christian Nahl set out to represent the Panama Route in 1867 in his "Incident on the Chagres River," the image he conjured up was not a railroad car but rather a bongo filled with foreign travelers being poled up the Chagres River by Panamanian boatmen—a sight that had not been seen in Panama since before the completion of the railroad in 1855. Over the brief span between December 1848 and the beginning of 1856, Panama was effectively transformed from a place that in the estimation of travelers from the United States was worthy of consideration in its own right, perhaps even of settlement and annexation, into little more than a whistle stop on the way east or west.

Yet the victory of the company over the locally controlled system of transport was not total. Even after the inauguration of the railroad and the introduction of the *Taboga*, a few boatmen continued to transport passengers between Playa Prieta and ships waiting in the Bay of Panama. In the very shadow of the railroad station, Playa Prieta and the adjacent neighborhood of La Ciénaga represented points of resistance to the domination of steam power. To understand how people living in La Ciénaga could resist the grasp of the railroad company, it is necessary to understand another revolution that took place in Panama during the gold rush—one that took place not in the realm of communication but sovereignty, and electoral politics in particular.

Chapter 3

Sovereignty on the Isthmus

Boosters of the transit route across Panama in the early nineteenth century imagined that the success of the route hinged on its openness to trade from all nations. But the dream of transforming Panama into an emporium left unanswered the question of how to govern a route whose success depended at least in theory on its freedom from the designs of any single state. The beginning of the gold rush forced Panamanians to confront this question with an urgency that they did not anticipate before 1849. So, too, did reforms legislated in Bogotá in the early 1850s, including the abolition of slavery in 1852, the establishment of universal suffrage in 1853, and the making of Panama into a federal state in 1855. The idea of the emporium as idealized by Panamanian elites assumed at least implicitly that political power, like economic power, was to remain in the hands of those same elites. Yet the early 1850s saw powerful challenges to elite political power in the realm of electoral politics as well as the streets of Panama City and rural areas of the isthmus located to the west of Panama City. These challenges arose from popular groups' efforts to navigate what Alfredo Figueroa Navarro has characterized as two revolutions that converged in Panama during the early years of the gold rush. The first of these revolutions was the gold rush itself, and more specifically the resurgence of Panama's transit economy and its subsequent industrialization at the hands of companies from the northern United States. The second was the liberal political revolution that overtook Nueva Granada as a whole in the early 1850s.[1]

Governing a "Universal Point of Transit"

The most influential work of elite political theory to emerge out of Panama during the gold rush came from the pen of Justo Arosemena: *El Estado Federal de Panamá* (The Federal State of Panama), published in 1855.[2] Arosemena's father, Mariano, had participated with other members of Panama City's elite in the creation of Panamanian independence and alliance with Colombia in 1821. These men turned to the Hanseatic League of medieval Europe as a model for how a small state with aspirations toward international trade could solve the problems of sovereignty. The league, which experienced its zenith in the 1400s, was essentially a commercial alliance among cities in northern Europe. As Panamanians understood the league's history, the commercial and political success of the alliance derived from the member cities' "neutrality," meaning their adherence to a set of trading rules that applied equally to all and thus fostered trade for members and nonmembers alike. Though small in size, the cities had avoided conquest by larger states because those same states recognized that they were themselves among the beneficiaries of the long-distance trade networks maintained by the league. To conquer the league or any city within it would be the commercial equivalent of killing the goose that laid the golden egg. Like others who shared the Hanseatic ideal, Justo Arosemena was a strong supporter of free trade, or the elimination of taxes on international traffic across the isthmus, as part of a broader commitment to neutrality—an orientation that reflected an engagement with liberal thought more generally in the Atlantic world. He argued that the peculiar challenges of governing an international trade route could be handled only by a government based in Panama City, one that was largely autonomous if not entirely independent of Bogotá.[3]

The first effort to transform Panama into a "Hanseatic" state took place in Panama City in 1826, when a small cadre of rebels including Mariano Arosemena declared independence from Colombia. The rebellion was quickly suppressed with little violence by Colombian army officers who apparently failed to appreciate the advantages of the Hanseatic scheme. Nevertheless, the rebels had broached questions that would continue to trouble leaders in Panama, and the Hanseatic ideal would have a powerful influence on Panamanian political thought through the rest of the nineteenth century and into the twentieth.[4]

Revolutions of 1848: Liberals and Conservatives in Panama

Questions related to Panama's political future as an emporium to the world arose at a time when practices of electoral politics in Nueva Granada were undergoing a broader transformation that opened up new opportunities for previously excluded groups, including the rural poor, people of African descent, and some indigenous peoples. Electoral politics in Nueva Granada by the period of the gold rush were defined by a contest between the Liberal Party and the Conservative Party (or the Ministerial Party, as it was also known in the early 1850s). The presidential election of 1848 was won by a Liberal general, José Hilario López. Liberals in Nueva Granada claimed the ideals of liberty, equality, and fraternity that were also espoused by revolutionaries in Europe and elsewhere in the Americas in that most revolutionary of years. Compared with their republican counterparts in Europe, however, Liberals in Nueva Granada proved more successful at translating those ideals into law and political practice in the early 1850s. Among their signal achievements were the final abolition of slavery in 1852 and the ratification of what was perhaps the most radical national constitution in the world in 1853, one that established universal manhood suffrage with no exclusions based on either property or color.[5]

Although ideological differences between Liberals and Conservatives were often less than clear, important distinctions between the parties existed with regard to the issues of slavery, the church, and the boundaries of citizenship. There was little Conservative opposition to abolition in Panama, but elsewhere in the country, in 1851, Conservatives rose up in armed revolt against the Liberal government in opposition to the coming emancipation. Conservatives had a far closer relationship with the Roman Catholic church than did most Liberals, whose more radical adherents were enthusiastically anticlerical. Generally speaking, Liberals in Nueva Granada were also much more willing than Conservatives to lower barriers to suffrage and to allow formerly excluded men within their ranks, including former slaves. In the wake of reforms passed in the early 1850s, elite leaders of both parties found themselves obliged to bargain for support with men who had

previously been excluded from electoral politics because they lacked sufficient property or because they were enslaved. In an era when parties commonly fought one another not only at the ballot box but also in the streets
and on rural battlefields, popular support became essential for the winning
and maintaining of political power.[6]

The Geography of Party, Color, and Class

By the early 1850s the dichotomy between San Felipe and the Arrabal
emerged as a dividing line between Conservatives and Liberals in Panama
City. Though each party claimed adherents on both sides of the city walls,
the existence of widespread support for Liberals among Arrabaleños was
a generally recognized fact among both Conservatives and Liberals, and
el arrabal was used by members of both parties as a synonym for the Liberal
Party's popular supporters, particularly men of color and castas more generally. Until at least the mid-1850s, however, the most prominent Liberal
leaders were elite residents of San Felipe who often had close family ties
with Conservatives of the same social class and parish. Conservatives existed in far fewer numbers in Panama City, and their support was located
almost exclusively within the fortifications of San Felipe. As in Panama
City, party differences in other parts of Panama corresponded with geographical differences. In the province of Azuero, peasants became the driving force behind the Liberal Party. But in the neighboring province of
Veraguas, where agricultural land was concentrated in the hands of relatively few families, Conservatives predominated.[7]

Liberal support for abolition contributed to a close bond between the
party and people of African descent in Panama, as was the case elsewhere in
Nueva Granada in places such as Cauca and the Caribbean coast. There
were less than five hundred slaves in Panama by the time abolition took
place on January 1, 1852. Nevertheless, the ceremonial emancipation of the
approximately fifty remaining slaves in Panama City was a significant event
for people living on both sides of Panama City's walls, in that it marked an
important step toward full citizenship and the disassociation of people of
African descent from the hated institution of slavery. The elaborate ceremony at the *cabildo* of Panama City was presided over by the Liberal
provincial governor of Panama, Tomás Herrera, who was also a noted general. The main speaker at the ceremony, Eladio Briceño, welcomed the former slaves to freedom with words that reflected on the larger significance

of emancipation for Nueva Granada as a whole: "Today, the Republic gains hundreds of *granadinos*." Yet even as he offered encouragement to those who had just gained "the precious rights of liberty," he also warned that freedom "is not unlimited—the line between liberty and licentiousness is very thin."[8]

Fears of Caste War

Shortly after the abolition of slavery, a Conservative newspaper in Panama City called *El Vijilante* warned of what the author perceived as a breakdown in the proper order of Panamanian society. The newspaper asked, "What would become of us in this country if the relations that govern our mutual survival were broken, and if the cook, the servant, the protector and the protected, the honorable man who pays the worker his due, were to become enemies?"[9] The newspaper noted furthermore that the apparent decay of social hierarchy corresponded with what it described as a "very marked difference" between the Liberal and Conservative parties in terms of color, with blacks siding with the Liberals and whites siding with the Conservatives. Both developments suggested that Panama was only a step away from a "caste war," which the newspaper defined as a conflict carried out "according to no other basis than color."[10]

Although elite Liberals were more circumspect than Conservatives in this regard, members of the elite from both parties perceived the politics of Panamanian society's lower orders to be driven by race and class hatred and the pursuit of white women. Like members of white elites in other slave-holding areas of the Americas after the Haitian Revolution, wealthy white men and women in Panama lived in fear of a repetition of what they incorrectly imagined was the wholesale slaughter of the white population of Saint Domingue by slave rebels, a nightmare that was often condensed into the two-word phrase "another Haiti." Other terms that members of the elite used to characterize the feared slaughter of whites by blacks were *guerra de castas* (war of the castes) or, less commonly, *guerra de razas* (war of the races). *Guerra de castas* was used elsewhere in the Americas as well, including Mexico, where elites branded the rebellion of Mayan peasants that began in Yucatán in 1847 as a "caste war."[11]

El Vijilante warned that a caste war, once under way, would result in the "carnal debasement of the spirit," which would have particularly dire consequences for "our dear daughters and sisters."[12] In a thinly veiled criticism directed at elite Liberals in Panama City, the newspaper decried those who "beguile and demoralize the masses instead of instructing them, planting the seed of discord between the races, making use of principles they do not understand and pretend to profess."[13]

At the same time that *El Vijilante* marked former slaves as unfit for electoral politics and government posts, it denied that racial categories based on color had any relevance in themselves. Ultimately, *El Vijilante* concluded, "all of us belong to one race, the human race, and we should seek to punish vice and crime wherever it occurs and to praise virtue, the love of work, and education."[14] The Conservative newspaper argued that differences among colors and classes derived not from distinct natures but rather from distinctions in levels of civilization, which could be altered through education. *El Vijilante* held out the promise of eventual equality for former slaves, people of color, and others engaged in menial occupations. Until the future moment of equality arrived, however, the newspaper admonished new citizens of the republic to maintain an attitude of patient subservience:

> Ingratiate yourself with the authorities, and they will give you justice against the white man if indeed you are in the right. All of us are equal before the law, and if you do not acquire government posts as lofty as our own, it is because in barbarous times that have fortunately passed, your education was neglected by the men who called themselves your masters, and you have not yet made sufficient effort to acquire what you lack to become equal with other men of the earth.[15]

Gen. José Domingo Espinar defended himself and members of the masses (*el pueblo*) of Panama City against accusations of caste war in his *Resumen histórico*, published in 1851, one year before the final abolition. The people whom Espinar categorized as el pueblo included men of color and castas who earned their living with their hands, in agriculture, as laborers, or as artisans. Espinar was himself a man of the Arrabal, which by the early 1850s had become identified with the Liberal Party. Nevertheless, Espinar's own relations with elite Liberal leaders such as Mariano Arosemena and José de Obaldía were cool if not openly hostile. These tensions were brought to the surface in October 1850 with the spread of a rumor in Panama City of a plot to make Panama independent from Nueva Granada in which Espinar was implicated along with the U.S. editor of an English-language newspaper named the *Panama Echo*. If such a plot existed, it did not get very far off the ground. The newspaper editor was arrested, and Espinar himself denied any involvement in any plan to "revolutionize" the isthmus.[16]

Espinar's denials did not prevent Obaldía from denouncing him as the author of "the only caste revolution in the former territory of Colombia," a disparaging reference to the revolt led by Espinar twenty years earlier, in 1830.[17] In response to Obaldía's calumny, Espinar defended himself and members of el pueblo against the accusation of having planned a massacre of the city's white population or transforming Panama into "another Santo Domingo [Haiti]." He readily acknowledged the lower orders of Panamanian society still lacked sufficient education to fulfill the requirements for participation in a "democratic Republic." Rather than call for revolution, he spoke in favor of "a conciliation between the great and small children of God's great family." Like *El Vijilante*, he attributed el pueblo's deficiencies to a lack of education rather than some innate characteristic, biological or otherwise. In contrast to the Conservative newspaper, however, he called for concrete measures for the uplift of el pueblo and criticized members of the elite for neglecting their duties to educate the more humble members of the population. Unlike *El Vijilante*, which adopted a tone of stern admonishment in its address to the lower orders of Panamanian society, Espinar posed as a paternalist defender of el pueblo. His parrying of the charge of caste war was hardly a rousing call to mobilize the city's masses of the kind that Liberals would articulate only a few years later. But Espinar roundly dismissed the notion of caste war itself as an unjustified calumny against both himself and the people of the Arrabal.[18]

"El 18 de Mayo"

As evidenced by the controversy between Espinar and Obaldía, the gold rush stoked fears among Panama City's elite about the possibility of caste war even before the final abolition of slavery in 1852. Tensions between Arrabaleños and residents of San Felipe culminated in a battle between the two sectors of the city in March 1850 and again, more dramatically, on May 18, 1850. According to a correspondent from *El Día*, a newspaper published in Bogotá, the conflict in March began when a white man from the United States killed a black man in Panama City and then was allowed by Gov. Manuel María Díaz, a Liberal, to walk away without punishment. The correspondent wrote that this reluctance by the governor to punish a white foreigner enraged "the blacks of the Arrabal," who directed their wrath toward both "americanos" and Gov. Díaz. Shortly after the incident, another man from the United States encountered the former governor, José de Obaldía, in San Felipe and knocked his hat off in a deliberate display of disrespect.[19]

Two months later, in mid-May, the French proprietor of a printer's shop in San Felipe accused one of his employees of theft and took it on himself to imprison the man in his own house. On May 18 residents of the Arrabal armed themselves with machetes and stones and invaded the neighborhood of San Felipe to liberate the accused employee. After they succeeded in their mission and withdrew beyond the walls of the city to the Arrabal, a more general melee broke out between people in both sections of the city. Some U.S. immigrants in San Felipe mounted the city's fortifications and fired their guns into the Arrabal.[20]

An uneasy truce was finally established through the mediation of Gen. Tomás Cipriano de Mosquera, whose work on the Panama Railroad and in the express business had brought him to Panama City. Standing in the main plaza of Santa Ana, the principal parish of the Arrabal, Mosquera appealed to residents of the neighborhood to cease hostilities. Along with ex-governor Obaldía, a Liberal, Mosquera ordered that soldiers be stationed at the Puerta de Tierra, the principal gateway between San Felipe and the Arrabal. A further order was given to gather up the wounded and to locate and remove any men from the United States who had strayed into the Arrabal.[21]

On the next day, according to the correspondent from *El Día*, some "rowdies" attempted to "excite the people of the Arrabal again, not only against the foreigners, but also against the [Panamanian] whites, and against General Mosquera." People described by the newspaper as "the blacks" prepared to attack the gold seekers once again before Díaz appealed to them directly to desist. Later in the day, residents of the Arrabal insulted Gov. Díaz to his face, denouncing him as the puppet of the foreign population.[22]

The correspondent from *El Día* blamed the conflict on the weakness of the governor, whom he regarded as incapable of containing either the foreign population or the "blacks of the Arrabal," whom he characterized as enraged by the insolent treatment they had received at the hands of the *yankees* in both Panama City and Chagres. In a letter written one week after the conflict of May 18, Mosquera interpreted the violence as "a collision between the Americans and the blacks [*negros*] of the Arrabal." Like the correspondent from *El Día*, he blamed both sides of the conflict and what he perceived as the weakness of the provincial government. Such conflicts, he speculated, might also be the work of investors promoting transit routes across Nicaragua and the Isthmus of Tehuantepec who sought to divert traffic away from Panama.[23]

Black Political Power and White Immigrants from the United States

Although tension between the Arrabal and San Felipe was hardly new, it took on a different character as San Felipe filled with immigrants from the United States. Some of these immigrants were only passing through, but the shortage of ships in the Pacific in the early 1850s often meant that these travelers spent weeks in Panama City. At times the city housed a population of as many as two thousand immigrants, primarily gold seekers from the eastern United States. The abrupt surges and precipitous declines in population that accompanied the arrival and departure of ships put a serious strain on a city that before the gold rush had a population of perhaps four thousand.[24]

White immigrants posed a real threat to the exercise of political power of men of color in Panama in the early years of the gold rush, when their population on the isthmus swelled. If white immigrants had difficulty grappling with the economic power wielded by people of color along the transit route, they were equally taken aback when they encountered such men in positions of political authority. John Forster, for instance, evinced some surprise when he came across a Roman Catholic priest in Chagres whom he regarded as most definitely of African origin. While passing through the town of Gorgona, he was profoundly impressed by his encounter with the town's *alcalde*, an office that combined functions of a mayor and a sheriff. He described the man as a "half-breed-Spanish-negro" and a "generalissimo in civil affairs—executive judge and jury." Coming from a nation where the voting rights of blacks had been drastically limited if they existed at all, he was surprised by the power enjoyed by this individual, whom he called "the wealthiest man in the place." Taking careful note of what he labeled as the man's "harem," he described the alcalde as if he were an African king or an oriental sultan rather than an official of a republic.[25]

Mary Seacole described a conflict in the early 1850s between white men from the United States and an alcalde of Gorgona who may have been the same man encountered by Forster in 1849. When the alcalde ordered soldiers to arrest a white man from the United States for stealing from a party of Chileans, the arrested man's "brother Americans" surrounded the soldiers, "abusing and threatening the authorities in no measured terms, all of them indignant that a nigger should presume to judge one of their countrymen." In response, the alcalde gave an impassioned address to the men from the United States. As Seacole wrote: "With an air of decision that puzzled everybody, he addressed the crowd, declaring angrily, that since the Americans came the country had known no peace, that robberies and crimes of every sort had increased, and ending by expressing his determination to make strangers respect the laws of the Republic, and to retain the prisoner; and if found guilty, punish him as he deserved." According to Seacole, the travelers from the United States were "too astonished at the audacity of the black man" to offer any resistance and retreated from their pretensions.[26]

Seacole attributed resistance by people of color to the racial impositions of whites from the United States principally to former slaves from the United States who had acquired their freedom and immigrated to Panama. According to her, such men from the United States had arisen to "positions of eminence in New Granada" in the priesthood, the military, and "all municipal offices."[27] She summed up her opinion both of African Americans in Panama and the people of Nueva Granada more generally as follows: "I found something to admire in the people of New Granada, but not much; and I found very much more to condemn most unequivocally. Whatever was of any worth in their institutions, such as their comparative freedom, religious toleration, etc., was owing mainly to the negroes who had sought the protection of the republic."[28]

Seacole's comments about African Americans in Panama raise interesting possibilities. Seacole herself was among a number of people of African descent who immigrated to Panama from Anglophone areas of the Americas, including the British West Indies and the United States. The "mulatto" William Hance, whose escape from prison is recounted in Chapter 1, immigrated to Panama and owned a hotel there, as did another man of African descent from the United States named Joe Prince, who operated a hotel along the transit route and later in Aspinwall. The captain of the *Gorgona*, one of the steamers on the Chagres River, was a black man from the United States. African Americans also immigrated to Nicaragua and established themselves in San Juan del Norte during the gold rush.[29] But the one account by an African American from the United States about Panama that I have been able to find, by James Williams, makes no mention of African American immigrants to Panama and lacks any reference to blacks from the United States in political or religious office. Williams crossed Panama in 1851 as a fugitive slave and worked briefly in Panama City as a porter at the American Hotel before continuing on his way to California.[30] Seacole's evident chauvinism in favor of English-speakers and her disdain for Panamanians in general may have led her to underestimate the degree to which Panamanians of color were capable of mobilizing the ideals of popular republicanism in the early 1850s or of mustering their own resistance to acts of intimidation by white immigrants from the United States.

For the alcalde described by Seacole, defense of his right to exercise political power became of a piece with the defense of local sovereignty from foreign pretensions. Many white immigrants, by contrast, interpreted what they perceived as the insolence of black workers and political officials as a threat not merely to their own persons but also to their liberties as white men. A petition written by a number of white men from the United States in the midst of the conflicts of March 1850 is revealing in this regard. The petitioners directed a complaint to the president of Nueva Granada in which they attributed the recent disturbances involving residents of Panama City and immigrants in part to attempts by officials of color to enforce the law against white men from the United States. They also decried the Panamanian practice of imprisoning white men from the United States in the same cells as men who were not white. The "prejudice arising from color . . . may or may not be unwise," the petitioners wrote, "but it exists . . . and it would seem to be the part of prudent and judicious legislators to remove as many causes as possible of needless irritation."[31]

The petitioners made a rousing defense of habeas corpus and the right to a trial by a jury of one's peers—which in this case meant a jury composed of other white men from the United States. As one possible remedy for the conflicts, the petitioners suggested that a special court be established in Panama in which white men from the United States accused of crimes could be judged by fellow white men from the United States rather than Panamanian judges. The petition thus used the defense of the rights of white citizens of the United States to justify what amounted to a proposal to deny rights to black people in Panama and to suspend the sovereignty of Nueva Granada with regard to judicial proceedings involving white men from the United States.[32]

Encounters between different concepts of rights and racial deference led to legal innovations that would have lasting consequences not only for Panama but also for Nueva Granada. In response to the above-cited petition, the provincial legislature of Panama established the right to trial by jury within the province of Panama in June 1850. In 1853, Liberals in the national congress led by Panamanian representatives made reference to the same petition in presenting their ultimately successful arguments in favor of incorporating the right to trial by jury and habeas corpus into the Constitution of 1853—the first constitution to guarantee such rights in the history of Nueva Granada or Colombia.[33]

Black Liberals

The same constitution that recognized the right of habeas corpus also established universal manhood suffrage throughout Nueva Granada. The battle of May 18, 1850, as well as the elite anxieties and the scolding that appeared in the pages of *El Vijilante*, are evidence of the growing power exerted by Arrabaleños even before universal manhood suffrage. But with the expansion of voting to include all adult men, Arrabaleños became a more potent force in party politics. A distinct group of elected officeholders emerged from the Arrabal in the early 1850s, including Buenaventura Correoso, Juan Mendoza, and others. By the early 1860s these men and other Arrabaleños would occupy political offices on the state level. In the early 1850s, by contrast, Arrabaleños' officeholding was limited largely to the municipal level, to offices such as *alcalde*, secretary, or a seat on the cabildo. But officeholding of this kind still represented a significant victory for people who had been largely excluded from electoral politics before the Liberal reforms of the early 1850s.[34]

Foreign observers sometimes spoke of Liberals in the Arrabal as if they constituted a distinct political party: *el partido liberal negro*, or "the black Liberal party."[35] But in the 1850s Arrabaleños themselves eschewed racially explicit terminology and denied that race was the sole basis of their political organization. Such an explicit orientation around color could only play into the hands of members of the elite who argued that people of color were motivated solely by race hatred. Using the term *negro* or *los negros* in print in the 1850s was generally considered derogatory and was purposely avoided by Liberals, who preferred racially neutral terms such as "citizens" or *hijos del país* (sons of the country). José de Obaldía, for instance, denounced *El Día's* account of the events of May 18, 1850, for deploying the term "negros," which Obaldía found degrading. That he could accuse Espinar in the very same year of having attempted to foment a caste revolution suggests how, in elite political discourse, rejection of explicit references to race or slavery such as "negros" could coexist with fears of caste or race war.

Liberals in the Arrabal claimed to represent the interests not of *los negros* but rather of el pueblo, a term that embraced people of color but was not in itself limited by color or race. El pueblo could also be used in a more generalized sense to refer to "the people" of Panama or Nueva Granada as a whole. The conflation of the two meanings of the word in Liberal political discourse suggested that the patriotic core of the nation lay not in the elite but rather with the common people of the isthmus, and in the Arrabal in particular.[36]

Nevertheless, foreign observers were onto something when they noted distinctions between Liberals from the Arrabal and those from San Felipe. Though united under the banner of the same party, popular and elite adherents to the party had significant differences, as would become clear during the gubernatorial election of 1856. Elite Liberals regarded themselves as the natural leaders of the party and frankly feared the increasing power of men of color in electoral politics, while Arrabaleños stressed their rights as citizens to equal participation in all realms of politics. In December 1855 Mariano Arosemena noted with alarm in a letter to Nueva Granada's diplomatic representative to the United States that all the fourteen people recently elected to the cabildo of Panama City had been *gente de color*. The fact that most people of color in Panama City called themselves Liberals apparently did not assuage his anxieties, for the same letter spoke fearfully about the possibility of a coming war between blacks and whites. According to Arosemena, race would trump nationality in any such conflict. Breaking with the established norms of Liberal discourse, which forswore the idea of race or caste war and the use of "negro" in print, Arosemena wrote, "If the blacks [*negros*] are against the white *granadinos*, they are also against the white foreigners."[37]

Governing a Universal Point of Transit

Arrabaleños' power in electoral politics grew at a time when government itself in Panama was becoming less stable, in large part because of challenges brought by the gold rush. The best diagnosis of this crisis came from Justo Arosemena. Justo's father, Mariano, was an important figure in his own right in Panamanian politics during the gold rush, as a leader of the Liberal Party and the author of unsigned articles in Panama City's most important Spanish-language newspaper, *El Panameño*, which was closely associated with the

Liberal Party. Justo had a more intellectual bent than his father. As a young man he had studied in Bogotá and traveled to Europe and the United States, and he was fluent in English as well as Spanish. Justo served as an adviser to the Sovereign State of the Isthmus, a brief experiment in independence that began in 1840 and concluded with reintegration into Nueva Granada thirteen months later. By 1848 he had published a treatise on morality and had helped in the negotiations between the national government of Nueva Granada and the Panama Railroad Company.[38]

Justo Arosemena's brief political treatise, *El Estado Federal de Panamá*, combined an analysis of the problem of sovereignty as it took form during the gold rush with a proposal for a solution to that problem. As he recounted in *El Estado Federal*, Panamanian boosters of the Hanseatic ideal had achieved a long-sought victory in 1849, when the national congress of Nueva Granada passed a law that turned Panama into what was essentially a free trade zone. National and local governments alike were forbidden from taxing international commerce that flowed across the isthmus.[39]

Boosters of the transit route embraced the principles of economic thought advocated by liberals throughout the Atlantic world in the mid-nineteenth century, including a commitment to free trade. But opposition to taxes and tariffs took on a special imperative for Panamanians, who had learned after decades of economic stagnation that geography alone was not sufficient to guarantee Panama's prominence as a point of transit. Panama needed to offer not merely the promise of quick communication between one ocean and the other but also trade policies that did not hinder the flow of traffic across the route; otherwise, the route became vulnerable to competing routes across Mexico, Nicaragua, and other points in Central America, and also conceivably elsewhere in Nueva Granada, to the east of Panama City in the region known as Darién. This vulnerability was made all the more acute because ships could move rapidly and inexpensively from one route to another with the turn of a wheel.

Arosemena recognized that free trade gave incentives to international commerce in Panama, but he lamented the failure of Nueva Granada to provide Panamanians with sufficient alternative sources of revenue for the sustenance of local government in the early 1850s. Deprived of the right to tax international commerce, the provincial government and the cabildo of Panama City attempted to shift much of the burden of taxation to intra-isthmian traders and local producers in the early 1850s, levying head taxes on peasants, boatmen, muleteers, and owners of shops and taverns. This policy was bitterly resisted and was also difficult to carry out because the government itself suffered from a chronic shortage of labor. The same rise in wages that bedeviled the Panama Railroad Company, rural *hacendados*, and urban elites also made it extremely difficult for the provincial government of Panama or the cabildo of Panama City to fill positions in the government bureaucracy, including not only tax collectors but also more menial jobs such as street cleaners, cemetery maintenance workers, and policemen.[40]

When local government officials sought to get around the prohibition on the taxation of international trade by levying tonnage taxes on ships or on foreign passengers crossing the route, the Panama Railroad Company, the steamship companies, and foreign consuls in Panama City refused to pay and lodged vigorous protests with local and national officials alike, citing in their defense the very commercial legislation that supporters of free trade in Panama had pursued so assiduously in the years leading up to the gold rush. The most vociferous resistance to local efforts at taxation came from U.S. officials, who based their arguments on their interpretation of the Bidlack-Mallarino Treaty of 1846 between the United States and Nueva Granada, by which the United States had promised to guarantee the sovereignty of Nueva Granada over Panama and the neutrality of the transit route in return for access to the route under the same terms granted to citizens of Nueva Granada. Exasperated by foreign refusals to pay local taxes, Arosemena quoted William Shakespeare in a warning that he delivered to his fellow Panamanians in November 1850: "Alert, Isthmians! To be or not to be, that is the question . . . to be or not to be an independent people, with its own laws and own customs; to be or not to be the owners of this portion of the earth that our fathers bequeathed to us; to be or not to be the humble servants of other proud races that will never concede to us the title of 'civilized peoples.' "[41]

On a more abstract level, the conflicts between the Panama Railroad Company and local officials in Panama represented a clash between two dimensions of sovereignty: Panamanians' efforts to govern their own territory, or domestic sovereignty, came to be undermined by the United States's insistence that Nueva Granada adhere to its obligations as the sovereign signatory to an international treaty. Officials of Nueva Granada in both Panama and Bogotá interpreted those obligations differently but had little power to back up their interpretation in the event of conflict with the United States. As a result, the provincial government and other local governments in Panama such as the cabildo of Panama City were close to collapse during the years of the gold rush, understaffed and insufficiently funded, even as the gold that infused economies in the United States and Europe passed under their eyes.[42]

The Federal State of Panama

Arosemena's solution to this quandary, as outlined in *El Estado Federal de Panamá*, was to unite the individual provinces on the isthmus into a "federal state" that would remain autonomous from Nueva Granada except in certain matters including foreign relations, military operations (*fuerza pública*), and matters related to the national treasury and railroad across the isthmus.[43]

When the gold rush began, in 1848, the Isthmus of Panama consisted of two provinces. The province of Panama embraced Panama City and the transit route and stretched eastward into the Darién. To the west the province of Veraguas included much of the agricultural heartland of the isthmus and extended all the way to the border with Costa Rica. This bipartite division of the isthmus was revised by the national constitution ratified by the Congress of Nueva Granada in 1853, which broke the isthmus into four new provinces. The province of Panama remained largely intact, but Veraguas was divided into three smaller provinces: Veraguas, Azuero, and Chiriquí. The new constitution also transformed the office of governor from a position appointed by the president of Nueva Granada to an elected office.

Arosemena criticized the division of the isthmus into four provinces. He complained that the political fragmentation, combined with an insufficiently prepared electorate, had led to chaos. Citing recent conflict in the province of Azuero, he argued that the individual provinces of the isthmus were too small to support stable governments and advocated their consolidation into a single state government to be based in Panama City. Thus at the same time *El Estado Federal* advocated increased independence for Panama from the central government in Bogotá, it argued for a centralization of power on the isthmus itself.[44]

Arosemena's proposal for the creation of a federal state drew on earlier articulations of the Hanseatic ideal in Panama as well as the writings of Alexis de Tocqueville and the debates over federalism in the United States in the late eighteenth century. Freed from the burden of national laws that were inappropriate for a transit route, Panamanian state government as envisioned by Arosemena could provide a conduit for commerce that would benefit not only Panama and the rest of Nueva Granada but the entire world. In return for protecting Panama from foreign conquest and representing its interests in the realm of diplomacy, Nueva Granada would receive a regular subsidy from the revenues of the Panama Railroad Company and increased access to foreign markets by way of its special relationship to the transit route. Relieved of the immense cost of its own defense, the Federal State of Panama would fund itself through means other than tariffs on trade, including the sale of public lands and taxes on maritime trade.[45]

Although Arosemena regarded political independence to be Panama's "*gran desideratum*," as he put it in *El Estado Federal*, he treated Panamanian independence from Bogotá in this essay not as an immediate goal but rather as the most likely of a number of outcomes that could result if the Congress of Nueva Granada failed to approve his plan for federalization.[46] This rather guarded approach to the topic of outright independence was undoubtedly rooted in part in the fact that *El Estado Federal* was written as an appeal to the Congress of Nueva Granada, whose members might have looked unfavorably on overt enthusiasm for a complete break with the national government, especially given Nueva Granada's significant interests in the isthmus, which included a potentially lucrative contract with the Panama Railroad Company. Arosemena was nevertheless insistent about Panama's right to disassociate itself from the republic if it so desired—a right that was grounded in the fact that Panama had freely joined Colombia only after winning independence on its own from Spain. This vision of the republic as an essentially voluntary association was by no means peculiar to himself or to Panamanians. As Arosemena reminded his readers, the Congress of Nueva Granada had itself declared in 1854 that any of the republic's constituent parts possessed the right to declare independence from the whole.[47]

Arosemena's doubts about the desirability of Panamanian independence in the present (if not in the future) arose not from concerns about Panamanians' right to self-rule but rather from his reservations about what latter-day scholars have come to call "Westphalian sovereignty," the ideal of an exclusive, one-to-one correspondence between territory and state power. Drawing on James Madison's concept of divided sovereignty, Arosemena advocated gradations of sovereignty within a single nation under a constitution that permitted as much autonomy as possible to states. He expressed grave doubts about what he referred to as *la gran nacionalidad*, the concept of "great nationality," which for him implied a large, centralized government that held sway over a number of small nationalities or communities (*pequeñas nacionalidades*) with disparate if not competing interests.

Arosemena criticized centralized governments for imposing their wills inappropriately on smaller communities and for reducing all interests within the nation to that of a single national government. A centralized government would be sorely tempted to privilege its own interests in ways that diminished or detracted from the mission of an emporium such as Panama, whose vitality depended precisely on its neutrality, or its freedom from the sovereign claims of any single government.[48]

Drawing inspiration from Tocqueville's *Democracy in America*, Arosemena attributed the strength of democracy in the United States in part to the flourishing of local government on the community level. In Arosemena's view, a state might relinquish certain forms of sovereignty to a larger confederation of states without losing other kinds of sovereignty.[49] The political unit that mattered most to Arosemena was what he called *la verdadera sociedad*, or "true society," which was embodied in what he referred to variously as *poder municipal* (municipal power), *el municipio* (the municipality), and *el común* (community): the power of cities, small nationalities, and other close-knit communities to rule themselves according to their citizens' own interests. According to Arosemena's vision, a given people's capacity to exercise self-rule at this most fundamental level would be strengthened, not weakened, by delegating certain aspects of government, notably defense and diplomacy, to a larger alliance of "small nations."[50]

The Foundation of the Federal State

Arosemena had first proposed his project for the transformation of Panama into a federal state to the Congress of Nueva Granada in 1853, but its consideration by the national congress had been interrupted by a civil war that shook much of Nueva Granada beyond Panama in 1854. After this revolt was suppressed, he attempted once again in 1855, this time achieving success as a senator to the national congress. The state's constituent assembly, held in September, elected Arosemena himself as Panama's first chief executive. Arosemena took office on July 18, 1855, and served as such until September 1855. Francisco de Fábrega, a Conservative who had served as governor of the province of Veraguas, was elected vice governor.[51]

Opinion on the isthmus was by no means universally supportive of this transformation, and Liberals in Azuero were right to fear for their political future. The national government that emerged in the wake of the 1854 civil war refused to recognize Pedro Goytía, a Liberal, after he claimed the province's governorship, and in March 1855, the Conservative national congress voted to abolish the province of Azuero altogether. The subsequent establishment of the Federal State of Panama sealed Azuero's fate by breaking the former province into two sub-units, or "departments," which were both subordinated to the state government in Panama City.[52]

Elections for the constituent assembly charged with the creation of the constitution for the federal state revealed more evidence of the growing independence of the Arrabal from San Felipe. In April 1855, the Spanish-language section of the *Star and Herald*, known as "La Estrella," reported considerable "electoral agitation" in Panama City as well as the foundation of two separate political societies, one of which was based in San Felipe and the other in the Arrabal. An effort by elites to subordinate the two societies to a larger "Unión Electoral" fell apart after members of the society in the Arrabal insisted on altering a slate of candidates that had been presented to them by the corresponding society in San Felipe. In its assessment of the tension between the two societies, *El Panameño* referred to the society within the city's fortifications as "esclusavists"—a term that highlighted efforts by elites in San Felipe to exclude or minimize the participation of Arrabaleños in the electoral process. This charge was vociferously rejected by the editor of "La Estrella," Bartolomé Calvo, a Conservative who had immigrated to Panama from Cartagena. The label "escluvistas" was especially incendiary because it was nearly identical to the term "esclavistas," a word that referred to defenders of slavery in the early 1850s. The clear implication of this usage was that the same men who had earlier supported the bondage of black men were now attempting to impose their will on their fellow citizens in the Arrabal.[53]

Popular Politics in the City: La Ciénaga and Playa Prieta

The conquest of Panama's transit route was not as complete as Robert Tomes had imagined it to be in *Panama in 1855*. In Panama City the railroad company found itself stymied by the one significant remaining portion of the indigenous transit system across the isthmus: the connection between the railroad station and ships waiting in the Bay of Panama. As if in a provocation to the locally controlled transit system, the railroad company had placed its terminus next to Playa Prieta, the principal point of embarkation and disembarkation for passengers and goods in the parish of Santa Ana.

The beach and the adjoining neighborhood of La Ciénaga, like other parts of the Arrabal, were hit hard by the completion of the railroad. Arthur Mackenzie, a British subject who testified to U.S. officials after the violence of April 15, 1856, recalled that Playa Prieta had long been a place of conflict between immigrants and boatmen, the blame for which he attributed to the conduct of both parties: "some of the passengers, when drunk being insulting to the negroes, and the latter on the other hand disposed to overcharge and otherwise impose upon the passengers."[54] Moses Brinkerhoff, a conductor for the railroad company, similarly testified that after the inauguration of the railroad, he had "observed an evident disappointment on the part of the natives at seeing the passengers pass from the [railroad] cars directly to the steamships, and vice versa, without stopping, consequently depriving them of their previous profits."[55] Mackenzie concurred and added that boatmen from the Arrabal had also been driven out of work by the introduction of another piece of steam-powered technology: the small steamship known as the *Taboga*, which was owned by the Pacific Mail Steamship Company.[56]

Despite these changes, a small number of boatmen continued to ply their trade on Playa Prieta by the spring of 1856, transporting passengers and cargo between the shore and ships in the Bay of Panama. In Colón the railroad company had solved the problem of transshipment by building a wharf with waters deep enough to allow steamships and other ships to tie up. On the other side of the isthmus, however, shallow water and extreme tides prevented the creation of a deepwater anchorage near shore. The company owned a wharf adjacent to the station, and when the tide was high, the *Taboga* provided transportation between shore and ship. But when the tide went down, the *Taboga* listed uselessly against the wharf. This connection was thus the last point in the transit system across Panama that still resisted the discipline of the clock and remained subject to the natural rhythms of the tides. Though boatmen could not compete with the *Taboga* in terms of speed or capacity for transporting cargo, they could offer lower prices to immigrants and they could also set forth at low tide.

But this was a slender basis on which to build a livelihood. When the tide rose high enough to permit the operation of the *Taboga*, boatmen could offer little to customers other than a lower price, and by 1855 most of the passengers had already purchased through tickets that covered their transportation from one coast of the United States to the other. The limited work that remained in the international transit economy was supplemented

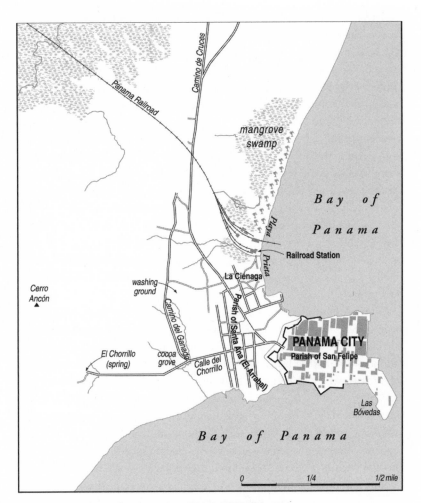

Map 5. Panama City and environs, circa 1856. By Philip Schwartzberg.

by the shipping of oysters, fruit, and other goods between Panama City and ports along Panama's own coast.

The plight of Panama City's boatmen was analyzed by no less a figure than Salvador Camacho Roldán, one of nineteenth-century Colombia's leading Liberal intellectuals, who served briefly as governor of the province of Panama in 1853. As he pointed out in a report on Panama's system of taxation, boatmen were squeezed not just by competition from the *Taboga* but also by new taxes adopted by the cabildo of Panama City to compensate for revenues it might otherwise have acquired through the taxation of international commerce. Camacho Roldán noted that there were approximately sixty bongos still at work in Panama's port, each with a crew of two men. Although as many as 2,500 travelers passed through the port every month, he guessed that far fewer were actually transported in these bongos, due to competition from the *Taboga* and sailing boats. Citing the recent arrival of a U.S. steamship as an example, he related that all 374 passengers had traveled from shore to ship in the *Taboga*, despite the fact that the boatmen had offered to transport passengers for as little as half a *real* per person. He doubted that the boatmen could hold on much longer if the cabildo did not move to lighten the tax burden on individual canoes.[57]

Two years later, on January 14, 1855, the boatmen themselves voiced similar concerns in a petition to the cabildo of Panama City. Though not all the petitioners could sign their own names, the petition exhibited a sophisticated analysis of the boatmen's plight that reflected their status as small proprietors with limited capital in a period of declining revenues. The petition protested a tax of two pesos per boat levied by the cabildo in 1854. This tax failed to recognize how the boatmen's business had suffered due to the *Taboga* and the completion of the railroad. A much more reasonable approach, they argued, was to tax their actual revenue rather than the value of their boats before business had gone bad. Without some relief, the signatories warned, they would soon be left with no legal way to sustain themselves.[58]

Although the course taken by the cabildo in response to this petition is unclear, the existence of the petition provides eloquent testimony to the boatmen's belief in their right to call on elected officials to defend their economic interests. Rather than address the members of the cabildo as supplicants, the boatmen presented themselves as citizens with the right to appeal to an elected governing body that was bound to protect the material interests of its constituents.[59]

Immediately adjacent to Playa Prieta was the neighborhood of La Ciénaga. Despite the marshy land located there, this small neighborhood was an attractive living space for working people. Located near the water, it was also only a short distance from San Felipe, where the majority of the foreign consumers of services resided. Best of all, the land in La Ciénaga was an *ejido* or communal land, governed by the cabildo. People who could not afford to live elsewhere in the city found in La Ciénaga a place where they could build a small thatched house without fear of being confronted by an owner of the property. These houses were called *casas de paja* or *casas pajizas*, meaning houses constructed of cane and roofed with palm fronds, or *paja*, as opposed to the ceramic tiles characteristic of buildings occupied by the city's elite in San Felipe. The presence of poor settlers in La Ciénaga and the proliferation of thatched houses in the Arrabal were controversial issues among members of the cabildo of Panama City. On one hand, some officials argued that the building of cane houses by the poor was an appropriate use of ejidal lands, so long as the residents were truly deserving of the cabildo's charity and paid a small rent of some kind to the cabildo. Others argued that the presence of thatched houses represented an intolerable fire threat in a city that had seen devastating infernos in the eighteenth and early nineteenth centuries. According to this view, settlers in La Ciénaga were squatters who had no right to build individual houses on the commons and whose presence kept the cabildo from earning a handsome sum by privatizing or alienating the land and selling it to private individuals at auction.[60]

The political hand of the settlers in La Ciénaga was strengthened by the weakness of local government in Panama, from the cabildo up to the provincial level. Elected officials could emit decrees, but that did not mean they could enforce them. This weakness was apparent from the start, when Governor José de Obaldía issued an order that made all casas pajizas illegal in the parishes of San Felipe and Santa Ana. Having made this decree, however, Obaldía faced a basic problem: no one could be found to enforce the law. A lack of police power in the suburbs of the city made the eviction of residents of ejidos extremely difficult to carry out. Even when police were available for the task, they were often loath to take drastic action against people who might easily be their own neighbors. This problem arose once again, in November 1852, after the cabildo outlawed thatched houses in La Ciénaga. In a letter written to the cabildo, the owner of a house with a tiled roof complained that the local police officer had refused to enforce the law. The police officer—one José María de León, nicknamed "Moñita"—had informed owners of thatched houses that they should have no fear of fines from the cabildo, and that in this regard he had the support of his patron, a wealthy land speculator from San Felipe and sometime member of the cabildo named Antonio Planas. The alcalde of Santa Ana offered his condolences to the irate homeowner but explained that he was powerless to convince Moñita to change his ways, despite the fact that he himself had appointed Moñita to his position.[61]

In October 1852 a group of women and men identifying themselves as *vecinos de la Playa de San José*, "residents of San José Beach," submitted a

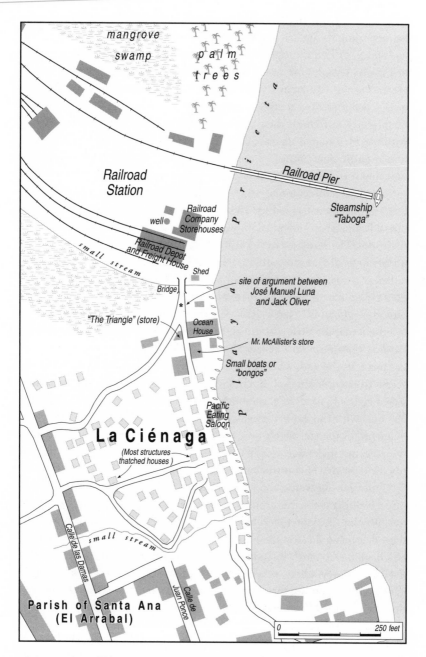

Map 6. La Ciénaga and the grounds of the Panama Railroad Station, circa 1856. By Philip Schwartzberg.

request for a postponement of their eviction from ejidal lands in the Arrabal, appealing to the cabildo to attend to the "clamor of suffering humanity" and to defend the rights of the "*pueblo*," meaning the common people of Panama City.[62] One month later, in November 1852, Governor Tomás Herrera wrote that "many women who live in the suburb called 'La Ciénaga' " had presented themselves at his office to protest an order by the cabildo either to remove their casas pajizas or to replace the thatched roofs with tile. He ordered the cabildo to grant the petitioners a grace period of four months, due to the difficulty of acquiring building materials during the rainy season as well as the high price of labor.[63]

In a fusion of colonial and republican political discourse, male and female petitioners begged for charity at the same time that they used the liberal language of individual property rights to defend their occupation of the ejidos. The result was a novel legal argument: petitioners defended the preservation of ejidos or communally held land not as an alternative to but rather as a guarantee of individual property in the form of buildings that they as individuals had constructed on land that belonged to the community as a whole. In March 1852 Saturnino Cano wrote in protest of an eviction order for a palm house he had constructed just outside the walls of Panama City near La Ciénaga. To bar casas pajizas from the beaches of Panama City, he said, would deprive men who made a living from the sea access to their livelihood. Such an order constituted a violation of "the sacred right of property," for as he pointed out, he had constructed his own building with the explicit permission of the cabildo. It was all the more shameful for the fact that it hurt the people who could least defend themselves against inclement weather, many of whom had not even managed to pay for their newly constructed homes.[64]

Confusion regarding the exact limits of the ejidos in the Arrabal also made it difficult for the cabildo to act against people it defined as squatters. Writing in September 1852, the alcalde of Santa Ana expressed his wish that he could stop the building of thatched houses along the eastern beach of the Arrabal, including the neighborhoods of Rajaleña and La Ciénaga. Nevertheless, whenever he confronted the owners of these newly built structures, they responded by thrusting crude deeds in his face that they claimed were proof of their rights. If he moved to expel people, he feared that his actions would be construed as an "attack against private property."[65]

In January 1853 the alcalde of Santa Ana wrote again to lament that he had been completely ineffectual in clearing the neighborhoods of La Ciénaga and

San José, whose residents informed him that they were prepared to pay "a thousand fines" rather than abandon their homes. In exasperation, he exclaimed against the "character of the *istmeños* [Isthmians]," who seemed hopelessly fractious to him.[66] One month later, another petition signed by the "residents of the neighborhood of La Ciénaga" issued a protest against attempts to fine them and push them to the outskirts of the city, away from their place of work. If they could afford to pay such a fine, they reasoned, they would not be living in La Ciénaga in the first place. In an attempt to shame the men of the cabildo, the petitioners asked the *cabildantes* to consider the effects of their actions on the children of La Ciénaga, who would no doubt starve if their mothers were put in jail because they were incapable of paying an unjust fine. If such a pathetic vision did not move the cabildo, then it could at least offer to pay the residents a compensation for the loss of their hard-won property.[67]

The struggle over La Ciénaga intensified toward the end of 1854 as a result of the Panama Railroad Company's decision to build its station immediately to the north of the neighborhood. The railroad company and the poor working population of Panama City had been drawn to the area around La Ciénaga by the same attractions: relatively cheap land and access to the waterfront. The railroad company's contract with the national government of Nueva Granada had given the company the right to claim any private or public land in Panama that was necessary for the completion of the railroad, provided that the company gave just compensation to the owner of that land. Citing this clause in the contract, the company presented a claim on La Ciénaga to the newly formed state government. Justo Arosemena made his own position on La Ciénaga clear when he gave his assent to the company's claim in July 1855. Finally, the people of La Ciénaga seemed to have met their match: both the new state government and the most powerful company in Panama were now aligned against them and their thatched houses. But when the company moved to make good on Arosemena's grant, it found its way impeded by counterclaims to the same land advanced by foes both small and large.[68] Members of the cabildo saw this move by the state government as a clear infringement on its own domain and contested the state's right to alienate the commons to any private entity. People who claimed to be property owners in La Ciénaga likewise protested.[69] They included not only poor owners of casas pajizas but also wealthier real-estate speculators, among them August Fretz and José María Alemán. Fretz, a U.S. citizen, adopted the same legal logic as the poor owners of thatched houses, claiming he had constructed buildings on ejidal land that he had rented from the cabildo. In January 1856 he accused the company of desiring the land for speculation rather than completion of the railway. Any alienation of land that deprived him of the ownership of buildings constituted a violation of his contract with the cabildo.[70] Alemán, in contrast, argued that he was the true owner of La Ciénaga, having purchased it in 1854, even as the cabildo of Panama City maintained that it was the legal proprietor of the land.[71]

The resulting stalemate benefited the poor residents of La Ciénaga in their efforts to retain control of the houses that they had built. As long as no single claimant prevailed, no one could contest their presence in what had become one of the most coveted areas of Panama City. Arosemena, president of the state of Panama, had ruled against them, but they still enjoyed the protection of at least some members of the cabildo: now popularly elected, it included men of color from the Arrabal itself and steadfastly defended the status of La Ciénaga as an ejido.

The railroad company's efforts to acquire La Ciénaga inspired considerable enmity among residents of La Ciénaga and the Arrabal more generally. This antagonism was sensed by Arthur Mackenzie, who remarked that "an ill feeling" that had been "created among the negroes by the fact that the Railroad company had made a demand on the General Government for that part of the suburbs of the city known as the Cienaga, and which is inhabited by them, and from which they feared they would be driven without compensation."[72]

That some of these "negroes" were themselves ex-employees of the railroad company, laborers who had been decommissioned on the railway's completion, was an irony that was not lost on Mariano Arosemena, who noted that the most vociferous enemies of the alienation of public lands to the Panama Railroad Company were people whom the company itself had brought to Panama to work as laborers.[73] As the boom time known as La California was banished to the past, many of the people who had migrated to Arrabal at the beginning of the gold rush either returned to their places of origin or departed for other points, leaving empty houses in their wake. The depleted ranks of the Arrabal were partially replenished by other newcomers: laborers whom the company had recruited to Panama from places such as Cartagena and Jamaica and who remained in Panama after the heavy work on the railroad was completed. By December 1855 Mariano Arosemena worried that these former workers and their allies in the Arrabal, who viewed the railway as "ruinous" for the entire isthmus, would soon join forces to destroy the railroad "with a single blow."[74]

Travails of the Federal State

From the very beginning, the Federal State of Panama experienced serious challenges to its legitimacy, starting with the resignation of its chief executive, Justo Arosemena, on September 28, 1856, some two months after beginning his term. The circumstances surrounding his abrupt departure are not clear. He had proved adept in the legislative struggle that culminated in the creation of the federal state, but he evidently proved less adroit at navigating local politics in Panama itself. On his resignation, Arosemena was replaced by Francisco de Fábrega, the Conservative landholder, or *hacendado*, from Veraguas.[75]

Despite Arosemena's hope that the creation of the federal state would provide a sound financial footing for government in Panama, the state that Fábrega inherited in the fall of 1855 was a financial disaster. As a condition of the state's establishment, the newly formed government inherited the debts of the provinces it had swallowed up, which were substantial. Even worse, Fábrega found it nearly impossible to raise new revenues using the means of taxation established in the new state's constitution. The national government offered no financial help—despite the fact that it received an annual payment from the Panama Railroad Company as part of its contract with the company. Panamanian efforts to establish a tonnage tax on ships visiting the isthmus were roundly opposed by both the steamship companies and the Panama Railroad Company. Fábrega could respond to these refusals with little more than paper exhortations to the companies in question and pleas for help from the executive power or the presidency of the republic.

On January 4, 1856, the fiscal crisis of the government had reached such a state that Fábrega found himself in the awkward position of writing to Gen. Pedro Alcántara Herrán, Nueva Granada's envoy to the United States, for help in securing a loan from a bank in the United States to reestablish the state's finances. As security, Fábrega offered to pledge the state's own government buildings in Panama City. If the state government defaulted, in other words, it would be cast literally into the streets. As he explained in one desperate letter to the central government, he was almost totally bereft of military force besides a small gendarmerie in Panama City whose already low salaries the state could barely afford to pay. Only about one hundred soldiers from the permanent army were stationed in Panama, and they were mostly employed guarding prisoners in jails around the state.[76]

Rebellion in Azuero

Fábrega's already difficult situation was made worse by a rebellion on the Azuero peninsula, an agricultural area west of Panama City. The Conservative Fábrega was the patriarch of the wealthiest and most prestigious family in the province of Veraguas, located to the north of Azuero. Before becoming vice governor of the federal state, he had been governor of Veraguas. In 1854 troops under his command had come into conflict with Liberal soldiers under the command of the Liberal governor of the province of Azuero, Pedro Goytía, who was himself from a landholding family of considerable wealth. The Goytías had a longstanding rivalry with Conservative families on the peninsula of Azuero concerning lands located in the area around Parita. Competition for land in the region may have been intensified by the demand for agricultural goods from the swelling population along the transit route.[77]

In his public pronouncements Goytía framed the conflict between himself and his Conservative foes as a battle over principles. The Liberals under his command consisted primarily of peasant smallholders, men of color and castas more generally whom he and other Liberals glossed as "el pueblo." Liberals won the first election for governor of Azuero in 1854 and then moved to consolidate their power in the province by ousting the Conservative vice governor. In response, Conservatives rallied support from the neighboring province of Veraguas and adherents of the Fábrega family. With support from Fábrega, a Conservative army sought to overthrow the Liberal provincial government but was beaten back by Liberal troops. Following their victory, Liberals expropriated lands claimed by Conservatives in the province, and Goytía declared himself governor.[78]

For Liberals in Azuero, then, the establishment of the Federal State of Panama and the ascent of Fábrega in 1855 represented frustrating defeats. The founding of the federal state resulted in the liquidation of the province of Azuero. The resignation of Arosemena led to the rise of the Liberal Goytía's worst enemy, the Conservative Fábrega, to the most powerful political office on the isthmus. Fábrega's Liberal enemies from the erstwhile province of Azuero did not take long to register their opposition to their old foe. On January 14, 1856, a state official in the interior wrote to inform Fábrega's government that Goytía was fomenting a revolt against the state government that was to begin with resistance to the payment of taxes imposed by the state treasury. According to the prefect, Goytía's forces had three hundred rifles and some cannons.[79] Six days later the citizens of the town of Parita submitted a petition protesting what they characterized as the exorbitant taxes levied by the state government. The petition claimed to the represent *el Pueblo de Parita,* "the people of Parita," and based its authority on the constitution of the republic and the principle that taxation without proper representation was a violation of the sovereignty that resided not in the state government but in the body of "el pueblo."[80]

The Phantom of Filibustering

As Fábrega struggled as the head of an impoverished state government to suppress a popular Liberal revolt in the interior, he faced what was conceivably a far greater threat, not simply to the state government but to the future of Nueva Granada's sovereignty over the isthmus itself. Toward the end of January, Fábrega communicated to Bogotá the existence of rumors that Col. Henry Kinney, the New Orleans–based filibuster, was contemplating an attack on Bocas del Toro, on the Atlantic coast of Panama near the border with Costa Rica. Rumors of filibustering were not new to Panama City: Juan José Flores, a former president of Ecuador with close associations to U.S. filibusters, had been a fleeting presence in the city in the early 1850s. But the danger of filibuster invasion took on a grim new reality following William Walker's conquest of Nicaragua at the end of 1855. Walker, a native of Nashville, Tennessee, had organized a filibustering mission that invaded Baja California and then Sonora in 1854. Walker declared himself president of Sonora but shortly afterward surrendered to U.S. troops, who carted him back to the United States to face charges of violating neutrality laws—charges of which he was soon acquitted by a sympathetic jury.[81]

In 1855 Liberals in Nicaragua invited Walker to aid them in a civil war against the nation's Conservatives. Walker arrived in June of that year with a number of recruits from the United States and quickly took control not only of the Liberals' military effort but also of the national government of Nicaragua. But Walker's seizure of power was soon contested. By the end of 1855 his forces faced a military alliance composed of troops from the other republics of Central America, Nicaraguan Conservatives, and many of Walker's erstwhile Liberal allies.[82] Though Nueva Granada was not officially a belligerent in the conflict, its envoy to the United States traveled to Costa Rica at the beginning of 1856 to pledge support for the Central American alliance.[83]

Filibustering and efforts in the U.S. South to expand slavery were intimately related in the mid-1850s, although not entirely synonymous. Walker himself vacillated before deciding to re-establish slavery as a way of attracting support from slaveholders and their supporters in the South. After officially pronouncing himself president of Nicaragua following a seriously flawed election in July 1856, he re-established slavery as a legal institution in Nicaragua on September 22, 1856.[84]

Walker's activities were reported in both the English- and Spanish-language press of Panama City, and rumors of filibuster expeditions permeated political commentary in the city in the early months of 1856. Though Fábrega's January letter stated that he no longer feared an imminent attack by Kinney on Bocas del Toro, he warned the central government that the pitiful number of national troops on hand in Panama was entirely insufficient for repelling any kind of foreign attack against Nueva Granada. The threat posed by filibusters, in his view, confronted not only Mexico and Nicaragua but Hispanic Americans as a whole: "The examples of Baja California and Nicaragua, etc., offer us ample evidence of a new kind of enemy against which the weak Hispanic American nationalities must prepare to defend themselves."[85]

¿Otro 18 de Mayo?

As if the impoverishment of the state government, the rural rebellion, and the threat of filibuster attack were not enough, Fábrega faced yet another challenge to his authority in February 1856. Panamanian officials arrested a U.S. sailor on liberty in Panama City from his ship, the USS *St. Mary's*, which was then in port. The U.S. consul, an ill-tempered veteran of the U.S.-Mexico War named Col. Thomas W. Ward, denied the Panamanian officials' right to imprison the man. With the threat of using U.S. naval forces to forcibly retrieve the sailor from jail, Ward demanded and received the sailor's release from the prefect of the Department of Panama, who was serving as acting governor in Panama City while Fábrega was repressing the Liberal revolt on the Azuero peninsula. Fábrega received the unwelcome news while he was in Santiago, the capital of the former province of Veraguas.[86]

On his return to Panama City, Fábrega found himself in an increasingly hostile environment. Conservatives were a distinct minority in Panama City, and the animosity of Liberal Arrabaleños to his administration was well known. Now he was confronted by the imperious demands of an irascible U.S. consul and officers of the U.S. Navy. Fábrega felt that the state government had no choice but to release the U.S. sailor, whatever his crimes. The military resources available to him as governor were entirely insufficient to stand in the way of either the consul or the USS *St. Mary's*. Yet he was even more fearful of the Arrabal and the likely reaction of popular Liberals to any attempt by the United States to use force to retrieve the sailor. From Fábrega's perspective, the existence of a considerable "foreign population" in Panama City was a positive thing, as it offered a buffer against a "class war" between the city's own residents. But the controversy over the U.S. sailor threatened to upset this delicate balance. Recalling the battle between Arrabaleños and U.S. immigrants in Panama City nearly six years before, he voiced his determination to avoid what he described as "the barbarous scenes that took place in Panama City in May of 1850," a reference to the conflict between Arrabaleños and gold seekers on May 18, 1850.[87]

By the end of March 1856, after Fábrega returned from his campaign in Veraguas and Azuero, Panama City was filled with tension. Having suppressed the revolt by popular Liberals in Veraguas, Fábrega now faced the enmity of popular Liberals in the Arrabal as well as the U.S. consulate. The decision by the prefect of Panama to relinquish the sailor to the U.S. consul had become a source of humiliation for Fábrega's government, with Liberals accusing Fábrega's administration of knuckling under to U.S. threats or, perhaps worse, acting in complicity with the U.S. consul and the U.S. Navy. Despite these rumors of a traitorous alliance, however, the hostility continued between Fábrega and the consul, who broke off all communications with Fábrega's government following the return of the sailor to his command.

Instability on the Isthmus

Justo Arosemena had hoped that the creation of the Federal State of Panama would put an end to the seeming chaos of Panamanian politics during the early years of the gold rush. During the first few months of the state's existence, however, the problems he had identified only worsened. The state government was no less impoverished than the provincial governments it had replaced and whose debts it had inherited. Rather than settle the problem of rural rebellion in Azuero, the state appeared to worsen it by placing Liberal peasants' most hated foe in the office of governor. The officers of transit companies and foreign diplomats treated Panamanian officials with no less disdain or disregard than had been the case before the federal state's creation. Liberal and Conservative elites were increasingly at odds with each other, even as they shared a fear of caste war and what they perceived to be its likely effects: murder, mayhem, and the rape of white women.

The tensions that beset Panama City in March and May 1850 and February 1856 were similar in many ways. In both instances, elite Panamanian officials found themselves caught between two contending pressures. On one side, there was the U.S. refusal to permit white men from the United States to be judged according to local law. On the other side, there was pressure from people of color from the Arrabal, who by 1856 had a long history of contending with the racialized impositions of white immigrants from the United States. In both 1850 and 1856 people of color from the Arrabal had insisted on the enforcement of local laws and the prosecution of U.S. citizens for crimes committed on national soil. And in both instances, elite Panamanian officials had ultimately conceded to U.S. demands to turn over the accused white men and thus opened themselves up to accusations of treason from the Liberal Arrabal. Although Fábrega was a Conservative, elite Liberals also felt caught between these contending pressures. Manuel María Díaz, the governor during the conflicts of March and May 1850, was a Liberal. As revealed by the private correspondence of Mariano Arosemena, elite Liberals did not necessarily welcome black political mobilization any more than their Conservative counterparts, even as they maintained what was at times a highly frayed alliance with el pueblo on the other side of the city's fortifications.

Yet important differences also existed between 1850 and 1856. In 1856, in contrast to 1850, men in the Arrabal had the right to vote, and they formed the most populous element of the Liberal Party's adherents in Panama City. The transformation of the governorship into an elected office in 1853, followed by the establishment of Panama as a federal state in 1855, made men of color and other castas even more important for the success of both Conservatives and Liberals at the ballot box and on the battlefield, as evidenced both by the election for the constituent assembly of the new state in 1855 and the battles between Liberals and Conservatives in Azuero in 1854 and 1855. Panama City's elite, meanwhile, had become increasingly divided along party lines. In May 1850 the Conservative Tomás Cipriano de Mosquera and the Liberal José de Obaldía had managed to put aside their partisan differences and had joined together at the Puerta de Tierra to persuade Arrabaleños to retire behind the city walls. But the possibilities of an elite white alliance across party lines had declined considerably by the early months of 1856 as the Conservative Fábrega led soldiers against Liberal troops in Azuero. The reforms that had weakened the bonds of patriarchy by placing men from the Arrabal on an equal plane in terms of citizenship with men from San Felipe also made it far less likely that Arrabaleños would defer to the commands or entreaties of elite men from San Felipe. Although women living in La Ciénaga had no right to vote, both they and the men in their midst had proved adept at mobilizing a republican language of rights to defend their property against the ambitions of the railroad company and elite land speculators. The combination of mobilization by resident men and women, support from elected members of the cabildo, and conflicts between the claims of the railroad company and elite speculators had kept La Ciénaga out of the grasping hands of the company even as it operated what amounted to a virtual mini-state on the other side of the isthmus in Colón.

The state of affairs that prevented any party from establishing a monopoly over La Ciénaga mirrored the stalemate that hovered over the state of Panama as a whole. The dispute in February 1856 over the prefect's return of the U.S. sailor had revealed Fábrega's precarious and increasingly untenable position. In arresting and imprisoning the U.S. sailor, Panamanian officials had enraged the U.S. consul and U.S. naval officers. By returning the sailor to his ship, the prefect and by implication Fábrega had aroused the ire of Liberals in the Arrabal. Fábrega found himself hemmed in by contradictory forces with incompatible demands: working-class Liberals in the Arrabal, their elite counterparts in San Felipe, Goytía and the Liberal peasants in Azuero, the Panama Railroad Company and the steamship companies, the U.S. consul, and the U.S. Navy. The national government, with its capital in Bogotá, offered little help: only a pathetically inadequate number of national troops and no funds from the national treasury. Meanwhile, rumors of a possible filibuster attack continued as Walker and his allies battled Central American troops in Nicaragua.

It is little wonder that Fábrega lived in fear of a repetition of the events of May 18, 1850. With neither the Conservative governor nor any one of these groups capable of monopolizing power over the transit zone, a stalemate of sorts had emerged by the beginning of 1856—one that permitted the railroad company to continue its operations but nevertheless was highly unstable.

Conclusion

Though connected to each other by the regularly scheduled departures and arrivals of steamships, California and Panama were different in important ways by 1856. Yet there were also significant similarities. Both were newly minted states located far from their respective national capitals. Women were excluded from the franchise in both places, as they were in every other republic in the world in the mid-nineteenth century. But in the United States and to a lesser extent in Nueva Granada, advocates of women's suffrage claimed a more significant place in national politics after 1848. In the United States the key event that year was the convention of abolitionists and suffragists in Seneca Falls, New York, whereas in Nueva Granada it was the rise of the Liberal Party, which raised the question of women's suffrage in the context of a broader effort to expand the boundaries of citizenship. A small number of radical Liberals called for women's suffrage, and the vote was granted at least briefly to women in the province of Vélez in 1853, although it remains unclear whether any women were able to take advantage of it before it was annulled by the supreme court of Nueva Granada. As the women of La Ciénaga had demonstrated, however, the deprivation of the right to vote did not mean that women could not lay claim to a language of rights in other domains, including the rights of women to property.[88]

As illustrated by the incorporation of habeas corpus and trial by jury into the Constitution of 1853, Panama was not merely the recipient of reforms mandated in Bogotá but was in itself an important laboratory of liberalism in Nueva Granada in the 1850s, as elites, popular groups, immigrants, and foreign-owned companies grappled with the problem of sovereignty in a place where different transnational, national, and local interests converged and often came into conflict. The erection of the Federal State of Panama in 1855 launched a period of federalism in Nueva Granada more generally that led to the de-centralization of sovereignty and creation of many other federal or sovereign states elsewhere in the nation during the mid-nineteenth century.[89]

Electoral politics in both Panama and California also excluded native peoples. No systematic efforts to exterminate indigenous people similar to those undertaken in California in the 1850s were attempted or even contemplated in Panama during the gold rush. Government officials and journalists in Panama City rarely wrote about Indians at all. When they did, they often spoke of indigenous people as if they were holdovers from the past and destined to disappear. Elsewhere in Nueva Granada, in the Cauca Valley, indigenous peoples became a more significant political force in the early 1850s, particularly among the ranks of the Conservative Party. But in Panama most native people who spoke indigenous languages and lived under indigenous leadership were in areas of the isthmus where the government of Nueva Granada was negligible.[90]

Panama's differences with California were starker with regard to *gente de color*. In California, the establishment of statehood had accelerated a process of Anglo-American conquest of the government that had begun even before 1848. Though California had been admitted to the Union as a "free state" in conjunction with the Compromise of 1850, slavery still persisted on a small scale in some parts of the state. California's new constitution denied African Americans and Native Americans the right to vote there as well as the right to testify in court against whites—an exclusion that was later expanded to include Chinese immigrants. Although elite *californios* maintained a hold on power in some parts of California such as Santa Barbara, other places where Mexicans had ruled just a few years before such as Sacramento or Monterey were now firmly in the hands of whites from the United States who trumpeted their commitments to freedom even as they denied the rights of citizenship to others. In parts of both northern and southern California, white vigilantes rode down and hanged other men who violated their own understandings of order, including other whites as well as Mexicans, Indians, and Chileans.[91]

Vigilantes sponsored by the Panama Railroad Company and the steamship companies had exercised extralegal power in Panama, but the Isthmus Guard was dismantled in March 1855. Though far more whites from the United States would cross Panama in 1856 than in 1849 or 1850, the time that these immigrants spent in Panama had been reduced to a few hours at most, and the expatriate population in Panama City and elsewhere in the transit zone had dropped precipitously since the early years of the rush. After 1853 all adult men in Nueva Granada possessed the right to vote. Color distinctions and extralegal practices of exclusion based on color or race still existed in Nueva Granada, of course, as white fears of caste war attest. But they were not written into laws that curtailed or eliminated the political rights of any group of men on the basis of color or any other distinction.

La Ciénaga, Playa Prieta, and the railroad station brought together a potentially explosive combination of immigrants from the United States, the facilities of the railroad company and its employees, and the members of Panama City's working population who were most aggrieved both by the company's policies and the depredations of passing immigrants. Not surprising, the railroad station and its immediate environs had acquired a reputation for frequent incidents of violence by the beginning of 1856.

The combination of impoverished black residents from Panama City and the latest in industrial technology struck some observers as incongruous, particularly when passengers were arriving or departing from Panama City. As an anonymous commentator lamented in the *Panama Star and Herald* of February 21, 1856: "There is not in or about the whole city so great a nuisance, or one which gives rise to so much mischief and disturbance, as that which arises from the privilege given to the very lowest grade of the negro population to hang around the station when passengers are there, ostensibly under pretense of selling fruit, but in reality to retail out the worst kind of rot-gut brandy, create rows and pick pockets when a chance offers. At every step, in every door-way, respectable people are insulted, jostled and frequently upset by these creatures, and even the Railroad employees are now frequently molested by them, while in the execution of their duty; but if any one attempts to retaliate or even to move them to one side, in order to pass bye, a whole troop of their darkey friends, who appear to be there for the express purpose, step forward with the most abusive and threatening language, and, armed with machetes, stones and other weapons, are all ready to commence a fight at once."[92]

The author of an anonymous article in the *Panama Star and Herald* similarly characterized the residents of La Ciénaga as "ready to start up at a moment's notice, and with torch and dagger, destroy and plunder the houses, conductors and passengers of an enterprise which is an honor to the age, and a benefit to themselves." Comparing the people of La Ciénaga to "the barbarous and savage races, generally," the author went on to observe that the sight of "the fruits of civilized industry" inspired in the neighborhood's residents not the "honest desire to labour and acquire by a course of continued and persevering industry" but rather "a murderous cupidity, [the desire] to possess."[93]

Yet La Ciénaga was no less a product of its age than the railroad station, and the woes suffered by the people who lived there were also "the fruits of civilized industry." Rather than the remnants of some archaic society doomed to disappearance, the thatched houses of the neighborhood, like the station itself, were recent constructions whose builders had sought to benefit from the tremendous potential for profit created by the surge in demand for transportation to California. If some residents of La Ciénaga now found themselves with no work to sustain themselves, it was not because of their own sloth but rather because their former livelihoods had been stripped away from them by the building of the railroad, the introduction of the *Taboga* into the Bay of Panama, and the dismissal of laborers by the company when the road was completed.

By first amassing a large concentration of laborers to push the railroad to completion and then turning most of those laborers away once the work was done, the railroad company had inadvertently contributed to the formation of a growing class of unemployed, increasingly impoverished people in the Arrabal who had many reasons to regret and resent the railroad that ran through their midst. Boatmen, muleteers, tavern keepers, washerwomen, seamstresses, and exlaborers for the railroad company had gathered in the transit zone for different reasons and at different times. They had come from many places, including other parts of Panama, Cartagena, Peru, China, and Jamaica. But by the early months of 1856 those who remained in the Arrabal shared not only a living space but also recent and painful experiences of economic disenfranchisement and abuse at the hands of white immigrants from the United States and the foremen of the Panama Railroad Company.

This economic disfranchisement was counterbalanced, however, by a political enfranchisement that made everyone in Nueva Granada free and gave all the nation's adult men the right to vote. In laying new kinds of claims on local government, the boatmen of Playa Prieta and the claimants to land in La Ciénaga combined different forms of what James Sanders has characterized as "popular republicanism"—novel modes of political discourse and bargaining that emerged out of the struggles of groups including indigenous peoples, migrants, and freedpeople in Nueva Granada more broadly after 1848. In Panama, these claims combined older colonial ideals of patriarchy with a newer language of property rights and an insistence on equality.[94]

The early 1850s were not years of unmitigated political gains for peasants and poor people on the isthmus. Though the establishment of the Federal State of Panama in 1855 had realized long-standing elite aspirations for self-government, it represented a blow to Liberal peasants in Azuero, who now complained of Panama City in refrains similar to those used by elites in Panama City to complain about Bogotá. Still, by 1856 the men of the Arrabal were citizens of a republic whose definition of citizenship was more expansive than that of any other constitution in the Americas. What is more, people in the Arrabal had increasingly translated those rights into concrete political power, as evidenced by the whispered warnings of the city's elite and the continued existence of thatched houses in La Ciénaga. The Arrabal thus contained within it a potential for collective mobilization that was based on a sense of shared living and working space—a small place that was defined in contrast to San Felipe in terms of not only color and economic activity or class but also allegiance to the Liberal Party. This potential would be realized, with tragic results, on April 15, 1856.

Chapter 4

"We Are Not in the United States Here"

The small but significant place that Panama had possessed in public consciousness in the United States at the beginning of the gold rush had largely disappeared by April 1856. This disappearance reflected in part the arc of the gold rush itself in public imagination in the United States: the gold discovery of 1848 was old news by 1856. But it was also a reflection of changes in Panama itself. No longer did the newspapers of New York City carry updates about the prices of transport across the isthmus or the number of days required to cross from one side to the other. For one thing, changes in price or travel time were less subject to dramatic ups and downs. The Panama Railroad Company had its set rates for passengers and cargo, and travel time did not vary significantly from day to day except for unexpected events such as a mechanical breakdown.

The conquest of the transit route by the Panama Railroad Company cost many in Panama City dearly, as people living in and around La Ciénaga were painfully aware. In contrast, immigrants who crossed Panama by train remained largely oblivious to the consequences associated with the relative comfort they enjoyed as they sped from one side of the isthmus to the other. After 1855, immigrants experienced Panama in much the same way that they might have experienced a train station while transferring from one train to another—Panama was a place immigrants passed through, pausing only briefly before continuing the journey.[1] That people in the United States did not have to think much about Panama for the Panama Route to serve its purpose was a sign not of the route's insignificance for the United States but rather of its efficacy as a conduit for the flow of people, information, and capital between the nation's two coasts. Only when the conduit ruptured or burst did people in the United States need take notice, and then only for a moment, before the flow was established once again.

The Filibusters Materialize

The likelihood of such a rupture was increased markedly at the beginning of April 1856 with the arrival in Panama City of the *Cortes*, a mysterious sidewheeler named after the Spanish conqueror of Mexico. The ship was owned by Cornelius Vanderbilt and had departed San Francisco on March 20, 1856.[2] On board were approximately forty men under the command of Horace Bell, all of them recruits for William Walker's filibuster army in Nicaragua. Captain Bell, as he styled himself, had immigrated to California during the U.S.-Mexico War, although he was not himself a war veteran. After the war he was by his own account an enthusiastic participant in the violent consolidation of Anglo-American power in Los Angeles and its immediate environs. During the early 1850s Bell had been a member of a vigilante force known as the Rangers, and he would later claim to have participated in the manhunt for Joaquín Murrieta, a Mexican immigrant to gold-rush California. Murrieta would later become a legendary figure in California history and a symbol of anti-Anglo resistance both for Chicanos in the United States and also for Chileans who recalled the abuse their fellow citizens had experienced in California during the gold rush years.[3]

Whether Bell actually participated in the hunt for Murrieta is a matter of some debate, and at least one historian has taken Bell to task for his proclivity to exaggerate and invent. It is true that Bell earned some renown in Los Angeles as a raconteur in the 1880s. Many of his tales of life on the California frontier are jocular in tone and syrupy with nostalgia for what, for Bell at least, were better days. In contrast, his writings about his experiences as a filibuster in Panama and Nicaragua have a more somber, regretful air about them. As Bell recalled long after the fact in an unpublished memoir, he had decided to join Walker's forces in early 1856, when the opportunities created by the gold discovery in California seemed largely to have disappeared for Anglo-Americans of slender means. Sensing the possibility of better prospects in Central America, Bell recruited a small company of forty men with the hope of attaining what he later described ironically as "distinction on the field of heroic deeds and desperate adventure."[4]

Walker's forces were faring poorly when the *Cortes* arrived at the port of San Juan del Sur, on the Pacific coast of Nicaragua. Earlier in the year, Walker had made a significant misstep by siding against Vanderbilt in a dispute over the ownership of the Accessory Transit Company, the U.S. concern that owned the right to operate the interoceanic route across Nicaragua. Walker revoked that right and gave it to Vanderbilt's bitter rivals, Charles Morgan and Cornelius Garrison, who were Walker's allies. In his rage over his ouster from the route, Vanderbilt mobilized all the resources at his disposal to undermine Walker and to direct traffic away from Nicaragua.[5] Previously, the *Cortes* and other ships owned by Vanderbilt had transported supplies and recruits to Walker's forces in Nicaragua. But when the *Cortes* arrived at San Juan del Sur with Bell and his men on board, the ship's captain was met by a representative of Vanderbilt who ordered him not to land any passengers and to continue instead to Panama City. Horace Bell and his recruits remained on board with the ship's other passengers as the sidewheeler steamed off for Panama.[6]

In his memoir, Bell claimed that he had attempted to seize control of the ship upon learning of the deviation to Panama but was thwarted by the *Cortes*'s captain.[7] Nevertheless, he and his men were probably fortunate that they were not allowed to disembark at San Juan del Sur. On April 11 Walker and his men would suffer a devastating defeat at the hands of the allied forces of Central America at the first battle of Rivas.[8] But at the time, Bell and his filibuster recruits were left "humiliated, chagrined, [and] crestfallen."[9] Deposited in Panama City, they found themselves with no return tickets to San Francisco and no immediately apparent way to continue to Nicaragua.

Bell later remembered that people in Panama City turned out in droves to watch him and his recruits walk from Playa Prieta to their lodgings in San Felipe at the Hotel Aspinwall: "The streets through which we passed from the beach to the hotel was [sic] thronged with people of all kinds, colors, sexes and conditions, eager to see the procession of the forty dreaded [filibusters,] who had made the first and farthest advance in the grand march of manifest destiny—a foreshadowing of the inevitable swooping down of the great nation of Northern barbarians, who, in two short years, had humbled the proud Aztec nation, and were stimulated thereby to march on with relentless tread to the conquest of the weaker nations inteverning [*sic*] between Mexico and Cape Horn." According to Bell, members of the crowd mistook him for William Walker. Though the aspiring filibusters may have been failures in California, they stalked about Panama City with an audacity that even Bell would later regard as foolishly provocative.[10] Miraculously, the hotel's guest register has survived into the present; it currently resides at the Bancroft Library, at the University of California–Berkeley, and its entry for April 8, 1856, bears the delicately written signature of Captain Horace Bell.[11]

Although Bell undoubtedly embellished his description of the filibusters' march through La Ciénaga and on into San Felipe, there is no doubt that the unexpected arrival of the filibusters caused considerable concern in Panama City, whose newspapers had carried ample reports of William Walker's progress through Nicaragua. The extent of this concern would be revealed a little more than a week after the arrival of the *Cortes*.[12]

The Rear Guard of Manifest Destiny

On April 15, 1856, with Bell and his men still marooned in Panama City, the New York City steamship *Illinois* arrived with nearly one thousand passengers at the port of Colón, on the other side of the isthmus. In contrast to the immigration from the United States across Panama at the beginning of the rush, which was almost exclusively male, the passengers aboard the *Illinois* included a significant minority of women and children.[13] After passengers disembarked at a wharf owned by the Panama Railroad Company, they boarded the train. By the afternoon of the same day, they found themselves at the railroad station in Panama City, facing the Pacific Ocean.[14]

Had the tide been high, the passengers could have immediately boarded the *Taboga* to be ferried to a San Francisco–bound steamship named for John L. Stephens, one of the founders of the Panama Railroad Company. But the tide was low, and the *Taboga* lay stuck in the mud beside the railroad company's wharf. While passengers waited for the ocean to lift the steamship from the muck, a number of them began to explore the environs around the train station. While some remained on the station grounds, others crossed the small bridge that led to La Ciénaga.[15]

José Manuel Luna: Seller of Fruit, Silversmith, and Citizen

On the other side of the bridge, a man named José Manuel Luna awaited the passengers from behind a small stand. On this stand Luna had laid out slices of watermelon that he hoped to sell to immigrants during the brief period between their arrival in Panama City and their departure aboard the *John L. Stephens.* Just a few yards away from Luna, bongos and other small watercraft listed in the sand, ready for any immigrants who did not care to wait for the tide to rise.

Although extant sources do not permit a precise reconstruction of the route Luna had followed to this juncture in his life, a few clues have survived. In his later testimony to judicial officials in Panama City, Luna described himself as twenty-nine years old, a bachelor, and a resident of Panama City. Judicial records in Panama conventionally made no mention of the race or color of parties to judicial cases in the mid-1850s, and Luna was not identified in such terms in his testimony. Officials and witnesses from the United States described Luna flatly as a "negro." We cannot know from his testimony whether Luna thought of himself as such, and if so, what such a color or racial denomination would have meant to him.[16]

Luna identified himself as a *platero*, or silversmith, and a native of the provincial town of Parita, a recent theater of armed conflicts between Liberals and Conservatives. It is possible that Luna conducted his apprenticeship with a local silversmith in his hometown, which had a history of silverwork in the colonial period. In the late 1700s, Parita had been the workplace of a well-known platero of color named Lucas Víctor Díaz whose nickname, "el zambo maestro" (the zambo master), identified him as a man of African and indigenous descent.[17]

Regardless of where he learned his craft, Luna was one of many in the Arrabal who had been born elsewhere and had immigrated to Panama City. The exact date of his arrival is unknown. But his capacity to speak English suggests that he had interacted with English-speakers for some time, either English-speaking immigrants or immigrants from the British Caribbean or perhaps both.

We know that he was in Panama City by 1851 because a list of voters for that year indicates that he cast his ballot in an election for the cabildo as a resident of the parish of Santa Ana in 1851. In 1853 his name appeared on the electoral list for the parish of Santa Ana, which indicated that Luna could both read and write. These poll records do not reveal any political affiliation for Luna. By 1856, however, the Arrabal had become thoroughly identified with the popular wing of the Liberal Party in Panama City. His presence on the list from 1851 indicates that Luna met the property requirements that limited the rights of citizenship even before the establishment of universal manhood suffrage in 1853. Although literacy statistics do not exist for Panama City in the early 1850s, he was also probably among the few men in the Arrabal who had learned to read and write.[18]

As a silversmith, Luna ranked considerably above most of his fellow residents of the Arrabal. Artisans enjoyed an economic and social status that was more prestigious than that of a boatman or a muleteer and certainly superior to that of street peddler or a fruitseller. The selling of fruit to passengers, furthermore, was an occupation that was strongly identified with women in Panama during the gold rush.[19] Why, then, would a silversmith be standing behind a fruit stand in one of the poorest areas of Panama City in April 1856? Luna's testimony offers no answer to this question. Perhaps he had been drawn into the service economy during the boom years of the gold rush, in 1849 or the early 1850s. But by 1856 the golden days of La California were long past. It seems more likely, then, that Luna had turned to selling fruit near the railroad station out of necessity rather than choice. He may have been one of the artisans in Panama City who had been driven out of work by the increased importation of manufactured goods to Panama that coincided with the gold rush—an increase that Gen. Espinar had predicted in 1851 would soon transform Panama into a place where nothing was made except, perhaps, for cigars.[20]

An Argument in La Ciénaga

At approximately 6:00 p.m., Luna found himself confronted by a group of three or four passengers from the *Illinois* whom he later described as "a little inebriated," and whom others would later describe as simply drunk. One of the men picked up a slice of watermelon. After Luna told him that the piece of fruit cost one *real*, or a U.S. dime, the man tasted the fruit. Then the passenger threw the fruit onto the ground and turned away without offering any payment.[21]

According to Luna's own testimony, he reprimanded the man and insisted on payment. The man responded in a vulgar manner, telling him, "Kiss my ass." But Luna again refused to acquiesce. Instead, he issued a rather formally phrased warning: "Careful, we are not in the United States here; pay me my *real* and we're even." The traveler then pulled a pistol and told Luna that he would pay with a gunshot, whereupon Luna told him, "If you have your pistol, I also have my knife," and then put his hand to his own weapon. According to Luna, the entire conversation between himself and the traveler was carried out in English.[22]

Dennis Shannon, one of three employees of the railroad company who claimed to have witnessed the argument, later testified to officials of the U.S. consulate in Panama City that he had witnessed the altercation while standing on the bridge that connected the company grounds to La Ciénaga. He recalled that he had seen "the Americans, one of them apparently inebriated, approaching the bridge, followed by a negro, who had a large knife in his hand, and was demanding a dime from one of the Americans for a watermelon."[23]

By this time a small crowd had gathered. According to Luna, one of drunken immigrants offered him a coin. Luna had already turned his back and was returning to his stand when one of the spectators, a man named Miguel Habrahan, jumped forward from the crowd and seized the passenger's firearm. The two wrestled for a moment in the dust before Habrahan managed to wrench the pistol free and then ran off with it away from the station, into the warren of thatched houses at the heart of La Ciénaga.[24]

The Drunken Passenger

The drunken passenger was not apprehended in Panama and never testified to officials from the United States or Nueva Granada. Nor was he among people later identified as dead or injured as a consequence of the violence that followed soon after his encounter with Luna. Presumably he continued on from Panama City to San Francisco aboard the *John L. Stephens*, but even this is unclear. The *Daily Alta California* of San Francisco, in its first report on the violence, identified the passenger as "Jack Oliver" and stated that he had been a passenger in steerage aboard the *Illinois* but did not report whether Oliver had actually made it to California.[25] Oliver's name appeared nowhere in the official U.S. report on the violence of April 15, which only identified the man in question as an "American" and a "passenger."[26] Bell, in his memoir, recalled that the cause of the fracas over the watermelon had been "a drunken, turbulent Irishman, who had given considerable trouble in the steerage of the New York steamer."[27] The British consul of Panama City, William Perry, claimed to have seen the passenger earlier in the same day and that he was already drunk at the time.[28]

The first mention of Jack Oliver's name in an official document produced by the government of Nueva Granada did not appear until June 28, 1856, in a letter by the secretary of foreign affairs, Lino de Pombo, who claimed that his information was based on accounts in English-language newspapers from San Francisco.[29] One U.S. official later claimed that "Jack Oliver" had never even existed. According to him, Oliver was a fiction concocted by the government of Nueva Granada to deflect blame from its own citizens.[30] Given the appearance of his name in the *Daily Alta California*, it seems unlikely that the figure of Jack Oliver was cut from whole cloth. Nevertheless, the identity of the drunken passenger remains somewhat mysterious.

Miguel

More information can be gleaned about the man who came to Luna's aid, Miguel Habrahan, whose testimony about the melee was published beside that of José Manuel Luna in the *Gaceta del Estado*. "Habrahan" is a variant spelling of "Abraham" or "Abrahán"—the father of Isaac in the Old Testament. Habrahan identified himself as twenty-five years old, a bachelor, and a native of the Peruvian port of Paita. Though the published text of Miguel's testimony spelled his last name "Habrahan," it was rendered in an article that appeared in *El Panameño* as "Abrán."[31] The Conservative newspaper known as *El Centinela* identified the same individual as a Peruvian named "Miguel Habran."[32] All three variations would have been pronounced identically by a speaker of Spanish.[33]

The name Miguel Abran, with no accent, had appeared on the boatmen's petition of January 1855 that was analyzed in Chapter 3.[34] With the bongos of Playa Prieta only a few feet away from Luna's stand, it seems almost certain that the Miguel of the altercation and the Miguel of the petition were the same individual. Another piece of evidence that supports the idea that the two were one and the same comes from the testimony of Ran Runnels, who witnessed the struggle over the drunken passenger's pistol in La Ciénaga and identified the passenger's foe as a "native boatman."[35]

Habrahan, Abrán, Habran, and Abran were not common last names in Panama in the 1850s—indeed, I have found no reference to any other individual with such a name in Panama City in this period. It is possible that Habrahan was a second given name for Miguel, and that he did not have a last name or "apellido," as was sometimes the case with poor men and also—before abolition—slaves. It is also conceivable that the multiple spellings of his name arose from uncertainty over how to transliterate the English surname "Abraham" into Spanish. If so, Miguel may have had connections to the English-speaking worlds of the British empire or the United States. Given the association of the name "Abraham" with Judaism, it is even possible that Miguel was Jewish.[36]

The Miguel of the petition was at least partially literate, for he was able to sign his own name. In that document the boatmen had called on the cabildo to reduce the tax levied on boats. Without this relief, the petitioners had warned, boatmen would soon be driven out of a trade that had already been damaged severely by the *Taboga* and the completion of the railroad. Perhaps this prediction had come true in Miguel's case, for he identified himself in his testimony as a carpenter. In contrast, the official U.S. report on the violence focused exclusively on Miguel's color or race, describing him as a "light-colored native" and a "colored man."[37]

According to Miguel's testimony, he had watched the argument between Luna and the drunken passenger and then stepped forward to demand that the passenger put away his weapon. When the passenger refused and prepared to fire the weapon at Miguel himself, Miguel grabbed the weapon and then wrestled with the gunman and other passengers. After Miguel freed himself, he fled with the pistol in his hand and then hid himself in a nearby house.[38]

In contrast, the official U.S. report accused Miguel of stealing the gun from its owner as the passenger was putting it away and then firing the pistol at the passenger. According to this version of events, Habrahan and Luna withdrew to the "huts in the Cienaga" and returned shortly thereafter with men armed with machetes before retreating once more to La Ciénaga. Soon afterwards, according to the report, "a large crowd of negros, armed with stones, machettes and other weapons, came down from the huts and commenced an attack" on people in the vicinity of the Pacific House and the Ocean Hotel.[39]

Official Narratives of April 15

Although there is much that can never be known with certainty about the events of April 15, the identification of commonalities and discrepancies between official records and other sources can help to reveal how official accounts produced by the United States and Nueva Granada obscured important aspects of the politics of the people who gathered in La Ciénaga during and after the argument between José Manuel Luna and the drunken passenger.[40]

In the aftermath of the violence, officials from both countries set about producing evidence that they hoped would serve their respective nations in any subsequent diplomatic disputes. The U.S. Department of State appointed a special investigator, Amos Corwine, to compile an official report on the event. A former U.S. consul to Panama City, Corwine was hardly a disinterested party: his brother, David, was an employee of the Pacific Mail Steamship Company and a long-time resident of Panama City. Corwine's final report blamed the instigation of the violence on Miguel Habrahan. According to Corwine, Habrahan's actions had served as a signal to "native negros" to launch a premeditated and unprovoked attack on innocent passengers "in connivance" with authorities from Panama. He accused the "colored population" of seeking to plunder and kill passengers and also to exact revenge for the damage done to the local transit economy by the completion of the railroad and the introduction of the *Taboga* into the Bay of Panama. His report alleged that participants in what he described as a "riot" had committed atrocities including the rape of female passengers by "colored men" and an attack on a mother with a small child.[41]

The most complete rebuttal of U.S. accusations by officials from Nueva Granada was authored by Lino de Pombo, the national minister of foreign affairs, and Florentino González. These two men served as commissioners for any claims against Nueva Granada arising from the violence of April 15. They portrayed the actions of people in Panama City as spontaneous acts of self-defense and placed the blame for initiating the conflict on Jack Oliver and other passengers as well as on previous acts of abuse directed at local inhabitants. In contrast to the official U.S. report, which failed to mention the presence of filibusters in Panama City, Pombo and González argued that fear of filibustering had played a central role in the actions of those who had participated in the tragic events of April 15. They also blamed the railroad company, which they accused of abandoning its former workers, whom they described as "destitute strangers, brought from the West Indies and other places as labourers on the Rail-road, and afterwards turned adrift by the Company to starve." To counter U.S. accusations that the violence had been premeditated, the commissioners portrayed the mobilization of Arrabaleños on the night of April 15 as an essentially spontaneous and unthinking reaction to assorted outrages committed by people from the United States in Panama. As they wrote, "New Granada is not to blame that the elements of a sudden and fierce conflagration should have been thus accumulated." In summation, they wrote, "The hour for retaliation, fixed by Providence, sounded, without New Granada being at all to blame."[42]

Although officials from the United States and Nueva Granada disagreed about whom to blame for the violence of April 15, they came to agree on an underlying narrative of events in Panama City on April 15 that was marked by a number of key turning points. The rudiments of this narrative were first put forth by the *Panama Star and Herald* on April 19, 1856. As the newspaper reported and officials from both governments subsequently concurred, the violence began with the dispute over a slice of watermelon at approximately 6 o'clock in La Ciénaga. Shortly afterward, the bell of the nearby parish church of Santa Ana began to sound the alarm for fire and hundreds of men converged on La Ciénaga, where they proceeded to trade blows with passengers from the *Illinois* and other immigrants from the United States who were in the area. The fighting soon focused on three buildings in La Ciénaga where passengers took refuge: the Ocean Hotel, the Pacific Eating House, and Mr. McAllister's store.[43]

Passengers in La Ciénaga who were able fled back to the railroad station, as did other passengers from the *Illinois* when they caught wind of the fighting. The station house was composed of two sections united under a single roof. Between the sections was a spur of track where trains waited while cargo was loaded on and off and passengers boarded or disembarked. South of the track, facing La Ciénaga, was the freight house, where luggage and cargo was stored. On the north side was the depot, which held company offices, a ticket booth, and a small waiting area. Most of the passengers took refuge inside the freight house, where they demanded arms from company officials to defend themselves and also loaded a cannon they found on the premises of the station. Some of the passengers wanted to leave the station to save women and children whom they feared were trapped in La Ciénaga, but they were restrained by company officials. Many passengers ran down to the end of the railroad company's wharf, where they clambered aboard the *Taboga*, which remained stuck in the mud. Railroad company employees also made efforts to shelter women and children on board the *vaporcito*. Meanwhile, hundreds of men from the Arrabal gathered outside the freight house, where they were soon joined by members of Panama City's gendarmerie, or police. Although officials from both countries disagreed about who the aggressors were—the people outside or inside the station—they concurred that insults were traded, rocks were hurled, and shots were fired.[44]

News of the fighting soon reached San Felipe. After arriving at La Ciénaga, the U.S. consul sent his secretary, Theodore de Sabla, to fetch Francisco de Fábrega, the vice governor and acting governor of the state, in the hope that he might be able to calm the situation. Fábrega was already on his way to La Ciénaga when the consul's secretary found him. As the secretary brought Fábrega to the place where the U.S. consul was located, the men came under fire. The secretary and another man who was accompanying the vice governor were wounded, and Fábrega's own hat was shot off. Although the origin of these shots would later be disputed by officials from the United States and Nueva Granada, Fábrega himself felt sure that they had come from inside the train station.[45]

Fábrega now faced an agonizing decision: should he hold the police at bay or should he order them to pacify the people in the station? According to his own subsequent account, he ordered the chief of the gendarmerie to take the station building and granted the chief permission to shoot back if the police found themselves fired upon by the people within.[46] The chief of the gendarmerie then ordered his men to march on the freight house. One of the policeman sounded a bugle at approximately half past seven o'clock, and gunshots were heard shortly thereafter. As the gendarmes struggled to force their way inside the building, they were joined by the members of the crowd wielding machetes, sticks, and other weapons. The firearms that passengers possessed were of little use now, and they were soon overwhelmed by the men rushing in. Most of the deaths of that night took place in the first minutes of confusion and violence inside the freight house.[47]

While the fighting was still going on inside the station, some of the gendarmes realized that the people inside were civilians and attempted to lead passengers including women and children to safety on board the *Taboga*. Seeing this, some men from the crowd ran to the end of the pier and demanded that the gendarmes let them come aboard the ship to confront the people on board, whom they claimed were intent on destroying the city. The police refused to let them pass, but the crowd did not disperse until after the police had disarmed all the passengers and removed two rifles and small cannon that were kept on board the *Taboga*.[48]

The fighting in and around the railroad station came to an end by dawn. In a letter dated April 18, 1856, the U.S. consul of Panama City informed the U.S. Department of State that fifteen U.S. citizens had been killed and at least fifty wounded.[49] The *Panama Star and Herald* of April 19, 1856, reported the deaths of fifteen people, including twelve unnamed passengers, a French expatriate who lived in Panama City named Octave Dubois, a railroad company watchman named Robert Marks, and Joseph Stokes, one of the filibuster recruits who had arrived aboard the *Cortes* a little more than a week before. Shortly afterward, a passenger named Alexander Sweet, a citizen of Maine, died of bullet wounds to his hip and puncture wounds to his face and his chest. The official newspaper of the state government of Panama, the *Gaceta del Estado*, reported the deaths of fifteen foreigners as well as two Panamanians, Lucas Prados and a man identified only as "Apolinar N." The *Gaceta del Estado* put the number of wounded Panamanians at thirteen and the number of wounded foreigners at sixteen.[50] A later report submitted to the U.S. government by two physicians in Panama City noted the death of one Panamanian and a total of eighteen foreign victims, including fourteen who died on April 15 and four who died afterwards of wounds they sustained on that day.[51]

The Desire to Pillage?

Amos Corwine argued that the "negros" of April 15 had been motivated by the desire to rob passengers, and his own report listed a large number of thefts from U.S.-owned buildings in La Ciénaga as well as from passengers at the railroad station.[52] Officials from Nueva Granada freely admitted that much property was stolen during the evening of April 15, but they denied that robbery was the primary goal of those who gathered in La Ciénaga after the conflict over the watermelon. Fábrega pointed out that if stealing valuables had been the overriding ambition of those who took part in the violence, they would have attacked not immigrants on their way west but passengers heading in the other direction, laden with gold from the mines of California.[53] Arthur Mackenzie, a British merchant living in Panama City, also noted that a much more propitious time to rob passengers would have been after the arrival of passengers from California or at a moment when the freight house was full of cargo.[54]

Gender, Race, and Honor

U.S. officials in Panama City claimed that "colored men" from the Arrabal had attacked female passengers. The idea that black men represented a special threat to the honor of white women was shared by many whites not only in the United States but also in Panama. Nevertheless, the official tallies of the killed and wounded produced by the U.S. government and the government of Nueva Granada included no women. The U.S. consul felt certain that women and children were slaughtered, but he could not point to any corpses and suggested that Panamanians might have secretly buried the bodies of women and children or thrown them into wells.[55] Corwine's final report cited the testimony of four witnesses who claimed to have seen the body of a murdered woman in the immediate aftermath of the violence, but no other evidence could be found to support their testimony, and Corwine was never able to attach a name to the woman who was allegedly killed.[56]

Despite the accusations of attacks on women and children, the available evidence suggests that gendarmes and members of the crowd saw themselves as protectors rather than attackers of women. After the gendarmes took the station, their chief set about immediately escorting female passengers and children away from danger and onto the *Taboga*.[57] At least some in the Arrabal apparently believed that the trouble in La Ciénaga had begun after a man from the United States had assaulted not a man but a woman. Sebastián Díaz testified that he had first been alerted to the trouble by a report that a passenger had stolen a pineapple from a female fruitseller.[58] T. B. Williams, a conductor for the railroad company, testified that unnamed people in La Ciénaga had informed him that a fight had occurred between a woman from Nueva Granada and "one of Walker's filibusters."[59] Similarly, a subsequent newspaper article in *El Panameño* claimed that Miguel Habrahan (or "Miguel Abrán") had been fired upon by a filibuster after Habrahan demanded a dime from him on behalf of a woman from whom the filibuster had sought to steal. According to this version of events, "el pueblo" was gendered as male, and Habrahan and other men in the Arrabal were figured as the true protectors of female honor and civilization more generally, in contrast to the filibusters from the United States who were so barbarous that they were capable of assaulting a woman. As *El Panameño* intoned, "The Panamanian people [el pueblo panameño] has made abundantly clear how much it values and esteems its dignity."[60]

Few women from the Arrabal seem to have participated directly in the conflicts of April 15, although in at least one instance, women conveyed a warning to a man from San Felipe who was on his way to the Arrabal. José María Rodríguez testified that he had been near La Ciénaga when some women had called out to him that he should leave because "el pueblo" had become "enraged" as a result of an injury to another Panamanian named Pedro Obarrio i Pérez. As they explained to him, "Since you are dressed like a foreigner they [members of el pueblo] could kill you."[61] Some women from the Arrabal were also observed in the aftermath of the violence in the process of looting the belongings of passengers left in the vicinity of the La Ciénaga and the railroad station.[62]

Writing in 1884, Carrie Stevens Walter recalled that she had seen women among members of "the mob," whom she characterized as drunken and infuriated. Walter was ten years old at the time of the violence, and she described one of the women she had seen as "a fiend incarnate" who carried "a large knife wet with blood." Walter had been caught with other members of her family on the upper floor of one of the buildings in La Ciénaga, most likely the Ocean Hotel. She described her reaction and that of her family members as one of terror and recalled that members of the "mob" had stolen valuables from them and others and even killed an unfortunate male passenger in their presence. But she also recalled that an employee of the railroad company who had taken refuge with them in the hotel had reassured her and her kinfolk that "the excited populace had sworn vengeance against all the men among the passengers; but they were not going to intentionally kill women or children."[63]

Jealousy?

The physical evidence left by the violence gives greater strength to the contention made by officials from the United States and Nueva Granada alike that members of the crowd were motivated to destroy the railroad company's property in retaliation for the damage done by the building of the railroad and the introduction of the *Taboga*. During the fighting, parts of the railroad track were uprooted, and the telegraph wire connecting the station to Colón was cut. Inside the depot, papers were scattered, and an attempt had been made to break open the company's safe. Almost all the baggage inside the freight house was either stolen or destroyed. In addition, businesses owned by U.S. citizens in La Ciénaga were ransacked, including the Ocean Hotel, the Pacific Eating House, and Mr. McAllister's store.[64] Witnesses who later testified to U.S. officials in Panama City also explained the violence in part as an expression of economic grievances against foreign companies as well as retribution for past acts of abuse by drunken immigrants. Arthur Mackenzie had witnessed fights on Playa Prieta between drunken immigrants and "negroes," and he also noted opposition by black residents of La Ciénaga to efforts by the railroad company to remove them without compensation from the neighborhood where they lived. In his testimony he also mentioned the negative effects of the building of the railway and the arrival of the *Taboga* on local transit workers.[65] Frederick Ansoatigue, the owner of a shop called the Triangle, also attributed the violence in part to revenge for the "conduct of dissolute persons crossing the Isthmus." He claimed that his shop was spared from pillaging because someone in "the mob" had noted that he was a "native of Panama."[66]

James Copeland, master of the *Taboga*, testified that boatmen from Panama City had previously expressed the desire to destroy his ship and also threatened his own life. According to Copeland, boatmen launched an attack on the *Taboga* only a month before, in March 1856, and had been prevented from boarding the ship with their knives by the ship's engineer, who had kept them at bay with the ship's hot water hose.[67] T. B. Williams noted what he perceived as an antipathy among Panamanians to the railroad company and people from the United States more generally, which he chalked up to jealousy.[68]

Officials from Nueva Granada blamed the violence primarily on foreign workers who had been abandoned by the railroad company, particularly immigrants from the West Indies.[69] Former workers would have had many reasons to resent the company, but the singling out of West Indians was likely an effort to deflect blame from citizens of Nueva Granada, who were clearly the chief protagonists in the crowd. Horace Bell reported that "Jamaicans" had acted heroically on the night of April 15—not against the company but rather in support of passengers. According to him, Jamaicans were left unmolested by members of the crowd "on account of their color and knowledge of the Spanish language" and were also able to gain the trust of passengers because of their ability to speak English. In cooperation with filibusters under Bell's command, "Jamaica men" managed to rescue several passengers who might have been killed or injured otherwise.[70] It is true that men from the Arrabal do not appear to have sought out West Indians for rough treatment. In testimony reprinted in the *Gaceta del Estado*, Alexander Henriquez, a Jamaican employee of the railroad company, stated that the crowd had spared him after he was identified by name by one of their number.[71]

Williams and others who attributed the violence to the envy of Arrabaleños treated the destruction of the livelihoods of boatmen, muleteers, and others involved in the transit economy as if this damage were an accidental byproduct of the railroad's opening, rather than an intentional consequence that was actively sought by company officials as a precondition for the railroad's completion. Efforts to attribute the violence primarily to

Arrabaleños' opposition to the railroad company and steamship companies also failed to explain the timing of the alleged "attack." If Arrabaleños were truly bent on destroying the railroad, as Mariano Arosemena had claimed, why did they wait until April 15, 1856, more than a year after the railroad was inaugurated? Although members of the crowd did significant damage to the railroad station and pulled up part of the track, the railroad was back in operation by April 17, and Arrabaleños apparently made no further sustained efforts to damage the track or other aspects of the company infrastructure. Far more damaging to the railroad than the events of April 15 was an accident that took place less than one month later, on May 6, 1856, in which more than forty people perished.[72]

Rumors of Invasion by Filibusters

A more likely explanation for the timing of the mobilization by men in the Arrabal lies in the apprehensions created by the arrival of the *Cortes* and its filibustering passengers. Many Arrabaleños appear to have perceived their own actions on April 15 not as aggressive attacks but rather attempts to defend themselves and their city from foreign invasion. This was the claim made by Fábrega, who wrote, "There were many . . . of little thought who imagined the country attacked by filibusters, and what contributed to engender that idea was not only the knowledge of the deeds of these adventurers in Lower California, Sonora, Nicaragua, etc., but above all the presence of many of them in this city."[73] If Fábrega later dismissed fears of filibuster invasion, his actions at the moment of the conflict indicate that he himself had been far from certain about what was taking place on the outskirts of the city on the night of April 15.[74]

In the hours after the argument over the slice of watermelon, many Arrabaleños seem to have believed that the filibusters had converted the buildings of the hated railroad into their personal fortress. This at any rate was the interpretation put forward in *El Panameño* on April 21, when the belief that filibusters had been behind the violence of April 15 was still apparently widespread in Panama City. According to *El Panameño*, representatives of el pueblo of Panama City had demonstrated on that night that they would no longer stand for the "barbarous manner" in which filibusters and others from the United States had treated them. In the process of defending themselves, they had also meted out just punishment to the railroad company: "In order to get to the [filibusters] . . . it was necessary to attack the station violently. The people had passed sentence on the company and saw it as an enemy, a terrible enemy. It was thus necessary for the *Fortress* [the station] to suffer along with many other things. The people sought to do damage to the company in proportion to the damage that the company had done to them."[75]

It appears, however, that Horace Bell and his men were mostly spectators to the events of that night, other than efforts they made after the worst of the fighting was over to shepherd passengers to safety in San Felipe. The exception was Joseph Stokes, the only filibuster who was listed among those who were killed on that night. Stokes was a personal friend of Horace Bell, who claimed that Stokes had won a considerable reputation as a "first-class desperado" in California, where he found ample opportunity to exercise his considerable skill with a revolver. As Bell later recalled with his typical hyperbole, "[Stokes] seemed to delight in broils and was only happy when mixed up in a first class fight, always refused to take an unfair advantage, and was never known to come out second best."[76] According to officials from Nueva Granada, Stokes was responsible for shooting two Panamanians to death in La Ciénaga.[77] Later, the filibuster found himself inside the train station, where he unsuccessfully exhorted passengers to venture back to La Ciénaga to rescue any passengers who were stranded there. According to Frederick Ansoatigue, "a man named Stokes, a passenger from San Francisco by the steamship Cortes, came up and addressed the passengers in an inflammatory strain, calling upon them to go out and assist the others of the passengers who were being murdered at the Pacific house and Ocean house by the mob."[78] According to Bell, Stokes then joined Robert Marks in loading a small cannon on the premises with rivets. The cannon was fired at members of "the mob" who stormed the freight house. Although Bell praised Stokes for defending the freight house with his revolver, he also acknowledged that gunfire from passengers inside the freight house had contributed to the confusion of that night. According to Bell, the passengers inside the station mistook the "soldiers" or police outside the building as members of the "murderous mob" and fired upon them. It was only then, he claimed, that the police had acted in concert with the crowd in taking the station.[79]

Xenophobia?

Arrabaleños apparently perceived themselves to be acting in defense of the city against certain foreigners—specifically, filibusters—rather than waging a pogrom of some kind against foreigners in general. Theodore de Sabla, Consul Ward's secretary, reported that while walking near the railroad station just before the violence began, he had heard people yelling, "Let's go kill Yankees."[80] Yet the commercial agent for the railroad company—a U.S. citizen named William Nelson–testified that men in La Ciénaga recognized him and specifically warned him to stay away from the railroad station if he wished to avoid being killed.[81] Edward Allen, another U.S. citizen, related how the police and the crowd had broken into his saloon and threatened to kill the individual he had left in charge, but then let him be once they realized that he was a "Chinaman."[82] Nor were Panamanians necessarily spared, particularly if they worked for the railroad company, as was the case with José María Bravo, who sold tickets in the office of the Pacific Mail Steamship Company inside the railroad station. Bravo had been inside the station when the confrontation began. After members of the crowd entered the building, he heard some declare that he should be killed while others argued that he was a mere employee and should be spared. In the end, he survived, but only after receiving a sharp blow with the flat side of a saber.[83]

The fact that many of the residents of the Arrabal were themselves from places other than Panama City also undermines any interpretation of the events of April 15 as xenophobic onslaught. Miguel Habrahan, the man who had come to the aid of José Manuel Luna, was himself a Peruvian. Sebastian Díaz testified to the *Gaceta del Estado* that he had seen *cartajeneros*, men from the Caribbean port of Cartagena, doing battle with an *americano* on the night of April 15.[84] Among those later arrested by Panamanian gendarmes for complicity in robberies were people whose names suggest that they almost certainly were not natives of Panama, including Eduardo Olier, William Douman, and Jhon [*sic*] Owen.[85] Places of residence suspected by Panamanian police to contain goods stolen during the violence included the house of "a Frenchman named Hoffman" and four rooms of a house located in San Felipe owned by a Carlos Cavalli.[86]

The Refusal to Disperse

The experience of Ran Runnels on April 15 and his efforts with Manuel María Díaz also illustrate the ways in which loyalties in Panama City could cut across lines of nationality, region, class, and color. In an apparent allusion to Ran Runnels and the Isthmus Guard, T. B. Williams noted that opposition to "foreigners" on the Isthmus had stemmed in part from efforts by the railroad company to establish its vision of order on the transit zone: "Foreigners do all the business of any importance on the Isthmus, and many of the Panameños and others object to this right. The Panama Railroad Company has caused to be removed all the leaders of those piratical gangs which formerly infested the Isthmus, and their friends who reside here, many of whom live within the walls of Panama [and] use their influence to the injury of foreigners and the Railroad Company in particular."[87]

Opposition to Runnels also existed outside the city walls, as was made clear by an incident in October 1854 that bore a resemblance to efforts by Arrabaleños to free one of their own from what they regarded to be unjust imprisonment in May of 1850. According to the *Panama Star and Herald*, the "negro population of Santa Ana became much excited" by a rumor that Runnels had arrested a "boy" from the Arrabal and deposited him in a jail located in San Felipe. As it turned out, the man from the Arrabal had been brought to the jail by two railroad company officials, not Runnels. Nevertheless, a large number of Arrabaleños entered San Felipe to procure the release of their neighbor from the jail. With Runnels absent at the time, the official in charge of the jail had no choice but to comply.[88]

According to his own testimony, Runnels first heard the commotion in La Ciénaga on April 15 while he was at the railroad station, where he was completing paperwork related to a shipment from Wells, Fargo & Co. He ran from the station to Playa Prieta and saw people he described as "boatmen" fighting passengers from the *Illinois*. After returning to the station to assess whether the company had any serviceable arms at hand, he was called back to La Ciénaga by David Corwine, Amos's brother, who hoped Runnels might calm the situation and "speak to the natives as I spoke Spanish and knew nearly all of them."[89]

On his way he came across Manuel María Díaz—the former Liberal governor—and entreated Díaz to join him. Then he and Díaz waded into the crowd of people from the Arrabal who had gathered outside the Pacific House and the Ocean Hotel and appealed to them to withdraw. According to Runnels, however, the members of the crowd "swore they would destroy the Hotel and kill the passengers." Yet despite the cries of some in the crowd who threatened him with their knives, Runnels was left unscathed as he walked among people of La Ciénaga. As he explained in his testimony, one of the members of the crowd outside the Pacific House had been a member of the Isthmus Guard before the dissolution of that body. According to Runnels, this member of the guard "raised me up in his arms and put me on the Beach, telling me I must leave or I would be killed."[90]

After Díaz again failed to convince the men in La Ciénaga to disperse, the two men withdrew toward a breach in the city walls known as the Puerta de Postigo, where they came upon the vice governor and informed him of the conflict in La Ciénaga. A moment later Runnels found himself attempting to calm not people in La Ciénaga but a group of men from the United States lodged in San Felipe who were rushing toward the scene of the conflict. He subsequently turned a group of fleeing passengers over to the protection of Horace Bell and some of his men, who had left the confines of San Felipe to investigate the goings-on in La Ciénaga.[91]

The Demise of Deference

The refusal of Arrabaleños to accede to Manuel María Díaz's entreaties to withdraw from La Ciénaga was just one of a number of moments on the night of April 15 in which Arrabaleños demonstrated considerable independence if not outright disdain for elite men from San Felipe from both the Conservative and the Liberal Party. Francisco de Fábrega was alternately cajoled, scorned, resisted, and ignored by members of the crowd. As a Conservative, Fábrega's political authority was already suspect in the thoroughly Liberal Arrabal. His credibility among members of the crowd could not have been improved by the fact that when he finally appeared in La Ciénaga, it was at the side of the secretary of the U.S. consul. Nelson would later recall that Fábrega found himself "in the midst of the negroes of the Cienaga, most of whom are said to be his personal enemies," and that these same negroes had "alarmed and frightened [Fábrega] into giving the order to the police to advance and fire upon the station."[92]

Fábrega also acknowledged the significance of party differences in the events of April 15. According to him, men in La Ciénaga accused him and other officials of treason when they attempted to convince them to stop the violence—an accusation that Fábrega believed was fed by "the deplorable political antipathies" that divided Panamanians.[93]

Another incident that revealed the fraying bonds of patriarchy took place on Playa Prieta after the police and members of the crowd had already entered the railroad station. As Fábrega and Nelson walked along the beach, they came across Dolores Urriola, a man who was preparing to fire a small cannon at the *Taboga* with the help of a companion. Fábrega ordered the men to stop, but they refused, claiming that the men on board the ship were planning to bombard the city as soon as the rising tide permitted the vaporcito to leave the pier. Urriola finally desisted only after Fábrega convinced him that there were two women from Panama on board the ship. But Urriola refused to surrender his cannon. As he informed Fábrega, the weapon was his personal property, and the vice governor had no right to take it from him. Urriola would later gain fame in Panama as a poet known by a nickname that referred to the color of his skin: "El Mulato Urriola."[94]

A Debate in the Plaza of Santa Ana

More evidence of tensions between people in the Arrabal and Fábrega over the right of Arrabaleños to take up arms against foreign invaders comes from testimony regarding a dispute that took place in the plaza of Santa Ana on April 16. Antonio Abad Monteser, a master mason from the parish of Santa Ana, was sitting in the door of his house that evening when he heard a commotion. When he went to investigate, another individual named Pedro Jiménes reproached him and others near him, telling them, "Here you sit without a care, while the filibusters are on their way from Colón to attack us." According to Jiménes, the news of the imminent attack had been brought by a "lengua azul" or "blue tongue"—a term used in Panama in the 1850s to indicate Jamaicans or English-speaking West Indians of African descent. Thus warned, Abad Monteser went to spread the word among other Arrabaleños that filibusters would soon attack.[95] Pedro Ramos, a tailor, testified that he had been in La Ciénaga when he had heard that filibusters were preparing to attack the city and that two other men had heard the same news, including a man named "Julián N," whose nickname was "Come-ñame," or "Yam-eater."[96]

Later on the night of April 16, Abad Monteser and Ramos joined a group of approximately one hundred Arrabaleños who met with the purpose of organizing the defense of the city in the plaza of Santa Ana, the principal religious and political gathering place in the Arrabal. Francisco de Fábrega and Manuel María Díaz were also there. Men from the Arrabal demanded that the vice governor deliver arms to them so that they could fight off the coming invasion. In contrast to the previous evening, when he had urged Arrabaleños to withdraw to their homes, Díaz now sided with the men in the plaza who demanded guns, while Fábrega delayed any decision and instead urged calm.[97]

After much cajoling from the men in the plaza, Fábrega finally agreed to distribute the weapons provided a person could be found who would make himself "responsible" for them. After Manuel María Díaz put his name forward, Fábrega issued an order for guns to be distributed to the men. The weapons had not yet been passed around when a report came that the rumor of a filibuster attack from Colón was untrue, and the order was quashed.[98]

Abad Monteser testified that he and others assembled in the Plaza viewed Fábrega's apparent hesitance to distribute arms to them as suspicious and speculated that a "hostile combination" or plot might exist between Fábrega's administration and the filibusters.[99] Pedro Ramos recalled that although members of "el pueblo" had confidence in Díaz, they distrusted the vice governor.[100]

Silversmith and Deputy

Another man who participated in the debate in the plaza of Santa Ana on April 16 was José Isabel Maitín, a Liberal deputy to the state's legislative assembly who testified that he had heard others express the opinion that Fábrega "showed little concern for the terrible fate that awaited the inhabitants of the city." Apparently unwilling to trust Fábrega's assurances, the men in the plaza had appointed Maitín and two other men to investigate independently whether the rumor of filibusters was true.[101]

Maitín identified himself in his own testimony as a thirty-one-year-old silversmith or platero. As silversmiths from the Arrabal, it is likely that José Manuel Luna and Maitín knew each another, perhaps through membership in a guild of silversmiths, or "gremio de plateros." Although a guild for masons existed in Panama City at the time, I have found no evidence of a guild of silversmiths in Panama City in the 1850s. But Ángeles Ramos Baquero has documented the existence of such a guild in Panama City as late as 1813, eight years before Panamanian independence from Spain.[102]

One thing, however, is clear: José Manuel Luna thought highly of José Isabel Maitín, because he had put Maitín's name first among the ten men for whom he voted in the election for the cabildo on December 8, 1851.[103]

Opposition to Freemasonry

As the testimony of Abad Monteser, Maitín, and others makes clear, anxieties of filibuster attack did not cease with the violence of April 15. Abad Monteser's testimony is also valuable for its inclusion of an element that is harder to explain in terms of the historical record. In relating the rumors he had heard, Abad Monteser referred to the foreign invaders both as filibusters and as "masones" or freemasons, which suggests that Arrabaleños' opposition to filibusters may have drawn on antimasonic ideas that circulated more broadly in the Atlantic world in the late eighteenth and early nineteenth centuries. Roman Catholic clergy condemned freemasons for their antagonism toward the Church, and masons were also feared more generally for their alleged plotting against and infiltration of legitimate political authority.[104] It is true that many prominent filibusters in the early 1850s were involved in freemasonry, although how Abad Monteser or other Arrabaleños would have known this is unclear.[105]

Memories of May 1850

The events of May 1850 provided a reference point for both elite and popular interpretations of the violence and its aftermath. For Fábrega the conflict involving Arrabaleños, U.S. immigrants, and men from San Felipe on May 18, 1850, represented a tragic episode whose repetition he was determined to prevent. As he wrote in his first official report on the violence to the national government in Bogotá, "Here May 18, 1850, is still remembered with horror."[106] In contrast, the memory of the battle of May 1850 appears to have been a source of inspiration to some in the Arrabal. The signal date for Arrabaleños, however, appears to have been not May 18 but May 19, 1850. When Pedro Obarrio i Pérez arrived in the Plaza de Santa Ana shortly after the tumult in La Ciénaga, he found a gathering of Arrabaleños, some of whom had armed themselves. When he asked what was going on, the men responded with the words, "Otro 19 de mayo."[107]

Arrabaleños' efforts to fit the fight in La Ciénaga on April 15 into a longer history of conflict between themselves and immigrants from the United States suggests that—contrary to the assertions of Fábrega and other officials from Nueva Granada—their actions on that night were not spontaneous and certainly not unthinking. It would have hardly been surprising if Arrabaleños had taken preparatory measures to defend the city after the arrival of the *Cortes*. In his report, Corwine pointed to two clues that support this idea. The first of these was the ringing of the bell of the parish church of Santa Ana shortly after the argument between José Manuel Luna and the drunken passenger. The second was the speed and apparent coordination with which men from the Arrabal converged on

La Ciénaga after the ringing of the bell and the spread of the news of a conflict between a man from the United States and a fruitseller.[108] It is possible that the proximity in time between the bell ringing and the fight was nothing more than a coincidence. The initial report on the violence in the *Panama Star and Herald* explained the ringing of the bell as an alarm prompted by the outbreak of a fire elsewhere in the Arrabal.[109] But if the bell was not in itself a signal, it appears that Arrabaleños were far from surprised by the news that a filibuster had attacked a fellow countryman or countrywoman in La Ciénaga. The preparations in the plaza of Santa Ana on April 16 indicate that Arrabaleños were prepared to work in concert to thwart any such attack in the future.

Conclusion

The events of April 15 exposed the costs of Panama's transformation at the hands of the railroad company. They also revealed the determination of Arrabaleños to defend rights only recently acquired, as well as a shared sense of both responsibility and entitlement to take up arms to defend their city against invasion by filibusters. There were indeed filibusters in Panama City on the night of April 15, as the accounts written by Horace Bell and others confirm. But except for Stokes, they were not leading figures in the violence of that night. In the confusion that followed after the fight in La Ciénaga, however, many Arrabaleños apparently came to see any white person from the United States whom they did not know as a potential threat. Any doubts that Arrabaleños might have had about the malign intent of those unfamiliar foreigners would have been settled by the actions of the passengers and Stokes himself, who responded to what they perceived as unprovoked attacks with gunshots and other measures that in their eyes constituted acts of self-defense.

In contrast to Stokes, however, the passengers from the *Illinois* represented a different face of U.S. expansion in the 1850s: not an advance guard of territorial conquest but a rear guard of immigrants on their way to a land that the United States had already annexed. They were armed principally with carpetbags rather than guns or swords. On the evening of April 15, these passengers tragically found themselves subjected to violence that they could only have perceived as entirely unprovoked and undeserved. It was this perspective that Corwine sought to represent in his final report rather than that of the filibusters, which he omitted entirely from his account.

In May 1850, when the elite Liberal Manuel María Díaz had been the provincial governor of Panama, Arrabaleños had accused him of being a puppet of immigrants and doing too little to defend his own people. Six years later, on the nights of April 15–16, Francisco de Fábrega was subjected to even harsher criticisms from the Arrabal, including the charge of treason. Díaz, meanwhile, found himself in a more ambiguous position. On the night of April 15, he had exhorted men in La Ciénaga to withdraw from the scene of the conflict in the company of Ran Runnels and had found himself largely ignored. On the following night, he took the side of men in the Arrabal who demanded arms from the vice governor. These apparent shifts in Díaz's position in relation to the Arrabal likely reflected broader changes in the arena of sovereignty over the previous six years. Whereas Arrabaleños' political power in 1850 had been largely limited to the streets, men from the Santa Ana now exercised the right to vote, and many if not most were members of Díaz's own Liberal Party. They were also potential supporters for his own pursuit of higher office, and Díaz would announce his candidacy for governor of the state only a few weeks later, in May 1856.[110] Díaz was thus a man who could ill afford to side against Arrabaleños at a moment when they feared that their own lives were in jeopardy, regardless of whether he believed that filibusters were truly on their way to attack the city.

Six years earlier, in May 1850, Arrabaleños had desisted in their fighting against U.S. immigrants after they were addressed in the plaza of Santa Ana by Gen. Mosquera, a Conservative leader and former president of Nueva Granada who wielded considerable local and national influence. The Conservative Francisco de Fábrega addressed Arrabaleños in the same plaza six years later, on April 16, with a similar goal—that of cooling tempers and reclaiming the political initiative for elite men such as himself from poor men of color in the Arrabal. In contrast to 1850, however, Arrabaleños refused to go home. Instead, they organized their own commission to investigate whether the reports of filibusters were true, and they insisted that the vice governor arm them so that they could take up the defense of the city themselves. Despite his evident terror at the idea of black men with guns, Fábrega had ultimately acceded to their demands, albeit with the proviso that Díaz would have to take personal responsibility for their use.

If the events of April 15–16 indicated a decrease in the deference that Arrabaleños showed elites of San Felipe from both parties, they also served to reinforce what was by 1856 a long-standing refusal on the part of working people of color in Panama to submit to demands for racial submission

15 one can only speculate. But a recognition of the hardships as well as the victories won by Arrabaleños over the course of the gold rush can help us appreciate better the range of meanings that could have accrued to the words of Luna's rebuke: "Careful, we are not in the United States here; pay me my *real* and we're even."

Chapter 5

U.S. Empire and the Boundaries of Latin America

The conquests of the late 1840s transformed the United States into a transcontinental nation. As novel as this territorial aggrandizement may have seemed to its own citizens, the United States was a latecomer to the list of transcontinental republics in the Americas. The other such republics in existence in 1848 included Mexico, Guatemala, Nicaragua, Costa Rica, and Nueva Granada. After the abolition of slavery in Nueva Granada in 1852, the United States was the only one of these six that still countenanced slavery as a legal institution within its borders. The sudden appearance of an aggressive slaveholding republic sitting astride North America proved disturbing to many observers located to the south. What could be done to halt the apparent advance of what the propagandists of Manifest Destiny touted proudly as an inherently expansionist "Anglo Saxon race"?

One answer to this question came in the form of calls to create diplomatic alliances or multinational confederations composed of states with a shared interest in preserving independence from the United States. Although these efforts ultimately failed to produce concrete results in the realm of diplomacy, they proved more successful in the domain of the political imagination by helping to call forth a new geopolitical idea: the concept of Latin America, or "América latina." Among the most prominent advocates for a specifically "Latin" political unity in Nueva Granada was Justo Arosemena. His writings and events on the ground in Panama after April 15 offer an opportunity to see connections between the emergence of ideas of Latin unity in the Americas, struggles over popular sovereignty, and the course of U.S. empire on the isthmus.

A Disputed History

According to Martin Lewis and Kären Wigen, "Latin America" is one of the oldest regional designations on the planet.[1] Nevertheless, the precise origins of the term remain controversial. In an essay published in 1968, the U.S. historian John L. Phelan credited the concept to pan-Latinist intellectuals close to Napoleon III, including Michel Chevalier, who sought to justify French intervention in Mexico in the early 1860s by asserting solidarity between France and Mexico based on a shared belonging to the "Latin Race." According to Phelan, it was only after the French coined the term that Spanish-speaking intellectuals in the Americas adopted the concept of Latin America for their own purposes.[2]

Although Phelan's account of the French origins of Latin America retains significant influence among English-speaking and French scholars of Latin America, his hypothesis was refuted almost immediately by Arturo Ardao, the Uruguayan philosopher and historian of ideas. Ardao credited the first use of the term "América latina" as a place that was distinct from the Latin countries of Europe to a *granadino* writer living in Paris named José María Torres Caicedo and specifically to his poem "Las dos Américas." Apparently written in September 1856, the poem appeared in February 1857 in *El Correo de Ultramar*, a Spanish-language newspaper published in Paris.[3] Miguel Rojas Mix subsequently suggested the Chilean Francisco Bilbao as another possible progenitor of the concept of Latin America, citing as evidence a speech delivered in Paris by Bilbao in June 1856.[4] The debate over who first articulated the idea of Latin America, and when, will undoubtedly continue. But the scholarship of Ardao and Rojas Mix and more recent contributions by Paul Estrade and Mónica Quijada have clarified both that the concept of Latin America as a geographical and political entity predates French intervention in Mexico and that 1856 represented if not the beginning then at the very least a watershed in the emergence of that concept.[5]

Against A Common Enemy

Following the U.S.-Mexico War, proponents of Manifest Destiny in the late 1840s and early 1850s created uneasiness throughout the hemisphere with boasts about conquering not only the rest of Mexico but also possibly the rest of the Americas. Walker's exploits in Central America and the violence in Panama of April 15 helped to galvanize a more general sense of urgency among intellectuals and diplomats from different points in the Spanish-speaking Americas. So, too, did a number of other encounters with the United States in the aftermath of the U.S.-Mexico War, including the Gadsden Purchase of 1853–54, disputes over guano islands in the Pacific, and filibuster plots directed at places such as Mexico, Cuba, and Nicaragua. In 1855, a conflict over the presence of a U.S. naval vessel in the Paraná River led to a protracted effort by the United States to extract compensation and commercial concessions from the Paraguayan government. In Chile, apprehensions of U.S. expansion arose in response to oppression of Chilean miners by Anglo-American vigilantes in California, competition between U.S. and Chilean grain producers, and tension with the United States and Ecuador over the control of guano deposits off the coast of South America.[6]

From the vantage point of the United States, these different episodes could easily have seemed largely unrelated to one another. But prominent diplomats elsewhere in the Americas interpreted these same flashpoints as the constituent parts of a constellation that portended further assaults on the rest of the hemisphere by the United States. The possibility of a continental treaty or alliance with the purpose of containing the United States was discussed by representatives from a number of different countries in the late 1840s and early 1850s, including Argentina, Bolivia, Brazil, Chile, Ecuador, Mexico, Nueva Granada, Peru, Venezuela, Mexico, and the republics of Central America. In July 1856, Venezuela proposed a conference among the Spanish-speaking republics in the Americas in Panama. This congress was never held. In Santiago, Chile, however, representatives of Chile, Peru, and Ecuador signed a "continental treaty" on September 15, 1856, which expressed the intention to form a union designed to preserve the independence of its member republics. In a similar spirit, Pedro Alcántara Herrán, the minister of Nueva Granada in the United States, called together a gathering of fellow diplomats from Hispanic American states in Washington, D.C., in November 1856. After a two-day meeting, representatives from Costa Rica, Guatemala, Nueva

Granada, Salvador, Peru, and Venezuela entered into a preliminary treaty or "plan of alliance."[7]

Neither of these conferences resulted in fully ratified treaties, and diplomatic efforts to establish alliances to stem U.S. conquest remained largely stalled throughout the rest of the 1850s. William Walker's surrender in 1857 eased much of the apprehension about filibustering in the Americas. But in 1856, observers from the Spanish-speaking Americas still had good reason to believe that projects for U.S. territorial expansion would continue to assault the rest of the hemisphere.

U.S. Narratives of April 15

For observers from Nueva Granada, U.S. reactions to the news of the violence in Panama City on April 15 proved particularly worrisome. Amos Corwine concluded his official report with a call for the United States to intervene forcibly in Panama as quickly as possible: "The interests our Countrymen have here are too great to be neglected, and left at the mercy of an ignorant, brutal race, such as infest the Isthmus, and who can neither be restrained nor subdued by the authorities of the country." The only solution, in his opinion, was U.S. military occupation or the "immediate occupancy of the Isthmus from Ocean to Ocean, by the United States." This call for "occupancy" stopped short of demanding annexation and instead portrayed U.S. military intervention as a temporary measure that could be withdrawn once Nueva Granada demonstrated its ability to safeguard the route.[8]

Corwine's justification for occupation presented a curious interpretation of the Bidlack-Mallarino Treaty of 1846, which obliged the United States both to protect the free flow of traffic across the route and to defend the sovereignty of Nueva Granada over the isthmus. At the time of the treaty's confection, negotiators from both countries had seen these two obligations as complementary. As Corwine read the treaty, however, the United States's role to defend the transit route gave it both the obligation and the justification to violate or infringe on the sovereignty of Nueva Granada if Nueva Granada itself could not provide adequate protection.[9]

Other calls were also made in the United States to take action to protect the route. In San Francisco, an anonymous writer for the *Daily Alta California* stressed the danger that events in Panama posed to California itself. According to his reckoning, overland transportation across the United States was vulnerable to harsh conditions and "bands of savages" while transport across the Nicaragua Route was seriously impeded by the ongoing war against William Walker. With the Panama Route now vulnerable to attack, the author argued, California had become dangerously isolated from the rest of the country. "We are thus, so far as safe communication is concerned, effectively cut off from the Atlantic States, and going to California after a seven years' settlement by Americans is assuming again its olden, attendant horrors. Unless something is done, and done quickly, we shall be greatly the sufferers."[10]

Frank Leslie's Illustrated Newspaper devoted the front page of its issue of May 17, 1856, to an account of the violence in Panama City of the previous month. An accompanying image purported to show the freight room of the Panama Railroad on the night of April 15. Black men armed with swords, machetes, and firearms assault an unarmed white family while another attacker makes away with what appears to be a piece of the family's luggage. Another image showed the battle under way outside the station, with bongos noticeably present in the foreground and the thatched houses of La Ciénaga looming menacingly on the fringes of the railroad's grounds. Two female passengers lie next to a bongo on Playa Prieta. The two women are clearly in distress, and one woman's chest is exposed. The obvious implication is that the women have been assaulted by male members of the crowd.[11]

Yet even this horrific scene could not compete for attention with the more generalized interest in stories of Walker's increasingly embattled campaign against the united armies of Central America. In May of 1856, the outbreak of violence between pro- and antislavery forces in Kansas over the question of slavery's expansion directed the attention of readers toward events within the United States's own borders. In San Francisco, meanwhile, incipient efforts to organize a private expedition to punish Nueva Granada for April 15 failed to move beyond a public meeting in the plaza of San Francisco on May 6 during which one of the speakers expressed his advocacy for "blowing Panama to h-ll."[12] Among the organizers was Charles Duane, or "Dutch Charley Duane." But Duane and others in San Francisco would soon be distracted by the murder later that month of the newspaper editor James King and the subsequent organization of a "committee of vigilance" that hanged two men accused of involvement in the murder.[13]

Rather than issue public calls to punish Nueva Granada or blow Panama "to h-ll," the directors of the Panama Railroad Company chose a quieter course. Outrage over a horrific slaughter could only have dampened the

Fig. 7. Anonymous. "Massacre at Panama." *Frank Leslie's Illustrated Newspaper*, 17 May 1856. Courtesy of the Newberry Library.

value of the company's stock and given hope to speculators with stakes in competing interoceanic routes across Mexico, Honduras, and elsewhere in Central America. In a private letter to the secretary of the navy, the president of the company urged that U.S. warships be sent to protect the route. But he made no demands, publicly or otherwise, for annexation or retaliation by the U.S. Navy against the population of Panama.[14] As he explained in a letter to Totten, his ideal resolution to the problem of sovereignty over the transit route was the establishment of a protectorate whose neutrality would be guaranteed not by a single nation but rather by mutual agreement between great powers with a stake in the route. As he wrote, "It has long been a favorite theory of mine that the great maritime powers of the world should unite in guaranteeing the neutrality of the whole Isthmus."[15]

Claims and Coercion

The U.S. diplomats charged by the administration of Pres. Franklin Pierce to negotiate claims arising from the violence of April 15 arrived in Bogotá with a proposed resolution that resembled Hoadley's "favorite theory." According to the scheme they presented in February 1857, the terminal cities of Colón and Panama City and the transit route were to become essentially self-governing and officially "neutral," or open to all. The transit route was defined as "a territory ten miles wide on each side of the Rail-road." The U.S. officials claimed that such an arrangement did not violate the sovereignty of Nueva Granada and compared the status of the ports and the route to "States in a federal compact." The neutrality of the transit route was to be guaranteed by the United States and any other nations who accepted the U.S. government's invitation to join it. In addition, the diplomats demanded that Nueva Granada cede to the United States the rights it had obtained through its contract with the Panama Railroad Company and two groups of islands in the Bay of Panama, which the U.S. government offered to purchase from Nueva Granada for the purposes of a naval station. In contrast to the transit zone, the United States was to enjoy total sovereignty over these islands and a U.S. naval station was to be established there. Finally, the United States demanded monetary compensation for all claims by U.S. citizens against Nueva Granada.[16]

The diplomatic strategy pursued in Bogotá by U.S. officials in early 1857 shared less in common with the annexationist policy that produced the Treaty of Guadalupe-Hidalgo of 1848 than it did with strategies of commercial empire that the United States had pursued earlier in Central America and East Asia, including the creation of treaty or free ports in which local sovereignty was curtailed or eliminated altogether in order to facilitate U.S. economic and military interests. U.S. officials in Bogotá sought to explain their plans for Colón and Panama City by explicitly referring to San Juan del Norte or Greytown as a precedent. Located on the Atlantic coast of Nicaragua, San Juan by the early 1850s was inhabited by a significant settler population from the United States. Acting largely on their own, these settlers declared the city to be a "free port," which meant both that the port was open for trade to all and also that it was to be governed by its own inhabitants independently of Nicaragua or any other state.[17] Seven years before, in 1844, the United States obtained commercial privileges from China that included the right to purchase land in five designated treaty ports and the right for U.S. citizens accused of crimes to be tried in U.S. consular courts. During his second voyage to Japan in 1854, Commodore Matthew Perry pressured the Japanese to concede commercial rights in designated ports as well as other privileges to the United States in the Treaty of Kanagawa.[18]

If U.S. officials imagined that their reference to San Juan del Norte would somehow calm the fears of officials in Nueva Granada, they were wrong. The national government rejected the proposed arrangement as a violation of its sovereignty and claims negotiations dragged until September 1857.[19] The general reaction in Bogotá to news of April 15, 1856, was one of outrage and concern. Rumors abounded of U.S. invasion and an attempt to annex Panama in the manner of Texas or California less than a decade before. Liberals generally called for resistance to U.S. demands and vowed to take up arms in the event of a U.S. invasion. Conservatives, by contrast, tended to be more resigned and expressed the fear that Nueva Granada might soon lose Panama to the United States through what they perceived to be a combination of U.S. acquisitiveness and the fecklessness of Panamanian officials.[20]

The American Question

Even before U.S. officials presented their demands to the national government of Nueva Granada, Justo Arosemena stepped into the debate over the significance of the violence of April 15 with an essay entitled "La cuestión americana i su importancia" (The American Question and Its Importance). This essay appeared in July 1856 in *El Neogranadino*, a Liberal newspaper published in Bogotá, where Arosemena was representing the state of Panama as a senator in the congress.[21]

Arosemena reminded his readers that their era was one in which "movement" or improved communication had created what he described poetically as a "formidable empire." This "cosmopolitan kingdom" of movement amounted to a new, accelerated state of being in which distance and physical barriers mattered less than in the past thanks to technological change and laws that favored the free circulation of trade, people, and ideas. The advent of the empire of movement was in Arosemena's view something to be celebrated. Like some latter-day prophets of globalization, he assumed that the increase in the speed and extent of communication among the world's peoples would promote progress and greater unity among members of the human species.[22]

According to Arosemena, there was no place on earth that was more important for the production of movement than the isthmus that linked Panama and Central America. That production was threatened, however, by the outrages of William Walker and other acts of aggression emanating from the United States. He portrayed the war against Walker and the brewing diplomatic controversy over April 15 as integral parts of a larger, epochal struggle between the "raza yankee" (Yankee race) and the "raza latina" (Latin race) over the future of "the American continent" and even the universe.[23] As evidence of the United States's designs, he cited events including the conquests of Texas and California, filibustering, the Pierce administration's official recognition of Walker's government in Nicaragua, Commodore Matthew Perry's expeditions to Japan, and recent events in Panama, including the depredations of Ran Runnels's Isthmus Guard, the U.S. refusal to support local government through the payment of taxes, and the insistence of U.S. officials on referring to the city of Colón as Aspinwall.[24]

Arosemena had already departed Panama City for Bogotá by April 15, 1856. But he assured readers that Panamanians were only bystanders to the violence of that evening and that the entire episode had been unplanned, accidental, uncoordinated, and devoid of any characteristics of a "popular movement." As he wrote, "El pueblo of Panama was not the protagonist [in the conflict with passengers] but rather a few of those upstart blacks ["negros advenidizos"] with origins in many countries, especially the Antilles." According to this interpretation, the violence of April 15 had resulted from the conflict between passengers from the United States and people of African descent whom Arosemena defined only vaguely but who had clearly stepped beyond what he perceived as their proper place.[25]

The struggle over the future of the isthmus was in Arosemena's view a matter of "interés latinoamericano" or "Latin American interest"—one with significance to all members of the Latin race on the American continent from Mexico to the tip of South America.[26] The adjectives that he used to describe the Latin race included "spiritual," "heroic," "chivalrous," "noble," and "sentimental."[27] In contrast, he described the Yankee race as "materialistic," "cold," and "industrial." The Yankee race was fundamentally corrupted, in Arosemena's view, by what he described as the "invasive spirit of conquest."[28]

Arosemena's characterization of the differences between the Yankee race and the Latin race bore certain similarities to the writings of proponents of Manifest Destiny in the United States such as James Buchanan, the Democratic politician and future president, or the journalist John L. O'Sullivan. Advocates of U.S. expansion also portrayed the "Anglo Saxon race" as fundamentally domineering or conquering by nature. But whereas expansionists in the United States celebrated this characteristic, Arosemena condemned it as unjust and ultimately self-destructive. U.S. descriptions of male members of the Spanish-speaking elite in the Americas, or "dons," often characterized such men as deluded by illusions of chivalry, effete, and effeminate. Arosemena conceded that members of the Latin race were more spiritual and sentimental than the Yankee race, but he reclaimed those characteristics as masculine virtues that would ultimately lead the Latin race to greatness.[29]

Arosemena's calls for a specifically "Latin American" or "Hispanic American" unity in the Americas resembled the writings of advocates of pan-Latin unity elsewhere, including Torres Caicedo. As early as 1850, while he was the editor of the Bogotá newspaper *El Día*, Torres Caicedo had warned of the United States's designs on the Isthmus of Panama. Six years later, in an article titled "Confederación de las naciones de la América española," he praised the "sons of Panama" for their actions on April 15 and then compared U.S. claims for damages from the government of Nueva Granada to Walker's aggression against Nicaragua.[30]

Like Torres Caicedo, Arosemena saw the ultimate salvation for the Latin race in the Americas in a confederation or an alliance of nations composed of members of the Latin race. As did some other federalists in Nueva Granada in the mid-1850s, Arosemena also called for the reconstitution of Colombia (or Gran Colombia), which he envisioned as the basis for the larger confederation he proposed. He articulated a similar aspiration to reinvigorate Colombia in a speech that he delivered in the same month of the publication of "La cuestión americana" in Bogotá. In contrast to his essay, however, in his speech Arosemena rejected the term "América" altogether and advocated instead for "Colombia" as the name of a confederation that would stretch from Panama all the way to Cape Horn. He did not state explicitly whether this vision of an expanded Colombia included Brazil. Given Arosemena's focus on the "Spanish race," however, it is likely that it did not.[31]

Torres Caicedo's and Arosemena's calls for a confederation among Hispanic American nations echoed earlier notions of political unity advanced by Simón Bolívar in the context of the Congress of Panama in 1826. But whereas Bolívar was chiefly concerned with threats to American sovereignty from Europe, Torres Caicedo and Arosemena identified the greatest danger to the independent republics carved out of the Spanish empire as the United States. Arosemena's and Torres Caicedo's characterization of the racial differences between the United States and the Latin peoples of the Americas owed less to Bolívar than to racial theories circulating in the 1850s and suggest the influence of French writers including Michel Chevalier and Félicité de Lamennais.[32]

Torres Caicedo articulated the racial nature of the struggle over the future of the hemisphere in his 1856 poem, "Las dos Américas," which is concerned primarily with William Walker and the struggle over Nicaragua:

> The race of Latin America [*América latina*]
> Finds itself confronted by the Saxon Race,
> Mortal enemy who now threatens
> To destroy its liberty and its banner.[33]

The "América latina" of Torres Caicedo's poem is no mere extension of a Latin Europe. Rather, it stands alone in its confrontation against the United States.[34] The same was true of Arosemena's portrayal in "La cuestión americana." Both France and Spain were too weak in Arosemena's view to offer any assistance, and Great Britain seemed to him too self-interested and too committed to trade with the United States to offer any support.[35]

Arosemena predicted the rapid decline of the Yankee race. Skeptical of racial mixing, he thought that immigration from Europe had vitiated the racial or national character of the United States and transformed the northern republic into "a living Babylon." He argued furthermore that the United States's territorial conquests had made it too large and unwieldy to survive for long as a nation. Most fatally, the United States's tolerance of slavery was in his opinion inimical to democracy. He anticipated with considerable prescience that the conflict in the United States between northern and southern states over slavery's expansion would soon lead to the disintegration of the country.[36]

For Arosemena, "raza" or race was essentially a synonym for nationality. Although he acknowledged the importance of the influence of the past, he did not regard racial characteristics as fixed in a biological or any other sense. The key differences between the Latin race and the Yankee race existed in the realm of temperament and the spirit rather than skin color or other physical traits. Although Arosemena sometimes used the terms "Spanish race" and "Latin race" as if they were synonymous, the adjective "Latin" located the origins of the race at least implicitly in Rome rather than Spain. Yet Arosemena presented both the Latin race in the Americas and the Yankee race as fundamentally new creations rather than holdovers from Europe. In his view, the Latin race only began to come into its own after throwing off the yoke of Spanish rule during the wars of independence and embracing "democracy," which Arosemena associated with republican government, free labor, free trade, and federalism. Although he conceded that the Latin race was relatively weak in the present, he assured his readers that democracy would ensure its growth in the future.[37]

Enemies from Within

The appearance of Arosemena's essay in Bogotá in July 1856—one month after Bilbao's pivotal speech and two months before the writing of Torres Caicedo's famous poem—indicates that the ideal of a specifically Latin American unity existed beyond the precincts of Paris much earlier than many previous scholars have allowed. What is perhaps more interesting about "La cuestión americana," however, is the evidence it provides of how Arosemena envisioned the Latin race in opposition not only to the "raza yankee" but also elements internal to "Hispanic American territory." Those who fell outside the bounds of Arosemena's vision of the Latin race included not only Yankees and others with origins outside the Hispanic American nations but also "black upstarts" in Panama City, particularly West Indians. If West Indians of African descent were clearly excluded from Arosemena's dreams of Latin unity, the roles of indigenous peoples and native people of African descent and *castas* more generally were less clear. He made no explicit reference to indigenous people in "La cuestión americana" except to note their destruction in North America by Yankees. One year before, in *El Estado Federal de Panamá*, Arosemena had written of indigenous peoples in Panama as if they had ceased to exist after the Spanish conquest—a destruction he regarded as a lost opportunity to educate and civilize native peoples to become productive members of the population.[38] In both "La cuestión americana" and *El Estado Federal de Panamá* Arosemena criticized the United States for its widespread discrimination against people of color.[39] By implication, then, people of indigenous and African descent might form part of Arosemena's Latin American polity, provided they were properly civilized and did not forget their place. But Arosemena sketched out no explicit vision for their inclusion or elevation in either work, and "La cuestión americana" makes it clear that his sympathies lay primarily with people of Spanish heritage or creoles such as himself. Like the vision of "el pueblo" articulated by Espinar or the more radical articles in *El Panameño*, the language of Latin unity provided a way of speaking about people in Panama and Nueva

Granada that glossed over the color or racial distinctions of the colonial caste regime, including distinctions between whites, blacks, *mulatos*, and Indians. But unlike the ideal of "el pueblo," it did so in a way that emphasized European origins at the expense of the indigenous or African heritage of the continent's inhabitants.

Renewed Fears of Caste War

The limits of elite Panamanians' visions of political unity would become more apparent in the months following April 15, 1856. On April 22, 1856, a ship bearing armed men from the United States anchored off Panama City. Rather than filibusters, these men were U.S. sailors and marines who arrived aboard the USS *St. Mary's*, under the command of Capt. Theodorus Bailey. Upon his arrival, Bailey directed an insulting letter to Fábrega in which he accused the local population of "outrages, robberies and murders" committed against "innocent and unarmed men, women and children, who were peaceably endeavouring to pass this great highway of nations." He demanded an immediate explanation from Fábrega so that he might determine "the necessity, of any immediate interference, for the protection of the persons and property of the citizens of the United States."[40] Two days later, he wrote an even harsher letter in which he accused Fábrega of sophistry and criminal inaction, if not complicity in the "frightful atrocity" of April 15.[41]

Bailey received a supportive welcome from the French consul, who warned Bailey that there were "2 to 5,000 blacks" in Panama who were "well armed." The British consul was more reserved, however, and expressed the opinion that there was no imminent danger to traffic across the isthmus. Although Bailey thought he could easily destroy Panama City, he doubted that he could seize the city and protect the railroad line with only two hundred men under his command.[42]

When Bailey ordered one of the gunboats of the *St. Mary's* to be stationed near the wharf of the railroad station in Panama City to greet the arrival of a train from Colón, Fábrega demanded that the U.S. consul of Panama City ensure that U.S. sailors committed no act "that could be interpreted as a violation of our territory." A U.S. military presence in Panama was entirely superfluous to the maintenance of order, he argued, and on April 28 he reassured U.S. officials that he had readied the city's police force to "prevent any collision between passengers and natives."[43]

Fábrega's insistence on the inviolability of national sovereignty began to change, however, in the face of increasing political organization of the Arrabal. May of 1856 saw the emergence of a new organization in the Arrabal named Amigos del Órden (Friends of Order). An admiring history of the Amigos appeared on May 17, 1856, in the *Panama Star and Herald*, which characterized the group as "the political society of the Arrabal." According to the anonymous Panamanian author, the Amigos had been founded after April 15 by "a party of the people living in the Arrabal" who had "offered their services to the Governor of the State" to protect passengers and others in the city against "the thieves who robbed, killed and committed various disorders against the undefended strangers" on that terrible day.[44]

Like the Democratic Societies founded in Bogotá, Cali, and other parts of New Granada in the early 1850s, the Amigos provided an institutional basis for the mobilization of the recently enfranchised, both at the polls and, when necessary, on the battlefield or in the streets. As rumors continued to circulate about the possibility of a foreign invasion, the Amigos del Órden took on the form of a militia whose dual purpose was to defend Liberal political interests and to protect Panama City itself against any foreign invaders. The choice of name for the club posed Arrabaleños not as revolutionaries but rather as defenders of order.[45]

The formation of the Amigos represented a further development in the political history of the Arrabal. During the elections for the constituent assembly in 1855, Arrabaleños had rejected efforts by elites to impose a slate of candidates upon them. During the nights of April 15 and 16, 1856, they had likewise exhibited considerable independence not only from elites in the Conservative party but also the elite leadership of the Liberal Party. At the same time, the society's own hierarchy suggested that within the Arrabal itself there still were limits to political voice for men of color. Even though the majority of the Amigos were from the Arrabal, the official leader of the society was an elite white man: Pedro Goytía, who had earlier led Liberals in the rural peninsula of Azuero against Fábrega and his Conservative allies in the region.[46]

On May 15, 1856, the U.S. consul of Panama City expressed his concern about the Amigos in a letter to Fábrega: "I am informed by reliable authority that the society named 'Amigos del Orden' have for some days past been making preparations for some event expected to take place on the arrival of the American passengers from New York, that the said society have some 300 muskets, and have lately put up about 1500 cartridges and are prepared to use these arms."[47] Fábrega responded that he was aware of the group and that their base of operations was the Arrabal.[48] According to the vice governor, the Amigos had been formed "with the object of repelling any attack by robbers or filibusters."[49] But he acknowledged that they were also opposed to his own government: "I am inclined to believe that these elements are destined to attack the government of the state, of which the leader [Pedro Goytía] . . . and a considerable number of individuals of the Arrabal have declared themselves to be irreconcilable enemies."[50]

The brief history of the Amigos that appeared in the *Panama Star and Herald* of May 17, 1856, made light of concerns expressed by unnamed foreigners in Panama City about the society. As the author explained, Pedro Goytía had stepped forward to provide the Amigos with munitions only after Fábrega refused to arm the organization properly. According to the author, Fábrega had tried unjustly to paint Goytía as if he were opposed to foreigners on the isthmus. The author denied this charge and described Goytía as a man whose republican ideals transcended national frontiers: "Sr. Goita [sic] has no country nor brothers—his country is the world and his brothers all republicans who, [at] heart, are friends of social guarantees and of industrial liberty."[51] Despite these assurances, however, the editor of the *Panama Star and Herald* had harsh words both for the Amigos, whom he linked with the people "who massacred our countrymen on the 15th April," and also for Fábrega, whom he ridiculed for tolerating an organization that had the clear intent to overthrow his own government.[52]

On May 24, Fábrega directed a letter to the U.S. consul in which he both warned against any effort by foreigners in the city to arm and organize themselves independently of his own authority and also suggested the possibility of forming an alliance between elites in Panama City and members of the expatriate population. The alliance that he proposed would consist "of all men of property and honor, without distinction among nationalities," and would be logically directed by the local government, apparently meaning himself.[53]

Fábrega directed similar letters to the French and British consuls in Panama City. Although the French consul expressed interest in some form of cooperation, the U.S. and British consuls both demurred. In his response to the vice governor, the U.S. consul argued that an alliance of the kind proposed by Fábrega might embroil U.S. citizens in the internal political struggles of Nueva Granada such as the current conflict between Fábrega and the Amigos.[54]

Meanwhile, provocative rumors continued to circulate in the city. On May 21, 1856, Fábrega wrote to the U.S. consul with a report that "a rumor is circulating in the city to the effect that the steamer 'Sierra Nevada' which is due to arrive soon from San Francisco brings two or three hundred filibusters with hostile intentions toward this country."[55] When the *Sierra Nevada* finally arrived, Fábrega ordered boatmen in Panama City not to transport any passengers from the ship to the land.[56]

In the end it was found that the *Sierra Nevada* had not brought an invading army to Panama. But there was good reason to fear such an invasion, for the *Sierra Nevada* had previously transported filibuster recruits to Nicaragua's Pacific coast and would continue to do so until early 1857.[57] The *Panama Star and Herald* dismissed rumors of filibuster attack as ridiculous. But on May 27, it published its own report on the meeting held in San Francisco of May 6, where speakers had spoken favorably of William Walker and promised to "avenge the blood of slaughtered women and children at Panama."[58]

On June 2, 1856, Capt. Bailey wrote that a recent shooting in San Felipe had given rise to a false rumor that "a foreigner had shot a native woman." According to Bailey, this rumor alarmed "the negroes in the suburbs." No further conflict took place, but Bailey stationed boats from the *St. Mary's* close to shore to prevent any disturbance.[59]

The tensions between the Intramuros and the Arrabal and rumors of attacks by filibusters continued with the approach of the election for the next state governor on June 29, 1856. As with the election of March 1855, Liberals found themselves divided by the city's fortifications. Initially, the Amigos del Órden supported Manuel María Díaz while Liberals in San Felipe expressed support for Justo Arosemena and Tomás Cipriano de Mosquera, a Conservative. Eventually, however, Liberals united around the candidacy of Díaz, which was in itself a testimony to the growing power of the Arrabal. Conservatives, meanwhile, rallied behind Bartolomé Calvo, a Conservative lawyer and journalist who hailed originally from Cartagena.[60]

On the eve of the election, Fábrega expressed despair over the state of affairs in Panama City. Rebuffed by the United States and the British, the Conservative vice governor came to feel increasingly beleaguered and isolated. In a letter to the secretary of foreign affairs of Nueva Granada, he portrayed Panama City as mired in a conflict among three antagonistic forces. On the one hand was the Arrabal, which in his view was "motivated only by its hatreds or racial preoccupations." The population of foreigners in Panama City, though composed of "diverse nations and antagonistic races," was united in Fábrega's view by its "disdain and dislike" for Nueva Granada. Meanwhile, the elite population of the Intramuros seemed maddeningly oblivious to the dangers posed by both Arrabaleños and hostile foreigners.[61]

Despite Fábrega's fears, the election was conducted without any major incidents of violence. This peace was soon broken, however, with the approach of September 15—the date on which votes were to be tallied and the winner of the election was to be announced. Conservatives responded to Liberal mobilization in the Arrabal by reviving the rumors of caste war or race war that had bedeviled popular Liberals in Panama City since before the establishment of universal manhood suffrage in Nueva Granada in 1853. In late August, *El Centinela*, a Conservative newspaper, accused an Arrabaleño named Manuel Hernández of running through the Intramuros shouting, "Down with tyranny! Long live the blacks, death to the whites!" Hernández denied the accusation, but the fact that he felt compelled to answer at all pointed to the obstacle that rumors of race war represented for black men who sought to exercise an independent voice in electoral politics.[62] The possibility of race war was also raised in the *Panama Star and Herald*, which suggested that only the presence of U.S. ships prevented the initiation of a "war of color."[63]

Warnings about the growth of the Arrabaleños' political power were complicated by the perception that the Conservatives' own candidate for governor, who came from a key port on the Caribbean coast, was himself a man of color. In his private correspondence, the elite Liberal Mariano Arosemena described Calvo in racially derisive terms as a "zambo" (a man of indigenous and African descent) and as an "orangután."[64] A memoirist in late nineteenth-century Panama recalled Calvo in similarly condescending if less inflammatory terms as "a man of color, but very intelligent."[65]

On August 31, the *St. Mary's* was joined in the Bay of Panama by the USS *Independence*, the flagship of the Pacific Squadron, which was commanded by Commodore William Mervine. Immediately on his arrival in Panama City Mervine entered into a heated dispute with Fábrega over a tonnage tax that Fábrega had attempted to collect from U.S. ships. The commodore accused Fábrega of deceit and then reminded Fábrega of his by now infamous order to the police to take the railroad station on April 15. As Mervine wrote sarcastically, "Probably better faith could not be expected from an official who could so outrage humanity, as to *order* the massacre of defenseless women and children."[66] Even before his dispute with Mervine, Fábrega had agreed to suspend a tax on U.S. mails. Now, in response to thinly veiled threats from Mervine, he agreed to suspend the tonnage tax as well.[67]

On September 1, 1856, the legislative assembly convened in Panama City with the purpose of determining the winner of the gubernatorial election and electing a vice governor. Liberals formed the majority of the legislature and immediately elected Mariano Arosemena as president of the assembly. On September 2, the *Panama Star and Herald* reported that although Calvo had won the majority of votes for governor, Liberals in the assembly had sworn that they would prevent him from taking his seat.[68] Liberal deputies proceeded to initiate a complicated series of parliamentary maneuvers. Manuel María Díaz was elected vice governor while the counting of votes for the gubernatorial election was postponed until October 10. Liberals apparently hoped that Díaz would ascend to the position of acting governor on October 1, the constitutionally mandated day for the transfer of power from the standing chief executive of the state to his successor.[69] Liberal legislators also proceeded to pass a resolution that officially accepted the "services" offered to the state by the Amigos del Órden, whom the editors of the *Panama Star and Herald* now characterized as a "a lawless and armed band from outside the walls."[70]

As the likelihood of an armed conflict between Liberals and Conservatives increased, some elite families sent women and children outside the city to places of relative security in the Pearl Islands and rural areas of the state, while the editors of the *Panama Star and Herald* charged Liberals in the legislative assembly with "raising up a war of caste."[71] The presence of U.S. ships in the Bay of Panama complicated the hostility between the two parties by raising the possibility of U.S. intervention and even annexation. William Nelson reported on this situation in a letter to the railroad company president, Hoadley: "A great deal of ill feeling exists between the Governmental and the opposition or so called liberal party. The whites inside of the walls fear they will be attacked by the blacks; the leaders of both parties are trying to unite [the population of Panama City] against the Americans, who, they say, wish to seize the Isthmus."[72]

Rather than unite Panamanians, however, the presence of U.S. ships led to divisions along lines of color and gender that cut across allegiances to political party. Conservatives in Panama City protested that the Liberal attempt to postpone the counting of votes was unconstitutional. Over one hundred Conservatives signed a petition that warned that if the law were not changed to ensure the announcement of a victor before October 1, a "civil war" could easily take place.[73] But when Conservatives attempted to present the petition to the legislative assembly on September 14, a number of Liberals deliberately absented themselves from the assembly to prevent the formation of a quorum.[74]

The Flight to the USS *St. Mary's*

Reports circulated around Panama City of an armed conflict between the two parties that was to begin on September 15. The Amigos del Órden took refuge in the Arrabal while Conservatives prepared themselves for battle in San Felipe. Members of elite families of both parties fled the city. In response to requests from people in San Felipe, U.S. naval officers allowed a large number of these refugees to take shelter on board the *St. Mary's*.[75]

Among those who went aboard the U.S. ship were members of the Arosemena family. Josefa Dolores Arosemena de Rice, the daughter of Mariano Arosemena and sister of Justo, gave her perspective on the turmoil in a letter she wrote aboard the *St. Mary's* on September 15, 1856. A member of the most prominent elite Liberal family in Panama City in the mid-1850s, Josefa was married to an expatriate from the United States who lived in Panama City. Yet as she related in her letter, her family connections to the Liberal Party did not stop her from seeking refuge aboard a U.S. naval ship once it became clear that Arrabaleños were not content to accept Conservative victory in the gubernatorial election. As she explained, she and her children as well as her mother and sisters had taken refuge on the ship in anticipation of a "conflict . . . between the two political parties on the governatorial [sic] question today." She noted that marines were mobilizing to protect "the whites" of Panama City and expressed the hope that her father, Mariano, would soon join the family on board. She claimed that his life had been threatened but did not specify the source of that alleged threat.[76]

Rather than join popular Liberals in the Arrabal, Arosemena had apparently decided to seek refuge in the French consulate. Upon being refused by the French consul, he proceeded to board the *St. Mary's*, where his daughter, wife, and others in his family were taking refuge from black men from the Arrabal.

Commodore Mervine expressed his reaction to finding Mariano—whom he misidentified as Justo—and other members of the Arosemena clan on board the ship: "I found the prime mover of all these troubles, Sr. Justo Arosemena with his family on board of the 'St. Mary's,' to which vessel this despicable coward fled for protection, after having been denied an asylum in the French consul's house. This man and his son are the editors of the Panameño—a public paper, one of the bitterest enemies our Country has in Panama, and the author of all the articles that have appeared in that paper against us."[77] Mervine noted with satisfaction that the presence of U.S. naval ships "appeared to paralyze all action of the Revolutionists." The lesson he drew from the day was that the "two races [white and black] can never live on terms of equality."[78]

U.S. Intervention

But the conflict was not over. Theodore de Sabla, who was by then the acting U.S. consul in Panama City, described the situation in Panama City on September 18, 1856, as follows: "Much excitement has been prevailing in this place and is still on the increase. Two political parties have been formed, one composed mostly of the black and colored population . . . the other, probably less in number, have amongst them the great part of the white natives and are led by the Acting Governor." Although de Sabla was acting as U.S. consul, he was a native of Panama, and his views about the correspondence between color and party were those of an elite man from San Felipe.[79]

Mervine reported on September 18 that there were "three thousand negroes living outside of the walls, who are armed and organized—the same persons who perpetuated the horrible massacre of the 15th of April last."[80] Meanwhile, Conservatives cobbled together what they claimed was a quorum by finding replacements for the missing Liberals, whose number included the Goytías as well as José Isabel Maitín—the silversmith who had received a vote from José Manuel Luna in the election for the cabildo of 1851.[81] Mariano Arosemena, the president of the assembly, also did not attend, although his absence was counted as being "excused," which suggests that he may have asked permission to absent himself from the session. At nine thirty in the evening, the recomposed assembly declared Calvo the victor by nearly 7,000 votes and proclaimed the restoration of peace after the "lengthy suffering caused by conflicts between the parties." According to the official results, Calvo won 10,205 votes compared with 3,393 votes for Díaz.[82]

On September 19, Pedro Goytía and other missing Liberals returned to claim their seats in the assembly and fighting broke out between deputies of the two parties.[83] According to de Sabla, both parties "rushed to arms: the 'black' party retiring outside the walls of the city."[84] The *Panama News and Herald* accused Liberal leaders of urging on the "negroes" outside the cabildo to attack their political adversaries. In an apparent reference to the Amigos del Órden, the editors of the paper claimed that "the Government has been threatened by an armed mob of organized negroes, who boast that they will sack the city and murder the white population."[85] According to the same newspaper, "armed negros" from the Arrabal entered San Felipe and retreated only after they were confronted by government troops and learned that the U.S. ships of war in the bay were prepared to attack in the event of any injury to foreigners.[86]

After it became clear that Arrabaleños were prepared to fight to secure victory for their candidate, Fábrega sent word to de Sabla on September 19 of his desire to have U.S. ships move closer to shore. At first de Sabla refused to consider anything less than a formal, written request.[87] But then Mervine himself asked the vice governor for "permission . . . to station some men at the Rail road depot and office." Apparently to allay accusations that the United States was acting unilaterally, U.S. officials asked Fábrega to make a written request in the presence of British, French, and U.S. consular officials for what amounted to the first U.S. military intervention in Panamanian history. Soon afterward 160 marines rowed to shore with a fieldpiece and took up a position at the railroad station.[88]

Conservative Repression

Conservatives took advantage of the U.S. military presence and moved quickly to arrest Pedro Goytía and his father, José María, who were both promptly sent into exile in Cartagena. Meanwhile, the legislative assembly met and officially proclaimed Calvo as the governor.[89] On September 22, Mervine ordered his men back to their ships. Not a single shot was fired during the entire episode.

Invasion from the United States had finally come—but in a form very different from what Arrabaleños had anticipated. Rather than an attack by filibusters bent on conquering territory, the intervention was a brief occupation that occurred with the consent of the vice governor and ended as soon as Conservatives reestablished control and U.S. officials felt sure that the railroad station was no longer under threat.[90]

Following the return of the marines to their ships, the *Panama Star and Herald* continued to warn of the possibility of an attack by Liberals and compared the efforts by Arrabaleños on behalf of Díaz to the Haitian

Revolution: "The populace outside the walls are no more subdued now than they were before the arrest of their political leaders—they still have their arms—they still have those men amongst them who, when the opportunity serves, will rouse their courage, and, still worse, those fiendish and brutal passions which always have characterised a rising of the negro race." Black men, the newspaper postulated, might easily revolutionize Panama and dissolve its bonds with Nueva Granada: "Should the negroes once gain possession of Panama—the most important point—we will have here a second San Domingo. Another Christophe may make his appearance amongst us, and thus the nationality of the Isthmus be lost." According to the newspaper, the proper response to this danger was U.S. military intervention, which it argued was fully justified by the Bidlack-Mallarino Treaty of 1846. The newspaper further urged Fábrega to declare martial law and take advantage of the presence of U.S. ships to disarm the "turbulent" elements of the local population.[91]

In contrast to Corwine, who had argued in his final report that the treaty entitled the United States to intervene even against the will of Nueva Granada, the anonymous author in the *Panama Star and Herald* portrayed the United States as a protector of the sovereignty of Nueva Granada. The greatest threat to that sovereignty, according to the author, came not from outside Nueva Granada but rather from within: "the negro race," and more specifically black supporters of Manuel María Díaz.[92]

Fábrega did not declare martial law. Once Conservatives had the state government firmly under control, however, they began to pursue Liberal activists, and many Liberals were forced to flee the Panama City. The Liberal party itself, meanwhile, splintered along lines of color, class, and neighborhood. Some Liberals switched to the Conservative side in the legislative assembly even as the Amigos del Órden retreated from the city. On September 25, the *Panama Star and Herald* reported that a "deputation" from the Amigos del Órden had met with Liberal deputies who had taken refuge in the countryside, including José Isabel Maitín. To complete the destruction of popular support for the Liberal Party, the *Panama Star and Herald* urged Fábrega to pass a vagrancy law in Panama City that could be used to quell "the present revolutionary spirit which now pervades the lower class of the population."[93]

On September 30, the Conservative-dominated legislative assembly passed a number of resolutions during a secret session that included a condemnation of the national government for failing to provide the state government of Panama with sufficient military force.[94] On September 29, in an apparent effort to promote reconciliation, the legislative assembly established a general amnesty for all individuals involved in conflicts of the preceding month. An exception was made for the Goytías, who had been sent into temporary exile. Mariano Arosemena chose voluntarily to exile himself and later joined the Goytías in Cartagena.[95]

The Conservative candidate, Bartolomé Calvo, was inaugurated as the new governor of Panama on October 1. Representing the United States at the ceremony was de Sabla, who was himself a citizen of Nueva Granada. Opposed to black power when organized en masse, Conservatives had proved themselves capable at least temporarily of overlooking skin color in the case of Calvo. De Sabla did not say in his own correspondence whether he perceived the new governor as a man of color. If he did, it would appear that he, too, was capable of overlooking color if it suited him.[96]

The Lie of Caste War

Although elite Liberals in San Felipe and Liberals in the Arrabal proclaimed their adherence to the same party, the sight of black men mobilizing in the Arrabal to defend their candidate for governor in mid-September apparently proved too much for Mariano Arosemena and the womenfolk in his family. Rather than join forces with his fellow Liberals in the Arrabal, he chose instead to take his place among his fellow inhabitants of San Felipe aboard the *St. Mary's*. Another sign of alienation between popular and elite Liberals had come in a change in the tone of the Liberal newspaper, *El Panameño*. Immediately after April 15 *El Panameño* had portrayed those who had joined in the violence as heroes who had defended the city from filibusters holed up inside the railroad station. By October, however, an anonymous author in *El Panameño* was offering advice that was remarkably similar to the patronizing suggestions the Conservative newspaper *El Vijilante* had directed toward freedpeople following the abolition of slavery four years before. The author opined that although Fábrega's actions in September had been "arbitrary," they had served valuable purposes, in that they had contributed to the reestablishment of order and demise of the "Amigos del Órden." As the author wrote: "For the vulgar class—the poor and the needy—to claim ownership of government and enter into politics is ridiculous. This class should concern itself with earning its daily subsistence—men born to be artisans and laborers can never be public leaders."[97] The expression of such an opinion in a Liberal newspaper in 1856 indicated that even among Liberals, the right of Arrabaleños and other working people to participate in electoral politics remained contested.

Rumors of race war resurfaced again two years later in the context of the following gubernatorial election. In order to rebut these accusations, a new Liberal newspaper in Panama City known as *El Elector* provided an account of the events of September 1856 that vilified Conservatives and defended the honor of Arrabaleños. An anonymous author with clear sympathies for popular Liberals in Panama City argued that the accusation of race war and the very idea of antagonism between blacks and whites in Panama were not only lies but also sources of national dishonor: "Since the evil hour when the Fábrega Administration and their henchmen traitorously invented the race question, that is, the question of whites and blacks—to their dishonor and the dishonor of the nation—something absolutely impossible among us—the germ of disunion that is killing us was also created." *El Elector* continued in a vein that anticipated arguments that would be made by Cuban patriots later in the nineteenth century. It accused Conservatives of exposing the nation to U.S. intervention and national humiliation by stoking an unjustified fear of blacks in both foreigners and elite women in Panama City: "Mr. Fábrega and his followers deceived the foreigners and women into the belief that the blacks [of Panama City] sought only to rob and kill, misrepresenting their principled actions as if they were motivated only by race. They triumphed in this way, having committed the treason of inviting foreign bayonets to violate our territory, and many of them asked for the Americans to make this land their own."[98]

El Elector's gendered logic of honor resembled that which they accused Conservatives of exploiting two years before. But *El Elector* altered the racial terms of that logic. Conservatives, according to *El Elector*, had argued that black men represented a threat to the honor of white women. In doing so, they had not only defamed their fellow citizens but also brought dishonor to themselves and to their country by provoking the intervention of foreign troops. The honor that was violated in *El Elector*'s account was not that of white women but that of a national territory gendered as female. As stalwart defenders of that territory, it was the Liberals of the Arrabal who were the true defenders of virtue, and white Conservatives who were the despoilers of honor, through their spreading of lies that had made them accessories to foreign soldiers and their bayonets.

As befit the newspaper's name, *El Elector* rejected the arguments of members of Panama City's elite that the time was not yet right for former slaves and the urban poor to participate in electoral politics. Black men were equals to white men in the present, and *El Elector* offered the actions of el pueblo during the election as proof:

> If between us there existed or ever could exist such a thing as hatred be-tween whites and blacks, if blacks have such a desire to rob and kill whites, as is vulgarly said, and if these accusations have some validity, then why is it that they do not rob and kill any day they please, instead of only on elec-tion day? The inventors of this infamous calumny know better than any-one, and el pueblo has demonstrated splendidly . . . that it is a lie.[99]

Sympathies of Race

Any Conservatives who hoped that the U.S. Navy or the Panama Railroad Company would become a consistent source of support would be roundly disappointed. As Mervine made preparations to order U.S. marines to shore, he made it clear that the purpose of the marines was solely to pro-tect U.S. citizens and property, and that he had no intention to interfere "with any domestic affairs." Hostile exchanges between the U.S. consulate over taxation of the transit route persisted throughout the next two years, and the Panama Railroad Company and the U.S. Department of State con-tinued to press claims for the destruction caused on April 15.[100]

Theodore de Sabla reported at the beginning of October 1856 that "several respectable natives" had communicated to him the desire to "see the U.S. Government interfere to relieve them from their uncertain and perilous situation." According to him, members of the "white" party had begun to assemble a petition asking that the United States "take possession of and protect this place should the efforts of the Acting Governor prove unavailing to repress the outbreak" that was expected.[101]

Nevertheless, the correspondence of U.S. officials in Panama and offi-cers of the Panama Railroad Company does not betray a special fondness for either the Liberal or the Conservative Party but rather an equal disdain for both. Despite the *Panama Star and Herald*'s and Amos Corwine's warn-ings about the danger posed by the "negro" population of the isthmus, the relative lightness of skin of most Conservatives apparently made little dif-ference to the company officials in their calculation of the company's interests. In a letter written on September 29, 1856, William Nelson indicated that he had learned of considerable support among the Conservatives for a movement to establish Panamanian independence from Nueva Granada with U.S. protection—Conservatives would rather live under the aegis of the United States, he thought, than see themselves ruled by Liberal men of color, or what Nelson himself vulgarly characterized as "a *nigger* government."[102]

Yet Nelson frankly doubted that Panamanian independence would serve the interests of the company. Not only might Great Britain object, but if the sovereignty of Nueva Granada over the isthmus were terminated, the company's own contract with the central government would be nullified. What would happen if Panama became independent and the contract for the railroad were put up for grabs? The company might easily lose the right to conduct the railway that the company itself had constructed. In the face of these dangers, Nelson counseled Hoadley to deal with Panamanian conspirators with great care: "I should not be surprised if some of the leaders approached you on the matter. It will be necessary to be cautious with these fellows—their plan looks very much like high treason."[103]

Hoadley, for his part, expressed the opinion that the company should conduct its business without any entanglement in party politics, lest it provide an opening for "British capitalists," who, he believed, were anxious to seize the route for themselves.[104] What opening this might be Hoadley did not specify. But clearly he recognized that even if the U.S. government could be persuaded to attempt to establish a protectorate, it could not act unilaterally without facing serious opposition from Great Britain, whose navy dwarfed that of the United States. Although Hoadley and Nelson did not themselves dwell on this fact, there was also the not insignificant matter of the United States's 1846 treaty with New Granada, which established the U.S. government as the guarantor of the sovereignty of Nueva Granada over the isthmus. But this was apparently of little concern to them compared with the threat posed by the British.

By the time of the next gubernatorial election, in 1858, the Conservative candidate for governor, José Marcelino Hurtado, had become convinced that the United States now favored the Liberals. In his private correspondence he revealed a complicated personal theory that the U.S. government had formed a secret alliance with Liberals in the Arrabal. This support was supposedly designed to convince blacks that they could act with impunity, provided they did not damage any U.S. property. Then the United States would seize on the rampage as an excuse to intervene and appropriate the isthmus, countering any recriminations from Great Britain or France with the excuse that occupation was necessary to prevent blacks from committing atrocities. As Hurtado wrote,

> We see great sympathies [among the Americans] for the party of the blacks; and I know from a good source that the Americans have assured the leaders of that party that their forces would not intervene as long as they only assault the persons and things of citizens of Nueva Granada. This infamy has the object of animating the blacks to commit excesses without fear of being impeded by the Americans, and then expose to the eyes of the whole world the methods they will take, for as I have said, under the pretext of giving guarantees, I fear that they will land their troops with the outbreak of the smallest disorder.[105]

Hurtado acknowledged that if such a disturbance occurred, it would be hard to avoid the temptation to request military assistance from the United States. Nevertheless, in an apparent reference to Fábrega's request for aid from U.S. troops two years before, he expressed his determination to avoid what he perceived as a trap set for him by U.S. conspirators: "Unfortunately, we do not have sufficient public force to enforce the authority of the law; but of one thing I can assure you, those who seek conflict so that we will be obligated to request the help of foreigners are mistaken, because this will not happen again in Panama."[106] What Hurtado feared most was not the presence of U.S. troops on Panamanian soil. On the contrary, he acknowledged that such a presence might well have advantages for his government, provided they eventually returned to their ships. What he sought at all costs to prevent was the appearance before the eyes of "the whole world" that U.S. intervention was somehow a necessity, for fear that it would provide the United States with an excuse to justify its aggression in the region before its imperial rivals. Hurtado explained the predicament in another letter written one year later: "The disembarkation of the American force, requested by local authorities, would have resulted in grave complications and might have resulted in the perpetual occupation of the Isthmus by American troops; and the whole world would have accepted this fact, because [the disorder] would have been caused by *granadinos*, and what is more, the very Panamanian authorities would have to admit as much."[107]

The possibility of U.S. intervention or even annexation also caused national leaders of Nueva Granada to ponder what they perceived to be the racial views of U.S. whites. Writing in 1858 as attorney general of Nueva Granada, Florentino González expressed his fear that the large concentrations of people of African descent on Nueva Granada's Caribbean coast might render that region vulnerable to assaults by filibusters from the U.S. South, who had already attempted to reimpose African slavery under Walker in Nicaragua. González wrote, "I have no doubt that the filibustering enterprises will continue, and that if we do not soon organize ourselves solidly we will become their target. The states of Magdalena and Bolívar would offer many advantages as slave states and could provoke the ambition of the entrepreneurs of conquest from Louisiana, Alabama, Florida, Tennessee, Indiana, Kentucky, and Missouri." He confessed that annexation to the United States might prove beneficial for the states of Santander, Boyacá, Cundinamarca, and Antioquia "since the white race is quite numerous in these, and they could maintain their importance if annexed to the Union." Nevertheless, he voiced his opposition to annexation because, as he put it, "I know what fate would await the race that populates the valleys of the Magdalena and all the hot lands."[108]

In 1859 Nueva Granada's Conservative president, Mariano Ospina Rodríguez, directed Pedro Alcántara Herrán, his representative in Washington, D.C., to explore the possibilities of the annexation of Nueva Granada to the United States. In his response Herrán was lukewarm about formal incorporation into the United States, but he expressed the hope that if Ospina's government could reenter the good graces of the Buchanan administration, the United States might offer assistance in suppressing Liberal revolts along the Caribbean coast of Colombia. As he explained, the belief among U.S. whites that the rebels were black might provide the hook that would draw Democrats in the United States onto the side of Conservatives in their struggles with Liberals on the Atlantic coast of Nueva Granada: "The belief here is that the scandals on the coast are the misdeeds of blacks. The fifteen states of the South [of the United States], out of their own self-interest, are ready to help directly or indirectly so that such revolts are repressed. The Democratic Party, which now has power in its hands, would not look on with indifference at a revolution of blacks led by white or half-white demagogues."[109]

Despite convictions in both Panama and Bogotá that U.S. policies were driven by an indelible commitment to white supremacy, events in Panama City itself reveal a more complicated story. Given the continued existence of slavery in the United States and laws that specifically disenfranchised men of color in states such as California and New York, it is not hard to see why observers in Panama City or Bogotá might think that fears of race war would propel the decisions of U.S. naval captains or determine the United States's support of Conservatives over Liberals. Nevertheless, U.S. hostility toward the state government appears to have been driven more by opposition to Panamanian efforts to impose taxes on international commerce than any love for "the party of the blacks," and Hurtado's suspect description of Liberals as mere puppets of the United States smacks of elite condescension.

Company officials were obviously not blind to differences in color or race, as Nelson's reference to "nigger government" makes clear. But they were also willing to put their pursuit of profit above issues of color or nationality. Rather than seek the annexation to the United States or territorial conquest of the kind envisioned by William Walker, the Panama Railroad Company took the more discreet course advocated by Nelson. A weak foreign government that left the company alone to do its business served it better than a change in sovereignty that might lead to war with Great Britain or the cessation of the company's rights on the isthmus. The skin color of the officials who manned that government meant little, or at least less than it had to the white immigrants who had streamed across the isthmus at the beginning of the gold rush. The fact that Calvo was perceived at least by some to be a man of color did not prevent the attendance at his inauguration of the acting U.S. consul, who was himself a citizen of Nueva Granada.

When relations between the company and Nueva Granada went wrong, the company sought to further its ends not by plotting annexation but by working with sympathetic officials such as Amos Corwine or the secretary of the navy. Rather than invaders bent on the conquest of territory, the marines who came ashore in September 1856 had a more limited agenda, one that focused on the preservation of U.S. property and lives. Although no record has apparently survived of Pres. Hoadley's opinion of the brief intervention, it seems likely that he would have approved.

Conclusion

Events in Panama and Walker's exploits in Nicaragua help explain the calls for pan-Latin unity made by Arosemena, Bilbao, Torres Caicedo, and others in 1856. The enlargement of the networks of steam combined with U.S. military intervention and filibustering transformed questions about slavery and territorial expansion from internal debates within the United States into compelling issues for the Americas as a whole. As Arosemena had foreseen in "The American Question," the answer to the question of whether slavery and freedom could coexist would be no, in both the United States and Nueva Granada. But the United States would first have to pass through the storm of civil war before its own constitution approached the principles proclaimed by Liberals in Nueva Granada in the previous decade. And even then the United States, with its own particular interpretation of federalism, would hold back from a declaration of a national right to universal manhood suffrage.

The return of the marines to the *Independence* and the *St. Mary's* did not put an end to fears that the United States would seek to annex Panama or reestablish slavery on the isthmus. Writing on March 18, 1857, Commodore Mervine informed the secretary of the navy of "occasional excitements among the people of Panama, owing in part to national characteristics and somewhat to rumors put in circulation to alarm their fears and foment prejudices against our citizens, by attributing to them the designs to take possession of the Isthmus of Panama and reduce the blacks to a state of slavery."[110] These fears may have been stoked by William Walker's official reestablishment of slavery in Nicaragua in September 1857. Writing again on April 2, 1857, Mervine informed the secretary of a "bad feeling" among the people of Panama City caused by "the belief that our Government intends to seize the City and Isthmus and enslave the colored race."[111]

Liberal perceptions of the differences between Nueva Granada and the United States were neatly summarized in a remarkable article that appeared in *El Elector* in Panama City in 1858. The article took the form of an imaginary dialogue between Nueva Granada and the United States. In the dialogue the United States appears as a hypocritical menace bearing down on the people of South America. Nueva Granada stands up to this menace, telling the United States, "Halt right there!" Nueva Granada then proceeds to dispense systematically with U.S. justifications for conquest: "What do you want? Political reforms? We already have them. Riches? We will acquire them. Liberty? You are no more free than we are. Fraternity? It is you who own slaves, despite your wealth, and we own none. Population? We shall obtain it." Shamed into "taking off the mask and stripping itself of sophistry," the United States is left with no alternative but to confess its naked ambition: "WE WANT YOUR TERRITORY."[112]

Such expressions of concern about U.S. expansion in the mid-1850s may seem odd to some historians of the United States. By 1856 the wind had largely fallen out of the sails for further territorial annexation in the United States itself, as conflict between opponents and supporters of slavery in the West came increasingly to consume domestic politics. But denunciations of U.S. conquest in 1856 and afterward make more sense when one looks beyond the continental United States toward the isthmus of the Americas, to the battlefields of Central America and the Arrabal of Panama City.[113]

Even as Justo Arosemena participated in the popularization of the idea of Latin America in print in the mid-1850s, his essay and the events in Panama City of September 1856 hinted at the racial limits of elite conceptions of political unity. Justo's father, Mariano Arosemena, had been willing to enter into alliances with men of color from the Arrabal despite the fears he expressed in his private correspondence about race war. But once Liberals and Conservatives picked up weapons in mid-September 1856, he fled to the safety of a U.S. warship.

Despite the convictions expressed in *El Elector*, the U.S. empire that had begun to emerge in Panama by 1856 was less concerned with control over territory than it was with the control of the flow of information, people, and capital across the isthmus or the "empire" of "movement," as Arosemena had put it so eloquently in "The American Question." Race was by no means irrelevant to this new order, but U.S. whites' racial views were not necessarily reliable predictors of the alliances that U.S. officials formed on the ground in Panama itself, as evidenced by the U.S. navy's aid to Calvo's cause in September 1856.

For elite Liberals, the election of September 1856 proved to be a dispiriting if not entirely crushing defeat. In a private letter written on September 22, 1856, Manuel María Díaz bitterly denounced Fábrega as a "tyrant" and condemned Conservatives for violating deputies' constitutionally guaranteed right of immunity from arrest.[114] From his exile in Cartagena, Mariano Arosemena wrote to his son, Justo, in November 1856 that he could not bring himself to return to Panama despite having received word that it was safe for him to do so. Referring to Calvo, the newly installed governor, he wrote, "The very idea of seeing that Orangutan in power makes me shudder."[115] In a supreme moment of despair, he even suggested that Panama might be better off if it were annexed by the United States.[116] Two years later, Justo Arosemena confessed his own discouragement in a private letter to Salvador Camacho Roldán in which he complained that all political debate in Panama had been reduced to "a single question: the question of blacks and whites."[117] For *El Elector*, by contrast, the portrayal of republican politics as a war between blacks and whites represented a slur against patriots who stood ready to defend liberty whatever the cost.

Conclusion

Conversations in the Museum of History

In the United States today, the dominant symbol of U.S. westward migration remains the covered wagon. But by 1856 the Panama Route was the preeminent path for people, letters, and gold in transit between the nation's two coasts. The prize that Panamanians won in return for this preeminence was a kind of invisibility that was peculiar to an era of railroads and steamships. Within the United States itself, people did not have to think about Panama or even know of its location on a map to benefit from Panama's advantages as a place of rapid transshipment of people, letters, gold, and other cargo. The transit had become routine, undistinguishable from train travel anywhere else except for details such as the views of tropical forests through the windows or the exotic fruits that could be purchased at either end of the route.

The gold rush had seemed at first to offer a return to the prosperity Panama had known in the colonial period. But the boom times of "La California" were long gone by the time Jack Oliver strode into La Ciénaga. By April 1856 Arrabaleños could see all too clearly the consequences of the conquest of Panama's system of interoceanic communication. Yet for those imbued with unprecedented rights of citizenship, Panama remained a place that was worth defending. Between May 1850 and April 1856 Arrabaleños

had translated reforms legislated by Liberals in Bogotá, including the abolition of slavery and universal manhood suffrage, into power in the arena of
sovereignty in Panama itself, power that could be gauged in terms of both
popular participation in local elections and physical force in the streets of
Panama City. The U.S. intervention and the Conservative repression of
September 1856 demonstrated that there were very real limits to the exercise of those rights. But those limits did not necessarily make the gains any
less precious.

Paths of Empire

For historians of the United States and Latin America alike, the events in
Panama during the gold rush offer an opportunity to rethink the course of
U.S. empire and its consequences for Panama and the Americas more generally. Scholars of U.S. expansion in the Americas long divided this history
into two stages. The first was the period of westward or continental expansion, understood to conclude with the "closing of the frontier" in 1890.
The second period was that of overseas empire, which began in earnest in
1898 with U.S. interventions in Caribbean and the Pacific, the so-called
Spanish-American War. Historians of Latin America in the United States
told a similar narrative of U.S. imperialism in the region. After making note
of the U.S.-Mexico War and filibustering in the 1850s, they picked up their
accounts of the "new imperialism" in the late nineteenth and early twentieth centuries.

   According to this division of the historical terrain, the California Gold
Rush was relegated largely to the history of continental expansion, whereas
discussion of Panama was mostly consigned to the second period of overseas empire, starting with the foundation of the Republic of Panama in
1903 and continuing to the building of the Panama Canal. When Panama
appears in U.S. histories of the gold rush, it is usually in the context of the
early stages of the story, in chapters that focus on gold seekers' journeys to
California, before what has become the defining moment of the gold-rush
era for Panamanians: La Tajada de Sandía in 1856.

   More recent scholars have questioned this stark opposition between continental expansion and overseas empire. Once anathema to historians who
insisted on the "exceptional" character of U.S. history, the idea of the United
States as an empire, comparable with other instances of empire in world history, has become increasingly prominent not only in academic circles but

on the pages of newspapers and news magazines in the United States. A rich and interdisciplinary literature has emerged whose exponents argue that "westward expansion" consisted no less of conquest than expansion anywhere else.[1] Others have built on Walter LaFeber's argument, first voiced four decades ago, that the "overseas expansion" of the 1890s represented a continuation of earlier projects of continental expansion rather than a peculiar aberration.[2] Recent books and articles have pointed out the linkages between imperial projects beyond the formal limits of the continental United States in the late nineteenth and twentieth centuries and developments within the United States itself, including the subjugation of Native Americans, the rise of Jim Crow, and Progressive reform.[3] Scholars working on the period of the 1840s and 1850s have begun to make similar arguments, noting the connections between filibustering expeditions abroad and the politics of conquest, slavery, and gender within the United States itself.[4]

A consideration of the gold rush as an event in Panamanian history can help us see more clearly how even "continental expansion" in the late 1840s and early 1850s hinged on extraterritorial or overseas empire. The making of U.S. empire in Panama was not a by-product or an aftereffect of the Anglo-American conquest of California that continued in the years after 1848. It was integral to and coincident with that conquest. This is not to say that the immigrants traveling west to California or the gold traveling east from California's mines could not have crossed someplace other than the Isthmus of Panama. But many of the immigrants and most of the gold did cross there, and the remaking of Panama into a passageway between the west and east coasts of the United States had important consequences that Panamanians still remember, even if people in the United States have largely forgotten.

The time of California in Panama was comparable in some ways to the gold rush as it unfolded in parts of California. Similar to what transpired in California's northern mines, Panama's transit economy went through a boom that in the late 1840s and early 1850s seemed to offer ample opportunities to those who were able and willing to take advantage of them. By 1856, however, many of those opportunities were gone. In both Panama and the northern mines, companies financed by capital from the northeastern United States and the introduction of steam-powered technology played leading roles in the consolidation and conquest of once-booming economies.

In the arena of sovereignty, there were similarities as well. The gold rush created new political opportunities that citizens of both California and

Panama seized on to win status as states within larger, federal republics. In both places, women were excluded from suffrage. No slaughter of indigenous peoples took place in Panama that can compare with the bloody events of California in the early 1850s. But indigenous peoples in both places were largely excluded from the realm of electoral politics. Men of African descent in Panama possessed rights in Panama by 1856 that had no correspondence in California, including the right to vote and a right to testify in courts that was in no way diminished or enhanced by the color of one's skin. It was no accident that Persifor Smith made his nativist decree barring "foreigners" from the goldfields of California in Panama City in 1849. At the beginning of the gold rush, the Panama Route became a funnel for people of many different nationalities headed to California with the hope of striking it rich. But no official, systematic effort to exclude or discriminate against non-Panamanians took place in Panama in the early 1850s that could compare with the efforts by U.S. whites to exclude "foreigners" in California in the early 1850s.

The Anglo American conquest of politics in California was by no means a total one—in certain regions of the state, *californios* still wielded considerable power in 1856.[5] In Panama, by contrast, the political power of "Anglo Saxon" immigrants waned over the early 1850s. At the start of the gold rush, immigrants from the United States had demanded their own courts from Nueva Granada and had often stalked about Panama City as if the place already formed a part of the United States. By April 1856, by contrast, white immigrants from the United States were a relatively fleeting presence, even as the fear of attack by filibusters remained very real. Short-lived vigilance committees became part of the political landscape of both Panama and California in the early 1850s. But while white vigilantes in California often targeted native peoples and so-called foreigners, Ran Runnels's Isthmus Guard was a thoroughly transnational, multiracial affair that was financed in large part by the Panama Railroad Company.

These broad strokes inevitably fail to capture the complexity of the similarities and differences between Panama and California as they were experienced by actual individuals in the late 1840s and early 1850s. But by April 15, 1856, it had become abundantly clear to José Manuel Luna that Panama was a place that was significantly different from the United States. No doubt those differences became more apparent to his drunken antagonist as well in the hours following his arrival in La Ciénaga.

Ironically, the diminished power of white immigrants in Panama derived in part from the economic conquest wrought by the Panama Railroad

Company and steamship companies in Panama. The empire created by the Panama Railroad Company has received far less attention from historians of Latin America and the United States than the brazen missions of conquest led by William Walker and his filibustering brethren. But in the end it was not Walker's vision of conquest but rather that of the Panama Railroad Company that would prove to be more indicative of the future of U.S. imperialism in the region. Rather than attempt territorial conquest, U.S. enterprises such as the United Fruit Company would seek wealth and power primarily through the kinds of strategies pioneered by the Panama Railroad Company, U.S. diplomats, and U.S. naval officials in Panama in the early 1850s.[6]

The growing importance of the Panama Railroad's more discreet form of empire was nicely symbolized by the departure of the defeated Walker from Nicaragua in 1857. Beaten on the field of battle, Walker and his associates were rescued from annihilation by the USS *St. Mary's*, the very ship on which Mariano Arosemena and others from San Felipe had taken refuge from Arrabaleños in the previous year. Many in Panama itself had seen U.S. naval ships and filibustering as part of the same phenomenon—a perception that was no doubt encouraged by the wavering policies of the U.S. government itself toward Walker and other filibusters. But when the *St. Mary's* arrived off Nicaragua's Pacific coast, the ship's objective was not to reinforce Walker but to pluck him out of Central America before he and his compatriots could cause any further trouble for the Buchanan administration. After the *St. Mary's* deposited Walker in Panama City, U.S. naval officials escorted him onto a train bound to Colón, where he alighted on Panamanian soil for another instant before being whisked away to the United States aboard another ship. The infamous and much-feared filibuster had finally arrived in person in Panama. When he set foot on the isthmus, however, he did so not as an invader but as a passenger.[7]

Despite the concerns of Governor Calvo, the railroad company whisked Walker from one side of the isthmus to the other. Reflecting on Panamanian fears in a letter to William Nelson, Hoadley expressed some amusement at Panamanians' perception of the company as somehow supportive of Walker's efforts in Nicaragua. On the contrary, he wrote, "Our sympathies run the other way."[8] Any success that Walker might achieve in restoring the operation of the transit route across Panama could only have hurt the Panama Railroad Company. As president of a company incorporated in the state of New York, Hoadley's allegiance to his company and its stockholders was greater than any affinity he might have felt for his wayward countrymen in Nicaragua.

Yet despite his lack of sympathy for Walker, Hoadley admonished Nelson to avoid embroiling the company with either the filibusters or their enemies: "[T]his Company is determined to avoid all complicity with either side [in the Nicaragua conflict]." Adopting a position that was oddly reminiscent of Justo Arosemena's insistence on neutrality, Hoadley was determined to keep the company focused on the business of transporting people and goods across the isthmus with as little entanglement as possible with political parties in Panama or the war that was being waged in Central America.[9]

The Panama Railroad Company carried on long after Walker finally fell before a firing squad in Honduras in 1860. The Panama Railroad was the first U.S. company to create a divided labor force on the Latin American continent through the importation of free workers from the British West Indies—a practice that was later pursued by the United Fruit Company and the builders of the Panama Canal, including the French attempts of the 1880s and 1890s as well as the U.S. construction effort that led to the completion of the canal in 1914. The new city the company created on Panama's Atlantic coast—Colón, or Aspinwall—became the first of a series of company enclaves or dense concentrations of U.S. economic and political power that sprouted up within the borders of other nations in Central and South America in connection with the banana industry and other forms of export agriculture and resource extraction.

Over the rest of the 1850s Panama City grew in importance as a nexus in steamship lines linking Europe, the Americas, and the Pacific. By the early 1860s the city had become more prosperous than it had been in the immediate aftermath of the completion of the railroad in 1855. But in terms of population and commercial activity, it was still far from the place it had been briefly in 1849 and 1850, and even farther from the emporium that elites had idealized. The Panama Route still derived most of its importance in the world economy from traffic between the east and west coasts of the United States until the completion of the transcontinental railroad across the United States in 1869 curtailed that traffic dramatically. The inauguration of this second transcontinental railroad in world history cast Panama into another period of relative economic isolation, one that was only partially relieved with the beginning of the ill-fated French effort to build a canal in the 1880s.[10]

The brief occupation of September 1856 was only the beginning of a history of U.S. intervention, which finally severed Panama from Colombia altogether in 1903. U.S. troops intervened in Panama thirteen times between 1856 and 1903.[11] The diplomatic conflict between the United States and Nueva Granada arising from the violence of April 15 led ultimately to the signing of a claims treaty in 1857. According to the terms of this treaty, Bogotá accepted blame for the loss of U.S. lives and property, and restitution was limited to a monetary payment. Over the ensuing years, the national government paid a total of $412,393.95 to the United States. The last of the payments was made in 1874.[12]

The U.S. intervention of September 1856 represented a transformative moment as U.S. officials and commentators came increasingly to see the Bidlack-Mallarino Treaty as a justification to intervene military in ways that disregarded or disrespected the sovereignty of Nueva Granada that the treaty had been created to protect. U.S. officials would take this logic even further into the realm of absurdity when they cited the 1846 treaty as a justification for U.S. intervention that enabled the separation of Panama from Colombia in 1903.[13]

The advent of what Arosemena identified in "The American Question and Its Importance" as the empire of movement signified in his mind a fundamentally positive development, and he would work for much of the rest of his life for a canal to be built across Panama. But his writings also expressed fears for the future of the people of Panama, Nueva Granada, and the Latin race in the Americas more generally if they did not succeed in turning those possibilities to their own advantage.

No doubt it is analytically useful to differentiate colonialism or the formal establishment of territorial control from informal or nonterritorial forms of domination. But there is also much to be gained from recalling the relations of mutual dependence that could exist among colonial metropoles, national territories, and nodal points in communication networks such as Panama, which may not have been colonized but were vital nevertheless for holding empires together. Panama was no colony of the United States in the mid-nineteenth century, but the order that emerged on the isthmus by the 1850s undeniably impinged on the sovereignty of the state of Panama and Nueva Granada, and the creation of that order was intimately related to conquests of native peoples, land, and resources in California and elsewhere within U.S. borders during the same period.[14]

The building of the Panama Railroad in the early 1850s did not foreordain the building of a canal across Panama in later years. Yet once the U.S. government selected Panama as the site for constructing a canal at the beginning of the twentieth century, its efforts to build that canal drew on earlier construction projects in Panama, not only the French attempts to finish a canal in the 1880s and 1890s but also infrastructural elements that had been created during the gold rush, including the city of Colón and the railroad line itself.[15] By 1903 the Panama Railroad was a very different entity from the one it had been during the gold rush, having passed through changes in ownership and other alterations. But the route across Panama itself remained very similar to what it had been in 1855. By 1903 the city of Colón had grown considerably, but it still retained the basic layout of streets created by the railroad company during the gold rush. In their constitution of the Canal Zone, U.S. officials in Panama attempted to resolve the problem of sovereignty over the route in a manner that resembled the proposal put forth by U.S. diplomats in Bogotá in 1856, by essentially removing the transit zone from the control of the nation that surrounded it—in this case not Nueva Granada but the newly independent Republic of Panama.

The U.S. government's direct involvement in the building of the canal, the foundation of the zone, and the shaping of the new Republic of Panama represented a level of intervention in Panamanian society beyond what even what the most wild-eyed expansionist could have imagined in 1856. Although Panama possessed importance for communication between the east and west coasts of the United States in this new era of U.S. imperialism, its primary role would be to enable greater access to overseas markets and communication between points in the U.S. empire, which now included formally claimed territories in both the Caribbean and the Pacific. Free from the restraint that the British had imposed on U.S. intervention in Central America in the mid-nineteenth century, U.S. intervention in Panama in the twentieth century would take on a formal character and a scale that would have been unimaginable in the mid-nineteenth century, most dramatically with the creation of the Panama Canal Zone.[16]

Racial difference figured in U.S.-Panamanian relations in the early twentieth century in ways that also differed from the mid-nineteenth century. The intense racial segregation for which the Panama Canal Zone would become famous had no equivalent in the 1850s. In September 1856, U.S. military intervention enabled a man of color, Bartolomé Calvo, to assume the office of governor of the state of Panama. In 1910, in contrast, U.S. officials successfully pressured Carlos Mendoza, the recently elected president of Panama, to resign because he was a man of color.[17]

While the more than five decades that span Calvo's inauguration and Mendoza's overthrow lie beyond the scope of this book, the difference between these two events may be explained in part by the intensification of scientific racism as the nineteenth century wore on, the more formal character of U.S. empire in Panama after 1903, and the presence of thousands of U.S. whites employed as canal employees in Panama in the early twentieth century. U.S. whites in the mid-1850s were not necessarily more disposed to look kindly at what William Nelson derisively called "nigger government" than they were in 1912. But Nelson, Runnels, and others who worked in the company's employ were capable of looking beyond their concerns about black political power when it suited them. In Nelson's case, at least, this capacity to set aside ideas about racial difference stemmed not from any belief in racial equality but rather a disdain for Panamanians that appears to have been close to universal. Although U.S. officials were capable of taking measures that might favor one political leader over another, they did not yet exercise anything approaching veto power over Panamanian politics. Efforts to exert power on that scale would have to await Panamanian independence in 1903.

U.S. Empire and the Making of a Latin America

The United States was not the only place to expand in the mid-nineteenth century—so too did Latin America, if only in the realm of political imagination. If subsequent U.S. historians have largely missed the connections among the making of empire in Panama during the gold rush, the Anglo-American conquest of California, and filibustering, the linkages among these three aspects of U.S. expansion were all too apparent to observers from Nueva Granada and elsewhere in the place we now know as Latin America. Assaulted seemingly from all sides, the Latin race's only remedy, in the minds of Arosemena, Torres Caicedo, and other advocates of Latin unity, lay in the formation of an alliance or confederation capable of withstanding what appeared from their perspective to be a concerted Anglo-Saxon onslaught. Arosemena's proposals for pan-Latin unity brought few practical results in 1856. The two diplomatic efforts to create defense alliances among Spanish-speaking republics in 1856—one in Washington, D.C., and the other in Santiago, Chile—bore little fruit, and Arosemena was not directly involved in either of them. But just as Arosemena and other pan-Latinists appropriated the ideas and writings of earlier political and racial theorists, their own attempts to articulate the differences between what they perceived as "two Americas" would be picked up and reworked by later advocates of Latin American unity in the late nineteenth and early twentieth centuries, including figures who are better known to scholars of Latin America today, such as José Martí and José Enrique Rodó.[18]

In this book I have focused on only one site in a far larger archipelago of pan-Latin theorizing that included other points in the Spanish-speaking Americas, Paris, and other places in Europe as well. Much work remains to be done to reconstruct the exchanges and interactions among these different sites. Arosemena's writings are significant for our understanding of that larger, transnational conversation not only because they stand among the earliest articulations of a specifically Latin American unity but also because they offer a window onto the interplay between racial theorizing in the realm of elite political thought and struggles on the ground, where purported differences in race or color could also emerge as dividing lines.[19] Just as the territorial expansion of the United States raised questions about the political significance of racial differences within U.S. borders as well as without, so, too, did the literary expansion of Latin America in the writings of Arosemena, Torres Caicedo, and other advocates of Latin unity.

The question of who counts as "Latin" American remains a vexed one in the Americas. While the debate has taken different forms over space and time, questions of color, ancestry, and linguistic difference have been central concerns since the emergence of the concept of Latin America itself. Scholars who seek to compare the workings of race in Latin America and the United States would do well to recall how the very units of analysis that frame such a comparison—the limits of both the United States and Latin America—were shaped by debates and struggles over racial inclusion and exclusion in the middle years of the nineteenth century.[20]

The Future of Panamanian Sovereignty

Rather than sour elite aspirations for mining the possibilities of Panama's geography, the disappointments of the gold rush helped rekindle an older dream: the quest for a canal. Long before the gold rush, elite Panamanian desires for self-rule had been linked to their determination to rebuild Panama's transit economy. By demonstrating the benefits of interoceanic commerce in the age of steam, and by revealing the perils that could ensue if the transit zone were inadequately governed, the gold-rush experience bound the quests for autonomy and emporium more tightly than ever.

In the realm of popular politics, the era of the gold rush saw the building of a foundation for mobilization in Panama City that would grow stronger in subsequent decades. In 1856 Arrabaleños' officeholding was limited largely to the municipal level, to seats on the cabildo or offices such as alcalde or judge. Yet the events of April 15 demonstrated that Arrabaleños were no longer willing to defer to elites in the way they had done in May 1850. The betrayal by elite Liberals during the September 1856 invasion came as a blow to Liberals in the Arrabal, but it also bespoke their growing independence from the elite leadership of their own party. By the early 1860s, Arrabaleños would rise to high office on the state level. The most successful of these leaders was Buenaventura Correoso, who had begun his political career as a judge who figured prominently in the gathering of testimony from witnesses following the violence of April 15.[21]

Arosemena's successful efforts to establish Panama as a federal state in 1855 marked the beginning of a history of federalism in Colombia that continued over the next three decades. Arosemena's brief time as head of the federal state in 1855 proved to be the zenith of his career as an elected official. But his efforts to find a form of sovereignty that was suitable for a universal point of transit continued, and he played an important part in future efforts to negotiate treaties and contracts for the building of canals across Panama. He played a prominent role in the drafting of Colombia's federalist constitution of 1863, and he would also remain active in efforts to promote political unity among the republics of Latin America.[22]

The same set of interrelated problems that plagued the federal state in the first year of its existence troubled government bodies in Panama in different forms for the rest of the nineteenth century: neglect by the national government, insufficient funds, and the frustration of efforts to extract revenue from the transit route itself. Whatever revenue the route produced was largely reserved by the national government for the national treasury.[23]

Although similar instability existed in other areas of Nueva Granada during the 1850s, the situation in Panama also reflected the peculiar challenges associated with the exercise of sovereignty by a single state over a transit route of international importance. In *El Estado Federal de Panamá* Arosemena had sought to imagine a form of government that could adapt the concept of sovereignty to a kind of commerce that by its very nature abhorred limits, whether those limits took the form of natural obstacles or man-made barriers such as tariffs or tolls. This abhorrence was a feature of capitalism in general, not just steamship or railroad companies. But it became particularly intense in a highly competitive market in which small differences in cost could result in huge profits for companies that were, by definition, highly mobile. Though the creation of the federal state did not solve this conundrum, Arosemena's writings were prescient in their diagnosis of the challenges that global capital poses to states with fixed borders.

The frustration of the quest for a canal over the remainder of the nineteenth century played a central role in the events that led to Panama's separation from Colombia in 1903. Far from a popular revolution, the almost entirely bloodless independence came as the result of a complicated alliance among a small and mostly elite group of Panamanian canal boosters, the U.S. government, and French and U.S. investors with financial interests in the Panama Route. One year later the United States essentially imposed a canal treaty on the new republic to provide the basis for the creation of the Panama Canal Zone—a colony in everything but name which ran through the center of the nation.[24]

After independence from Colombia in 1903, Arosemena's writings and the events of the gold rush in Panama were invested with new meaning as Panamanian historians in search of a national past looked back to the era of La California as a watershed in the making of the Panamanian nation. Though contemporaries in the 1850s often spoke of La California as the boom period of 1849 and the early 1850s, the term was later used by historians to embrace the entire period between 1848 and the completion of the transcontinental railroad across the United States in 1869.[25]

Even as La California took on different temporal dimensions, the defining moments of the period remained the founding of the federal state in 1855 and La Tajada de Sandía in 1856. Nationalists looked to the writings of Arosemena as the ideological foundation of Panama's independence from Colombia, and critics of the United States drew on these same writings for a vocabulary of resistance in a new era of U.S. imperialism. As Panamanian efforts to retake the canal began to show a more explicitly popular character in the 1960s and 1970s, La Tajada de Sandía underwent a transformation from an event that Justo Arosemena regarded as a tragedy into a laudatory example of popular, patriotic resistance to U.S. imperialism. Today Justo Arosemena holds a place in Panamanian culture similar to that of José Martí in Cuba and George Washington in the United States. José Manuel Luna's place in public memory is far less elevated. But the date of April 15, 1856, is still recalled today in Panama as the anniversary of the event that Panamanians have come to know as La Tajada de Sandía.[26]

The Path of the Nation

The nationalist interpretation of the Tajada de Sandía in the present is neatly summed up in a monument erected on the campus of the University of Panama to commemorate the one-hundred-and-fiftieth anniversary of the storied event in April 2006. "The Path of the Nation" is a series of plaques that commemorate important moments in the history of Panamanian resistance to U.S. imperialism from the Tajada de Sandía to the transfer of the Panama Canal to sole Panamanian control in 2000. The plaque devoted to the Tajada de Sandía reads as follows: "Incident of the Slice of Watermelon. Reaffirmation of the National Dignity. April 15, 1856." The clear implication of the plaque is that José Manuel Luna's actions represented an effort to defend a specifically national dignity and that the nation in question was Panama rather than Nueva Granada. Although it would be hard to dispute that José Manuel Luna acted in a way that defended a sense of dignity, the assertion that his dignity was a specifically national one, let alone a specifically Panamanian national dignity, is harder to sustain. Miguel Habrahan, the man who came to Luna's defense, was not a Panamanian but a Peruvian. Although Arrabaleños were anxious to defend themselves against invasion by filibusters, there was nothing in their actions that day that bespoke a desire for political independence from Nueva Granada.

Although many questions remain about the different motivations of those who took part in the events of April 15, the actions of Arrabaleños suggest a broader conception of rights that extended beyond national borders—one that might befit "a man with no country," as Pedro Goytía was described by his admirer in the *Panama Star and Herald* in 1856.[27] Such rights could have included the right to live free from slavery, to earn a decent living, and to receive just compensation for one's labor. That this more universal sense of rights could emerge out of the crucible of a neighborhood is no paradox—it is rather a reflection of the ways in which people of different origins living in a shared space developed similar concerns and ideals that extended across the boundaries of any single nationality. The corpses that littered the ground around the railroad station on April 15 indicated the potential limits of Arrabaleños' conceptions of rights and the tragic consequences that can result from efforts to use violence to defend even the noblest of ideals.

If the "Path of the Nation" can be criticized for its anachronism, it is harder to fault its makers' efforts to invest the past with meaning for people in the present. Nationalist histories can be criticized for distorting the past, but they also have much to teach. For historians concerned primarily with the United States, learning about the gold rush as Panamanian history offers an opportunity to rethink answers to questions as fundamental as when and where the gold rush took place, and with what consequences and for whom. The reverse is true for Panamanian historians, although because of the differences in power relations between the United States and Panama, historians of Panama are much more likely to know U.S. history than vice versa. The recognition of differences and commonalities opens up in turn the possibility of worthwhile conversations that might not otherwise take place.

In the Museum of History

As I concluded the writing of this book, I accepted an invitation from the Republic of Panama's Instituto Nacional de Cultura (INAC) to speak at the national commemoration of the one-hundred-fiftieth anniversary of the Tajada de Sandía in April 1856. On the day before the commemoration, INAC employees placed replicas of José Manuel Luna's fruit stand in different points around Panama City, and reenactors dressed in nineteenth-century costumes. The reenactors sold slices of watermelon to passersby for *un real*—a slang term that in Panama today means a five-cent coin rather than a dime. I helped stack watermelons at a stand that was set up outside the National Museum of Anthropology, in downtown Panama City, and I was invited to play the role of Jack Oliver as bystanders looked on.

As I wrote the book, I frankly had come to detest Jack Oliver's actions on April 15, and I had imagined that on some level or in some way my book might act as a counterweight, however small, to the national arrogance of the United States that Oliver has come to represent for Panamanians today. And so I accepted the offer to play Jack himself with some ambivalence. The reenactor and I joked as I requested a piece of fruit using my most formal Spanish. I passed a nickel to him, and he gave me in return a slice of watermelon in a small plastic bag. I thanked him. "We gringos are better behaved nowadays," I said in Spanish. But then, from across the street, a man called out to the reenactor, "Watch out for that gringo!" I looked up. The man across the street was not smiling.

The commemoration itself took place the next day in Panama City's city hall—the same building that holds the municipal archive, where I had come across José Manuel Luna's name on two lists of voters a few years before. Next to the front door of the city hall, a reenactor dressed in nineteenth-century costume stood next to another cart filled with watermelons and greeted people. This time, however, the reenactor was a woman—a fitting choice, given the confusion regarding the fruit seller's gender on April 15.

The event was held in an elegant room across the hall from the room that holds the city's Museum of History. The ceremony began with observations by dignitaries in attendance, including officials of INAC and a representative of the papal nuncio. An oil painting of watermelons by a well-known Panamanian artist was unveiled. Then I stood up and took my place next to a wooden cart laden with melons. The juxtaposition of a gringo historian with watermelons may have seemed incongruous to some in the audience, but no one cracked a smile as I approached the microphone.

I began by expressing my thanks for the invitation and then proceeded to present to the audience some of the things that I had learned over the course of my research. Without belaboring the differences between my own research and what the audience might have learned from other historical narratives, I took note of aspects of the event that nationalist accounts in Panama itself have sometimes underplayed or omitted, such as the importance of differences not only between Panamanians and people from the United States but also among Panamanians themselves, the significance of the recent abolition of slavery for the events of April 15, the presence of José Manuel Luna's name on lists of voters, and the fact that many observers from the United States had perceived Luna to be a man of color. At the end, I earnestly asked the audience to remember with me not only the heroism of José Manuel Luna but also the lives that were lost on that day.

After the talk, a reception was held in the small museum across the hall. I accepted a glass of watermelon punch and exchanged ideas about the Tajada de Sandía with members of the audience. One man told me that he thought I should make class more central to my analysis and pointed out an aspect of the event that I had neglected in my talk. A radio newscaster asked me whether I would like to offer a defense of Jack Oliver, and I demurred. I shook hands with a woman who thanked me for drawing attention to the importance of people of color in Panamanian history.

I felt a little deflated when some of the people in the museum approached me and complimented my Spanish—an implicit acknowledgment that I was no native speaker. As I reflected more on the nature of the event we were commemorating, however, I consoled myself by thinking that perhaps being able to speak in Spanish about Panamanian history was not such a small thing. I had imagined before the commemoration that my participation in the event would feel like a culmination of some kind. Instead, the experience of speaking with others in the Museum of History felt more like a beginning.

Along with posters detailing different aspects of the event and a few artifacts was an exhibit of paintings that schoolchildren in Panama City had made to commemorate the event. One picture featured a map of the Republic of Panama superimposed on a watermelon with the words "Panamá 150." Another picture included a letter addressed in Spanish by the young artist to the drunken man who assaulted José Manuel Luna:

> Dear Mr. Oliver:
> You shouldn't have eaten that slice of watermelon and then started that fight. You shouldn't have done that.
> Respectfully, the Author.

The letter calls to mind Luna's own response to Jack Oliver: "Careful, we are not in the United States here; pay me my *real* and we're even." What meaning will these words have in a new era of empire? The answer to this question is one that only Panamanians can know.

Coda

With Dust in Our Eyes

I was wrapping up my work in the National Archive of Panama when an archivist walked over to my desk in the reading room. In his hands he held an unmarked cardboard box. I reached inside and removed a small stack of loose papers. My eyes opened wide when I saw the date on the first document: April 23, 1856. It was a letter written by Capt. Theodorus Bailey of the USS *St. Mary's* to Francisco de Fábrega only eight days after the Tajada de Sandía. I made my way through the stack and found other communications between government officials in Panama and representatives from the United States, including consuls and naval officers, from the 1850s through the 1890s.

Slowly, it dawned on me that these were the documents I had been searching for on my first visit to Panama, four and a half years before. At first I felt too stunned to think or feel anything. Then a wave of joy and relief passed over me. No longer would I have to wonder what secrets the documents might contain. As I reflected more, I also began to feel anger as I imagined how my life might have been simpler had I found the documents during that first research trip. Most of all, I felt intense curiosity: what was the history of this box and its contents?

A later conversation with the archivist offered an answer to this riddle. Five years before I set foot in Panama, in the months before the U.S. invasion that began on the night of December 19, 1989, officials in Gen. Manuel Noriega's military government had begun to prepare the civilian population for the possibility of an attack of some kind from the United States. The military government brutally repressed its critics among the civilian population, government officials delivered nationalist, anti-imperialist speeches on television and radio, military leaders vowed courageous acts of resistance, and paramilitary citizens' organizations called Dignity Battalions prepared to repel any invasion of the country.

It was at some point during these desperate days that the director of the National Archive, an appointee of the military government, began to prepare a public exhibit about the history of U.S. imperialism in Panama, one that was to consist of original documents from the archive's collection. The director ordered the members of her staff to remove documents related to conflicts involving the United States from the archive's holdings. Employees removed bound documents from their bindings with blades and attached a note to each one with a citation so the document could later be returned to its proper location. Before the documents could be mounted for public display, however, U.S. airplanes began to drop bombs on Panama City. The imperialism that was to be subject of the exhibit overtook the exhibit itself.

Panamanians paid a horrific price for the removal of a leader who had been a long-time recipient of covert U.S. aid.[1] In the hours and days that followed the beginning of the invasion, many people died. Although the U.S. government first placed the number of casualties resulting from the invasion at 516, more reliable estimates by human rights groups and nongovernmental organizations ranged from one thousand to as many as four thousand people or more. Fires and fighting in the streets destroyed significant portions of parts of the city, and looting led to the theft and destruction of millions of dollars' worth of property. The most devastated area of the city was the poor, largely black neighborhood known as El Chorrillo—a place located not far from the National Archive that in the 1850s had formed the outskirts of El Arrabal.[2]

What happened to the documents I had sought between the invasion and the time that I finally saw them? I do not know, and I did not ask. Instead, I said simply, "Thank you." That I had been permitted to see the documents at all seemed explanation enough.

As dispiriting as my first research trip to Panama had been, the problem posed by the missing documents had proved in time to be a blessing of sorts. Denied the documents I had sought in the first place, I found myself reading what I might otherwise have ignored but what in the end proved crucial for the book. To understand those documents, I plunged more deeply into Panamanian history and literature than I had planned. I sought out guidance from Panamanian scholars and archivists, attended undergraduate history classes at the University of Panama, and spent long hours in conversation with other students over coffee and ice-filled pitchers of beer.

The effort to think about the gold rush as Panamanian history required me to reconsider the assumptions about time and space I had originally brought to my study of the past, as well as my assumptions about what was important about that past. Panama's links with the United States still mattered. But they mattered as part of a larger web of relationships forged during the gold rush, a web that connected Panama not only to the United States but also to Bogotá, Jamaica, Nicaragua, China, Liverpool, Parita, Paita, and other places in new ways.

Over the course of many visits to the National Archive, my conversations about the past with archivists had often turned to more recent history, especially the invasion of 1989. I struggled to explain the factors that had led to the invasion that President George H. W. Bush had dubbed "Operation Just Cause." Mostly, however, I stayed quiet and listened as people told me stories of what had happened to them and their families in the days after December 19. One day, an archive employee mentioned offhandedly that U.S. Marines had briefly taken up a position within the archive itself during the invasion. Even in my most angst-full reflections on the complexities of studying the history of empire from within, I had not imagined soldiers pointing machine guns out the windows of the reading room where I had spent so many hours thumbing through old pieces of paper.

The history of the unmarked box with its loose leaves offers a reminder that the practices of patriotic devotion and disciplinary history are not as separate as they might seem. I had come to the archive in search of evidence that I might use to support or undermine one hypothesis or another. But the documents inside the box had been gathered together to serve another purpose. In my frustrated imaginings as a researcher from the United States, the documents that I could not find in the National Archive were all "smoking guns" filled with secrets and intrigues of the past. In the end, however, the contents of the box spoke little to the questions that had drawn me to the archive in the first place. Like the letter from the U.S. naval captain to the Panamanian governor, they were principally mundane missives written by government officials in the course of their duties. But for those who had lived the history of invasion, and who unknowingly were soon to live that history again, those same documents were relics that provided physical links to a sacred past.

Despite the differences between the priorities that led me into the archive and those of the people who had assembled the contents of the box, we had worked under the roof of the same archive. In ways that were obvious from the start and other ways that became apparent to me only over time, patriotic acts had begun to condition my access to evidence long before I even stepped through the archive's door. Yet because the National Archive was itself a battlefield—both figuratively and (as I later learned) literally—that same building had also become a refuge of sorts for fugitive fragments or facts that fit uneasily into national histories of Panama or the United States.

That an invasion in 1989 could have shaped my access to the history of the nineteenth century might seem at first a reversal of the order in which knowledge about the past is supposed to accrue. One of the fictions of the bureaucratic archive, after all, is that events in the present do not alter access to events of the past, whose material residue in the present sits neatly organized in boxes or microfilm reels or tomes, available to the researcher who seeks them. Historians may bring different questions or interpretations or prejudices to the past, but the evidence in the archive, the documents, ideally remain the same.

But the ideal of a past that can be bundled up and stored away as in a vault, safe from the ravages of the present, is easier to sustain in some places on the planet than it is in others. That such an illusion has often seemed more plausible in the United States than in Panama is not merely a coincidence—it is also a reflection of the nearly inverted relations of power in which the United States has long maintained the upper hand. Panamanian soldiers have never taken up positions in the U.S. National Archives.

To recognize the inseparability between historians and the objects of their research is no longer a novelty. But to observe that a historian never steps into the same archive twice is not to provide a justification for not stepping into the archive. All archives, it is true—and not just in Panama— contain elisions or silences created in the past as well as the present.[3] There will always be questions that historians bring to the archives that the archives themselves will not be able to answer. But who is to say that the value of reading old pieces of paper lies only in finding the answers to the questions we bring to them? Just as valuable, perhaps more, are the questions that the archives themselves pose—questions that blow us off course and in the process cause us to rethink our deepest assumptions about a past that is never merely ours.

Like the documents that eluded me in the National Archive, the gold rush as an event has no permanent binding or natural home. But the acknowledgment of this multiplicity need not lead to despair. On the contrary, such an acknowledgment creates the opportunity to write histories that analyze those different possible pasts in relation to one another by drawing comparisons and retracing connections that no single binding can contain. If this endless process of unbinding and rebinding leaves us with a more acute sense of the struggles over the meaning and definition of an event such as the gold rush, we will have perceived the past more clearly rather than less.

The path to global history leads not to an Olympian perspective but through the dust cast up by contending claims on the past. With that disorienting dust in our eyes, we may see more readily how the United States and Latin America emerged in relation to each other in the mid-nineteenth century, in contention and yet defined in part, as in the present, by the existence of the other.

Notes

Prelude: April 15, 1856

1. *Gaceta del Estado*, 29 April 1856.

2. On the history of the meanings of the Boston Tea Party, see Alfred F. Young, *The Shoemaker and the Tea Party: Memory and the American Revolution* (Boston: Beacon Press, 1999).

3. E. Taylor Parks, *Colombia and the United States, 1765–1934* (Durham: Duke University Press, 1935), 219.

Introduction: In the Archive of Loose Leaves

1. On the Panama Route in the mid-nineteenth century and its place in the longer history of Panama as a nodal point in global transit networks, see the path-breaking scholarship of Alfredo Castillero Calvo, including "El transporte transístmico y las comunicaciones regionales" in *Historia General de Panamá*, ed. Alfredo Castillero Calvo (Panama City: Comité Nacional del Centenario de la República, 2004), vol. 1, and "La economía hasta mediados del siglo XIX," in *Historia General de Panamá*, vol. 2. Also see Aims McGuinness, "Aquellos días de California: El Ferrocarril de Panamá y la transformación de la zona de tránsito durante la Fiebre del Oro," in *Historia General de Panamá*, vol. 2. The classic and still invaluable history of the Panama Route in English is John Haskell Kemble, *The Panama Route, 1848–1869* (1943; reprint, with a new preface, Columbia: University of South Carolina Press, 1990). The most comprehensive maritime history of the California Gold Rush is James P. Delgado, *To California by Sea: A Maritime History of the California Gold Rush* (Columbia: University of South Carolina Press, 1990).

2. Kemble, *The Panama Route*, appendix 2, "Passengers by the Isthmian Routes, 1848–1869," 254; John D. Unruh, *The Plains Across: The Overland Emigrants and the Trans-Mississippi West, 1840–1860* (1979; 1st unabridged paperback ed., Urbana: University of Illinois Press, 1993), 119. Kemble and Unruh arrived at these totals by adding up references to immigrant populations found in newspapers and other contemporary records such as customs house reports and travelers' accounts as well as secondary sources. Unruh calculated his best estimates for each year and then rounded them. In contrast, Kemble sought to establish an "assured minimum" number of immigrants and chose not to round. Although Kemble and Unruh went to

great lengths to develop accurate estimates, both were keenly aware that the data they presented were only approximations.

3. The significance of the Panama Route for intercoastal communication in the United States and communication between the Atlantic and Pacific more generally is summarized by Kemble, *The Panama Route*, 200–209 and Delgado, *To California by Sea*, 65–73.

4. See Ferol Egan, *The El Dorado Trail: The Story of the Gold Rush Routes across Mexico* (New York: McGraw-Hill, 1970) and David I. Folkman Jr., *The Nicaragua Route* (Salt Lake City: University of Utah Press, 1972).

5. By far the most influential theorist of the relationship between communication and sovereignty in Panama has been Justo Arosemena. See his classic treatise, *El Estado Federal de Panamá* (1855; Panama City: Editorial Universitaria, 1982). For a wide-ranging discussion of the history of ideas of sovereignty, see Thomas Blom Hansen and Finn Stepputat, introduction to *Sovereign Bodies: Citizens, Migrants, and States in the Postcolonial World*, ed. Hansen and Stepputat (Princeton: University Press, 2005).

6. For important contributions toward an understanding of the gold rush as world history, see the essays collected in Kenneth N. Owens, ed., *Riches for All: The California Gold Rush and the World* (Lincoln: University of Nebraska Press, 2002). Owens's introduction offers a comprehensive review of the historiography of the California Gold Rush including the outpouring of works published in association with the one hundred and fiftieth anniversary of the beginning of the rush in 1848. On the gold rush and the politics of historical memory, see Susan Lee Johnson, *Roaring Camp: The Social World of the California Gold Rush* (New York: W. W. Norton, 2000).

7. Works that address the transregional dynamics of gender during the gold rush include Johnson, *Roaring Camp*; Brian Roberts, *American Alchemy: The California Gold Rush and Middle-Class Culture* (Chapel Hill: University of North Carolina Press, 2000); and Malcolm J. Rohrbough, *Days of Gold: The California Gold Rush and the American Nation* (Berkeley: University of California Press, 1997).

8. Although histories of the gold rush have long considered the experiences of gold rush immigrants in Latin America, recent histories have paid closer attention to the gendered and racialized aspects of interactions between immigrants and local peoples. See Albert F. Hurtado, "Crossing the Borders: Sex, Gender, and the Journey to California," in *Intimate Frontiers: Sex, Gender, and Culture in Old California* (Albuquerque: University of New Mexico Press, 1999) and Brian J. Roberts, "A Great and Perverse Paradise," in *American Alchemy*.

9. For an influential comparative study of the California Gold Rush and the Australian Gold Rush, see David Goodman, *Gold-Seeking: Victoria and California in the 1850s* (Stanford: Stanford University Press, 1994). For an overview of the importance of the California Gold Rush for subsequent rushes, see Jeremy Mouat, "After California: Later Gold Rushes of the Pacific Basin," in Owens, ed., *Riches for All*.

10. Kenneth N. Owens, introduction to *Riches for All*, ed. Owens, 13.

11. For a classic history along these lines, see C. L. R. James, *The Black Jacobins: Toussaint L'Ouverture and the San Domingo Revolution* (1938; New York: Vintage, 1963). Also see Frederick Cooper, Thomas C. Holt, and Rebecca J. Scott, *Beyond Slavery: Explorations of Race, Labor, and Citizenship in Postemancipation Societies* (Chapel Hill: University of North Carolina Press, 2000); Walter Mignolo, *The Darker Side of the Renaissance: Literacy, Territoriality, and Colonization* (Ann Arbor: University of Michigan Press, 1995); and Ann Laura Stoler and Frederick Cooper, "Between Metropole and Colony: Rethinking a Research Agenda," in Stoler and Cooper, eds., *Tensions of Empire: Colonial Cultures in a Bourgeois World* (Berkeley: University of California Press, 1997).

12. For a collection of essays that helped to launch the new scholarship on U.S. empire, see Amy Kaplan and Donald E. Pease, eds., *Cultures of United States Imperialism* (Durham, N.C.: Duke University Press, 1993). For a similarly influential work that focuses on U.S. empire in Latin America, see Gilbert M. Joseph, Catherine C. Legrand, and Ricardo D. Salvatore, eds.,

Close Encounters of Empire: Writing the Cultural History of U.S.–Latin American Relations (Durham, N.C.: Duke University Press, 1998).

13. For a comprehensive sample of these new approaches to Panamanian history, see the essays collected in Castillero Calvo, ed., *Historia General de Panamá*, vols. 1–3. Alfredo Figueroa Navarro's classic history of nineteenth-century Panama is *Dominio y sociedad en el Panamá colombiano (1821–1903)* (Panama City: Editorial Universitaria, 1982).

14. Recent works that address popular politics in nineteenth-century Colombia include Nancy P. Appelbaum, *Muddied Waters: Race, Region, and Local History in Colombia, 1846–1948* (Durham, N.C.: Duke University Press, 2003); Aline Helg, *Liberty and Equality in Caribbean Colombia, 1770–1835* (Chapel Hill: University of North Carolina Press, 2004); Marixa Lasso, "Race War and Nation in Caribbean Gran Colombia, Cartagena, 1810–1832," *American Historical Review* 111, no. 2 (2006): 336–361; Alfonso Múnera, *El fracaso de la nación: Región, clase y raza en el Caribe colombiano (1717–1810)* (Bogotá: Banco de la República, 1998); and James E. Sanders, *Contentious Republicans: Popular Politics, Race, and Class in Nineteenth-Century Colombia* (Durham, N.C.: Duke University Press, 2004). On the place of Panama in Colombian historiography, see Heraclio Bonilla and Gustavo Montañez, eds., *Colombia y Panamá: La metamorfosis de la nación en el siglo XX* (Bogotá: Universidad Nacional de Colombia, 2004).

15. Thomas Bender, *A Nation among Nations: America's Place in World History* (New York: Hill and Wang, 2006), 10. On global or transnational approaches to U.S. history, see Thomas Bender, *La Pietra Report* (Bloomington, Ind.: Organization of American Historians, 2000); Thomas Bender, ed., *Rethinking American History in a Global Age* (Berkeley: University of California Press, 2002); and "The Nation and Beyond," a special issue of the *Journal of American History* 86, no. 3 (December 1999). For reflections on recent trends in transnational history more generally, see C. A. Bayly, Sven Beckert, Matthew Connelly, Isabel Hofmeyr, Wendy Kozol, and Patricia Seed, "AHR Conversation: On Transnational History," *American Historical Review* 111, no. 5 (2006): 1440–1464.

16. See, for example, Nancy P. Appelbaum, Anne S. Macpherson, and Karin Alejandra Rosemblatt, eds., *Race and Nation in Modern Latin America* (Chapel Hill: University of North Carolina Press, 2003); Ada Ferrer, *Insurgent Cuba: Race, Nation, and Revolution, 1868–1898* (Chapel Hill: University of North Carolina Press, 1999); Greg Grandin, *The Blood of Guatemala: A History of Race and Nation* (Durham, N.C.: Duke University Press, 2000); Brooke Larson, *Trials of Nation Making: Liberalism, Race, and Ethnicity in the Andes, 1810–1910* (Cambridge: Cambridge University Press, 2004); Florencia E. Mallon, *Peasant and Nation: The Making of Postcolonial Mexico and Peru* (Berkeley: University of California Press, 1995); Mark Thurner, *From Two Republics to One Divided: Contradictions of Postcolonial Nationmaking in Andean Peru* (Durham, N.C.: Duke University Press, 1997); and Samuel Truett and Elliott Young, eds., *Continental Crossroads: Remapping U.S.-Mexico Borderlands History* (Durham, N.C.: Duke University Press, 2004).

17. My thanks to Jorge Mitchel for this and other fruitful conversations in the archive.

1. California in Panama

1. On the importance of isthmus as a migration route before the Spanish conquest, see the contributions to Anthony G. Coates, ed., *Central America: A Natural and Cultural History* (New Haven: Yale University Press, 1997), including S. David Webb, "The Great American Faunal Interchange," Paul Colinvaux, "The History of Forests on the Isthmus from the Ice Age to the Present," and Richard Cooke, "The Native Peoples of Central America during the Precolumbian and Colonial Times." On the increased importance of the isthmus as an interoceanic route after the Spanish conquest, see Alfredo Castillero Calvo, "Reorganización económica y política del espacio: 1519–1581. Fundación y función de los pueblos de españoles e indios," *Historia General de Panamá*, ed. Castillero Calvo, vol. 1, tomo 1, 115.

2. Alfredo Castillero Calvo, "El transporte transístmico y las comunicaciones regionales," in *Historia General de Panamá*, ed. Castillero Calvo, vol. 1, tomo 1, 355–398. Also see Christopher Ward, *Imperial Panama: Commerce and Conflict in Isthmian America, 1550–1800* (Albuquerque: University of New Mexico Press, 1993).

3. Alfredo Castillero Calvo, "Decadencia de las ferias, crisis comercial y nuevos soportes económicos," in *Historia General de Panamá*, ed. Castillero Calvo, vol. 1, tomo 2. Also see Ignacio Gallup-Díaz, *The Door of the Seas and Key to the Universe: Indian Politics and Imperial Rivalry in the Darién, 1640–1750* (New York: Columbia University Press, 2004).

4. Alfredo Castillero Calvo, "Despegue comercial pre-independentista" and "La independencia de 1821: Una nueva interpretación," in *Historia General de Panamá*, ed. Castillero Calvo, vol. 2. Also see Celestino Andrés Araúz, *La independencia de Panamá en 1821: Antecedentes, balance y proyecciones* (Panama City: Academia Panameña de la Historia, 1980) and Figueroa Navarro, *Dominio y sociedad*, 140–142, 239–242.

5. Simón Bolívar, "Reply of a South American to a Gentleman of this Island [Jamaica]," 6 September 1815, trans. Lewis Bertrand, in *Selected Writings of Bolívar*, ed. Harold A. Bierck Jr. (New York: Banco de Venezuela, 1951), 119.

6. Alfredo Castillero Calvo, "La economía hasta mediados del siglo XIX," in *Historia General de Panamá*, ed. Castillero Calvo, vol. 3, 47; Figueroa Navarro, *Dominio y sociedad*, 28–33.

7. Castillero Calvo, "La economía," 53.

8. Figueroa Navarro, *Dominio y sociedad*, 243–244; Marixa A. Lasso, "La crisis política post-independentista: 1821–1841," in *Historia General de Panamá*, vol. 3, 71.

9. Figueroa Navarro, *Dominio y sociedad*, 245–246; Lasso, "La critis política," 66–72.

10. Alfredo Castillero Calvo, "La esclavitud negra," in *Historia General de Panamá*, vol. 1, tomo 2, 451.

11. Castillero Calvo, "Reorganización económica y política del espacio"; Figueroa Navarro, *Dominio y sociedad*, 82–84; Marixa Lasso, "Race War." On the use of racial categories in official records in Panama in the first half of the nineteenth century, see Alfredo Figueroa Navarro, "Seis aproximaciones a la historia social y demográfica de Panamá (siglos XVIII y XIX)," *Humanidades* ser. 3, 2 (April 1994): 131–152.

12. On Kunas in the nineteenth century, see James Howe, *A People Who Would Not Kneel: Panama, the United States, and the San Blas Kuna* (Washington, D.C.: Smithsonian Institution Press, 1998), 10–20.

13. Castillero Calvo, "La esclavitud negra," 450–451.

14. On the formation of Panama City's social geography during the colonial period, see Alfredo Castillero Calvo's *La vivienda colonial en Panamá: Arquitectura, urbanismo y sociedad; Historia de un sueño* (Panama City: Biblioteca Cultural Shell, 1994). On the organization of space and race in the mid-nineteenth century, see Figueroa Navarro, *Dominio y sociedad,* 79–90. On race and space on the level of the region in nineteenth-century Colombia, see the work of Nancy Appelbaum, including "Whitening the Region: Caucano Mediation and 'Antioqueño Colonization' in Nineteenth-Century Colombia," *Hispanic American Historical Review* 79, no. 4 (1999): 631–667, and *Muddied Waters*.

15. José Domingo Espinar, *Resumen histórico . . .* (Panama City: Imprenta de José Angel Santos, 1851), 5–6. All translations are by the author unless noted otherwise. On caste regimes in colonial Latin America more generally, see George Reid Andrews, *Afro-Latin America* (Cambridge: Harvard University Press, 2004), 44, 48–52.

16. Robert A. Naylor, *Penny Ante Imperialism: The Mosquito Shore and the Bay of Honduras, 1600–1914* (Cranbury, N.J.: Associated University Presses, 1989), 168–181.

17. Michael Conniff, *Panama and the United States: The Forced Alliance,* 2d ed. (Athens: University of Georgia Press, 2001), 19–20.

18. Kemble, *The Panama Route*, 20–22.

19. Fessenden Nott Otis, *Isthmus of Panama* (New York: Harper Brothers, 1867), 17–18; Gerstle Mack, *The Land Divided: A History of the Panama Canal and Other Isthmian Canal Projects* (New York: Knopf, 1944), 149; Victor von Hagen, *Maya Explorer: John Lloyd Stephens and the Lost Cities of Central America and Yucatán* (Norman: University of Oklahoma Press, 1947); John Lloyd Stephens, *Incidents of Travel in Central America, Chiapas, and Yucatan*, 2 vols. (New York, Harper & Brothers, 1841).

20. George Muirson Totten to J. P. Adams, 2 January 1849, U.S. National Archives (hereafter USNA), Record Group 185 (hereafter RG 185), Letters of G. M. Totten (hereafter, "Totten Letters"), vol. 1.

21. Egan, *The El Dorado Trail*, 8–25.

22. Rohrbough, *Days of Gold*, 25–28; Unruh, *The Plains Across*, 402–403.

23. Kemble, *The Panama Route*, 28, 33–34.

24. On the organization of the transport across Panama at the beginning of the gold rush, see Kemble, *The Panama Route*, 166–178.

25. Jay Monaghan, *Chile, Peru, and the California Gold Rush of 1849* (Berkeley: University of California Press, 1973), 108–109.

26. Ibid., 113.

27. Ibid., 114.

28. Monaghan, *Chile, Peru, and the California Gold Rush*, 114–115; Rohrbough, *Days of Gold*, 222.

29. Monaghan, *Chile, Peru, and the California Gold Rush*, 115–122.

30. Jefatura Política del Cantón de Taboga, 9 January 1855, Archivo Nacional de Panamá (hereafter ANP), Sección Judicial (hereafter SJ), box labeled "Juicios Criminales 1855, 1854, 1844, Notaria No. 1 de Circuito de Panamá, Vol. 2, Año 1855, Juicios Criminales."

31. Lara Putnam, *The Company They Kept: Migrants and the Politics of Gender in Caribbean Costa Rica, 1870–1960* (Chapel Hill: University of North Carolina Press, 2002), 234 n. 2.

32. *El Vijilante*, 9 January 1853.

33. Mary Seacole, *Wonderful Adventures of Mrs. Seacole in Many Lands* (1857; New York: Oxford University Press, 1988).

34. Mary Jane Megquier to daughter, 24 February 1849, reprinted in Mary Jane Megquier, *Apron Full of Gold: The Letters of Mary Jane Megquier from San Francisco, 1849–1856*, ed. Polly Welts Kaufman (Albuquerque: University of New Mexico Press, 1994), 24. On women's labor and the gendering of work more generally in California during the California Gold Rush, see Susan Lee Johnson, "Domestic Life in the Diggings," in Johnson, *Roaring Camp*.

35. William Penn Abrams, diary, BANC MSS C–F 65, Bancroft Library, University of California, Berkeley. On immigrant perceptions of women in Panama and Latin America more generally, see Roberts, *American Alchemy*, 135, and Amy S. Greenberg, *Manifest Manhood and the Antebellum American Empire* (Cambridge: Cambridge University Press, 2005), 112–123.

36. On elite real estate speculation during the gold rush, see Figueroa Navarro, *Dominio y sociedad*, 276–298.

37. Charles Toll Bidwell, *The Isthmus of Panamá* (London: Chapman and Hall, 1865), 344–345.

38. Arosemena, *El Estado Federal de Panamá*, 75–76.

39. Juan García to Manuel Echeverría, 9 October 1851, ANP, Período Colombiano (hereafter PC), cajón 849, tomo 2145, 220.

40. Roberts, *American Alchemy*, 6–7, 120–121.

41. On the gendered and racialized dynamics of interactions among U.S. travelers and local peoples in Panama and elsewhere in Latin America, see Roberts, "A Great and Perverse Paradise"; Greenberg, "An American Central America" and "Sex and Violence in the Latin American Travelogue, in *Manifest Manhood*; and Hurtado, "Crossing the Borders." On minstrelsy and the role of violence in racist humor in the antebellum period, see Eric Lott, *Love and*

Theft: Blackface Minstrelsy and the American Working Class (Oxford: Oxford University Press, 1993), 141–142, as well as Lott's discussion of minstrelsy and the gold rush (169–210 passim). On U.S. views of Mexicans and Latin Americans more generally in the late 1840s and 1850s, see Reginald Horsman, *Race and Manifest Destiny* (Cambridge: Harvard University Press, 1981), 229–248, and Frederick Pike, *The United States and Latin America* (Austin: University of Texas Press, 1992), 86–111. On sensational literature and U.S. empire in the 1850s, see Shelley Streeby, *American Sensations: Class, Empire, and the Production of Popular Culture* (Berkeley: University of California Press, 2002).

42. Greenberg, *Manifest Manhood*, 84–85.

43. James [McMurphy] to "Household of Robt. McMurphy," 7–25 April 1849, Huntington Library, HM52733.

44. Ibid.

45. Ibid. See *Kemble, The Panama Route*, 177.

46. John H. Forster, "Field Notes of a Surveyor in Panama and California" (unpublished manuscript, 1849), John Harris Forster Papers, Michigan Historical Collections, Bentley Historical Library, University of Michigan, 19 March 1849.

47. Roberts, *American Alchemy*, 120–121; 129; Greenberg, *Manifest Manhood*, 106–107.

48. Charles Frederick Winslow to "Lydia," 26 April 1849, Charles Frederick Winslow letter book and miscellany, MS 1734, California Historical Society, San Francisco. Courtesy of the California Historical Society.

49. Forster, "Field Notes," 13 March 1849.

50. Forster, "Field Notes," 23 March 1849.

51. Theodore T. Johnson, *Sights and Sounds in the Gold Region, and Scenes by the Way* (New York: Baker and Scribner, 1849), 12.

52. *Panama Herald*, 26 May 1851.

53. Robert Tomes, *Panama in 1855* (New York: Harper and Brothers, 1855), 215.

54. *Panama Herald*, 18 April 1851; 16 June 1851; 7 July 1851.

55. *Panama Herald*, 2 June 1851.

56. Forster, "Field Notes," 12 May 1849.

57. Affidavit of Frederick Ansoatigue, July 11, 1856, USNA, General Records of the Department of State (hereafter DS), Record Group 59 (hereafter RG 59), Microfilm Series 139 (hereafter M–139), roll 5.

58. Arosemena, *El Estado Federal*, 74–75.

59. On the use of racial categories in official records in Panama in the first half of the nineteenth century, see Alfredo Figueroa Navarro, "Seis aproximaciones a la historia social y demográfica de Panamá." On patriotism and race, see Lasso, "Race War and Nation in Caribbean Colombia."

60. Johnson, *Sights and Sounds in the Gold Region*, 17.

61. Frank Marryat, *Mountains and Molehills* (London: Longman, Brown, Green, and Longmans, 1855), 14.

62. James L. Tyson, *Diary of a Physician in California* (New York: D. Appleton, 1850), 19.

63. Bayard Taylor, *El Dorado* (New York: G. P. Putnam, 1850), 11–12.

64. Kemble, *The Panama Route*, 178.

65. Sarah Merriam Brooks, *Across the Isthmus to California in '52* (San Francisco, 1894), 37.

66. Forster, "Field Notes," 12 March 1849.

67. Johnson, *Sights and Sounds in the Gold Region*, 21.

68. Forster, "Field Notes," 14 March 1849.

69. Mary Jane Megquier to Milton, 14 May 1849, *Apron Full of Gold*, ed. Kaufman, 29.

70. Brooks, *Across the Isthmus*, 63. On the journey west and white U.S. fears of contact between white women and black men, see Hurtado, "Crossing the Borders," 55–55. On women's

immigration across Panama more generally, see Glenda Riley, "Women on the Panama Trail to California, 1849–1869," *Pacific Historical Review* 55, 4 (1986):531–548.

71. Seacole, *Wonderful Adventures*, 41.

72. Taylor, *El Dorado*, 16.

73. Brooks, *Across the Isthmus*, 93.

74. Seacole, *Wonderful Adventures*, 41.

75. Taylor, *El Dorado*, 11–21.

76. Johnson, *Sights and Sounds in the Gold Region*, 74–75.

77. *Panama Herald*, 4 August 1851.

78. Seacole, *Wonderful Adventures*, 52–53.

79. *Revisor de la Política y Literatura Americana*, 16 March 1850.

80. See Johnson, "Mining Gold and Making War," in *Roaring Camp*; Rohrbough, *Days of Gold*, 16–20.

2. The Panama Railroad and the Conquest of the Gold Rush

1. Historical understanding of the early years of the Panama Railroad has been unfortunately clouded by Joseph L. Schott, *Rails across Panama: The Story of the Building of the Panama Railroad, 1849–1855* (Indianapolis: Bobbs-Merrill, 1967). Schott presented his book as a work of history based on investigation in primary sources. Throughout the book, however, he interlaced references to actual historical personages and events with fictional persons and extensive scenes that were completely of his own invention. To take only one example, Schott opened the book with an extended account of a conversation aboard the *Falcon* in 1847—the year before the ship was launched. Unfortunately, Schott's book has been cited by many subsequent historians as if it were a reliable secondary source. For a fuller discussion of these inventions, see McGuinness, "Aquellos tiempos de California."

2. John L. Stephens to Benjamin Stephens, 27 December 1848, Bancroft Library, John L. Stephens Papers (hereafter Stephens Papers), box III, folder 202.

3. Kemble, *Panama Route*, 170–171.

4. Ibid., 171. For a discussion of the impact of the introduction of steam power and other aspects of the politics of labor and water transport along the Nicaragua Route, see Miguel Angel Herrera C., *Bongos, bogas, vapores y marinos: Historia de los 'marineros' del río San Juan, 1849–1855* (Managua: Centro Nicaragüense de Escritores, 1999), 175–207.

5. Charles Frederick Winslow to "Lydia," 26 April 1849, Charles Frederick Winslow letter book and miscellany, MS 1734, California Historical Society, San Francisco. Courtesy of the California Historical Society.

6. Ibid., 6 May 1849.

7. Kemble, *The Panama Route*, 151.

8. Kemble, *The Panama Route*, 167–168; Robert M. Lapp, *Blacks in Gold Rush California* (New Haven: Yale University Press, 1977), 45; Jorge E. Patiño, "El acuerdo istmeño-norteamericano de 1851," *Revista Lotería* 336–337 (March/April 1984): 50–57.

9. Stephen Chapin Davis, *California Gold Rush Merchant*, ed. Benjamin B. Richards (Westport, Conn.: Greenwood Press, 1974), 38–44. Patiño, "El acuerdo," 55–56.

10. Otis, *Isthmus of Panama*, 1.

11. Totten to Thomas L. Ludlow, 13 February 1850, Totten Letters, USNA, RG 185, vol. 1.

12. Ibid.

13. William H. Aspinwall to Stephens, 13 May 1850, Bancroft Library, Stephens Papers, box 1, folder 11.

14. Aspinwall to Stephens, 3 August 1850, Bancroft Library, Stephens Papers, box 1, folder 11.

15. Francis Catherwood to Stephens, 4 July 1850, Bancroft Library, Stephens Papers, box 1, folder 40, and Aspinwall to Stephens, 13 June 1850, Bancroft Library, Stephens Papers, box 1, folder 11.

16. See Thomas C. Holt, *The Problem of Freedom: Race, Labor, and Politics in Jamaica and Britain, 1832–1938* (Baltimore: Johns Hopkins University Press, 1992), 33–41.

17. Totten to Ludlow, 13 February 1850, Totten Letters, USNA, RG 185, vol. 1; Otis, *Isthmus*, 27.

18. Totten to Ludlow, 13 February 1850, Totten Letters, USNA, RG 185, vol. 1; Otis, *Isthmus*, 25–26.

19. Totten to J. P. Adams, 11 April 1849, Totten Letters, USNA, RG 185, vol. 1.

20. Totten to Stephens, 25 August 1850, Totten Letters, USNA, RG 185, vol. 1.

21. Otis, *Isthmus*, 26.

22. Ibid.

23. Ibid.

24. Totten to Spies, 29 January 1852, Totten Letters, USNA, RG 185, vol. 1. Otis, *Isthmus*, 27–28.

25. Totten to Stephens, 25 August 1850, Totten Letters, USNA, RG 185, vol. 1.

26. Totten to Stephens, 21 September 1850, Totten Letters, USNA, RG 185, vol. 1.

27. Totten to Stephens, 11 December 1850, Totten Letters, USNA, RG 185, vol. 1.

28. Totten to Stephens, 22 December 1850, Totten Letters, USNA, RG 185, vol. 1.

29. Ibid.

30. Peter Peirce to Totten, 23 December 1850, Totten Letters, USNA, RG 185, vol. 1.

31. John Borland to Totten, 23 December 1850, Totten Letters, USNA, RG 185, vol. 1.

32. Totten to Stephens, 6 January 1851, Totten Letters, USNA, RG 185, vol. 1; Totten to Stephens, 23 January 1851, Totten Letters, USNA, RG 185, vol. 1.

33. Totten to Stephens, 8 February 1851, Totten Letters, USNA, RG 185, vol. 1.

34. Totten to Stephens, 23 January 1851, Totten Letters, USNA, RG 185, vol. 1.

35. Totten to Stephens, 26 August 1851, Totten Letters, USNA, RG 185, vol. 1.

36. Totten to Stephens, 8 February 1851, Totten Letters, USNA, RG 185, vol. 1.

37. Totten to Stephens, 11 December 1850, Totten Letters, USNA, RG 185, vol. 1.

38. Totten to Stephens, 24 February 1851, Totten Letters, USNA, RG 185, vol. 1.

39. Totten to Stephens, 9 August 1851, Totten Letters, USNA, RG 185, vol. 1.

40. John A. Liddell, "Upon the Medical Topography and Diseases of the Isthmus of Panama," *New York Journal of Medicine* 8 (1852): 242–259.

41. Totten to William C. Young, Esq., 31 January 1853, Totten Letters, USNA, RG 185, vol. 1.

42. Totten to Stephens, 24 February 1851, Totten Letters, USNA, RG 185, vol. 1.

43. Totten to Stephens, 9 August 1851, Totten Letters, USNA, RG 185, vol. 1.

44. Totten to Stephens, 24 February 1851, Totten Letters, USNA, RG 185, vol. 1.

45. Otis, *Isthmus*, 32.

46. Totten to Francis Spies, 8 December 1851, Totten Letters, USNA, RG 185, vol. 1. Otis, *Isthmus*, 32–33.

47. Totten to Spies, 9 February 1852, Totten Letters, USNA, RG 185, vol. 1.

48. Otis, *Isthmus*, 33.

49. Totten to Alexander Center, 14 July 1852, Totten Letters, USNA, RG 185, vol. 1.

50. Delgado, *To California by Sea*, 64.

51. Totten to Center, 20 July 1852, Totten Letters, USNA, RG 185, vol. 1.

52. Tomás Cipriano de Mosquera to Stephens, 11 March 1851, Bancroft Library, Stephens Papers, box II, folder 129.

53. Kemble, *Panama Route*, 173.

54. Conniff, *Panama and the United States*, 21–23.

55. Mack, *Land Divided*, 179–187.

56. Kemble, *Panama Route*, 73. On the Nicaragua Route, see David I. Folkman Jr., *The Nicaragua Route* (Salt Lake City: University of Utah Press, 1972), and Herrera C., *Bongos*. On gold-rush routes across Mexico, see Ferol Egan, *The El Dorado Trail: The Story of the Gold Rush Routes across Mexico* (New York: McGraw-Hill, 1970).

57. Totten to Young, 19 August 1853, Totten Letters, USNA, RG 184, vol. 1.

58. Totten to Young, 20 December 1852, Totten Letters, USNA, RG 184, vol. 1; Kemble, *Panama Route*, 188.

59. Totten to Young, 20 December 1852, Totten Letters, USNA, RG 185, vol. 1.

60. Totten to Young, 31 December 1852, Totten Letters, USNA, RG 185, vol. 1.

61. Totten to Spies, 17 February 1853; Totten to Young, 17 April 1853; Totten to Young, 15 May 1853, Totten to Young, 17 July 1853, Totten Letters, USNA, RG 185, vol. 1.

62. Totten to Young, 2 June 1853, Totten Letters, USNA, RG 185, vol. 1.

63. Totten to Young, 3 June 1853, Totten Letters, USNA, RG 185, vol. 1.

64. Totten to Young, 17 August 1853, Totten Letters, USNA, RG 185, vol. 1.

65. Otis, *Isthmus*, 35.

66. Totten to Young, 1 September 1853, Totten Letters, USNA, RG 185, vol. 1.

67. Totten to David Hoadley, 22 December 1853, Totten Letters, USNA, RG 185, vol. 1.

68. Joseph Schott, in *Rails across Panama*, provided an account of mass suicide by Chinese workers that he claimed to base on quotations from an account written by Totten. But the correspondence between Totten and the company that is preserved in the U.S. National Archives is silent on the question of Chinese workers except for some brief mentions of the possibility of supplementing the force with Chinese laborers at the end of 1853. The correspondence does not even cover the period in 1854 when the indentured workers were employed by the company. See Schott, *Rails across Panama*, 176–182.

69. Walton Look Lai, *Indentured Labor, Caribbean Sugar: Chinese and Indian migrants to the British West Indies, 1838–1918* (Baltimore: Johns Hopkins University Press, 1993), 94–95; Otis, *Isthmus*, 35–36.

70. Hoadley to Messrs. R. Morrison & Co., 9 September 1854, Panama Railroad Company Letterbooks, USNA, RG 185, vol. 7, 491.

71. Totten to Hoadley, 30 December 1853, Totten Letters, USNA, RG 185, vol. 1. On the establishment of universal male suffrage and the local election of provincial governors, see Bushnell, *Making of Modern Colombia*, 108.

72. Totten to Young, 29 October 1853, Totten Letters, USNA, RG 185, vol. 1.

73. Totten to Hoadley, 12 November 1853, Totten Letters, USNA, RG 185, vol. 1.

74. Ibid.

75. Totten to Hoadley, 30 December 1853, Totten Letters, USNA, RG 185, vol. 1.

76. John L. Stephens to Henry Chauncey, 21 February [1852], Stephens-Chauncey Collection, Special Collections Division, Georgetown University Library, Box 1, Folder 14; Otis, *Isthmus*, 33; Ernesto J. Castillero Reyes, *La isla que se transformó en ciudad: Historia de un siglo de la ciudad de Colón* (Panama City: N.P., 1962), 69–86. Although Castillero Reyes attributed the suggestion of the name to Paredes, the letter by Stephens cited above indicates clearly that it was Stephens who proposed the name to Paredes.

77. Kemble, *Panama Route*, 187.

78. *Panama Herald*, 25 March 1852.

79. "Contract between the Republic of New Granada and the Panama Railroad Company," 28 December 1848, USNA, RG 185, "Panama Railroad Legal and Fiscal Documents," box 1, folder 17.

80. *Panama Herald*, 22 April 1854.

81. *Weekly Panama Star and Herald*, 8 May 1854.

82. A. R. Orton, "*The Derienni*"; *or, Land Pirates of the Isthmus* (New Orleans, N.P., 1853).

83. On crime along the transit route in the early 1850s, including a sensational robbery of the treasure train of the Pacific Mail Steamship Company in September 1851, see Kemble, *Panama Route*, 175.

84. On the disastrous expeditions of the Darién in 1854, see Todd Balf, *The Darkest Jungle: The True Story of the Darien Expedition and America's Ill-Fated Race to Connect the Seas* (New York: Crown Publishers, 2003) and Mack, *Land Divided*, 246–259.

85. See Ernesto J. Castillero Reyes, "Ran Runnels en la ruta de 'El Dorado,' " *Lotería* 23 (October 1957), 88–97. Also see Juan A. Susto, "La personalidad de Ran Runnels," *Lotería* 23 (October 1957), 97—99.

86. *Weekly Panama Star and Herald*, 31 July 1854.

87. Horace Bell, *On the Old West Coast: Being further Reminiscences of a Ranger*, ed. Lanier Bartlett (1930; New York: Arno Press, 1976), 54. Also see Hubert Howe Bancroft, *California Inter Pocula* (San Francisco: The History Company Publishers, 1888), 183–184.

88. Testimony of "Ran Runels" [*sic*], 23 February 1855, and Juan Bautista Trujillo, 17 February 1855, "Averiguación sobre un robo hecho a Je. Ramphy," ANP, SJ, box labeled "Juicios Criminales 1855 1854 1844," tomo labeled "Notaria No. 1 de Circuito de Panamá, Vol. Nu. 2, Año 1855, Juicios Criminales."

89. Kemble, *Panama Route*, 175.

90. Hoadley to Edward Flint, 18 December 1854, Letterbooks of the Panama Railroad Company, USNA, RG 185, vols. 8–9 (September 16, 1854–December 5, 1855), 103–104.

91. On the famous vigilance committees in San Francisco of 1851 and 1856 see Philip J. Ethington, *The Public City: The Political Construction of Urban Life in San Francisco, 1850–1900* (Cambridge: Cambridge University Press, 1994). Also see Johnson, *Roaring Camp*, 218, and Rohrbough, *Days of Gold*, 86–90. On filibustering, see Robert E. May, *Manifest Destiny's Underworld: Filibustering in Antebellum America* (Chapel Hill: University of North Carolina Press, 2002), and Greenberg, "William Walker and the Regeneration of Martial Manhood" and "The Irresistible Pirate," in *Manifest Manhood*.

92. On the progress of the year leading up to the inauguration of the line, see Kemble, *Panama Route*, 188–189, and Otis, *Isthmus*, 36.

93. Kemble, *Panama Route*, 189–195.

94. On William Walker's intervention in Nicaragua and its effects on the transit economy, see E. Bradford Burns, *Patriarch and Folk: The Emergence of Nicaragua, 1798–1858* (Cambridge, Mass.: Harvard University Press, 1991), 160–237, passim, and Michel Gobat, *Confronting the American Dream: Nicaragua under U.S. Imperial Rule* (Durham, N.C.: Duke University Press, 2005), 21–41.

95. *New York Herald*, 29 January, 6 and 26 February 1855, cited in Kemble, *Panama Route,* 190.

96. Arosemena, *Estado Federal*, 75–76.

97. Espinar, *Resumen histórico*, 5–6.

98. Tomás Martín Feuillet, "Cuánto tiene?" (1856), quoted in Figueroa Navarro, *Dominio y sociedad*, 341–342.

99. Pío Luna to Cabildo de Panamá, 1855 [no day], Archivo del Consejo Municipal de Panamá (hereafter ACMP), tomo 14. On the economic impact of the gold rush on Panama, see Alfredo Castillero Calvo, "El oro de California en la vida panameña," in *Relaciones entre Panamá y los Estados Unidos* (Panama City: Biblioteca Nuevo Panamá/Ministerio de Educación, 1973), 117–128.

100. Tomes, *Panama in 1855*, 200–214, passim.

101. Ibid.

102. Otis, *Isthmus*, 18.

103. On the emergence of Chicago as an emporium similar to that idealized by boosters

of Panama's transit route in the mid-1800s, see William Cronon, *Nature's Metropolis: Chicago and the Great West* (New York: W. W. Norton, 1991). The language of boosterism deployed in mid-nineteenth-century Chicago, including the ideal of the emporium, was strikingly similar to that used by Panamanian elites in the same period. See Cronon, *Nature's Metropolis*, 41–46.

104. Johnson, *Roaring Camp*, 239–249; Rohrbough, *Days of Gold*, 197–203. The classic history of mining in gold-rush California is Rodman K. Paul, *California Gold: The Beginning of Mining in the Far West* (Cambridge, Mass.: Harvard University Press, 1947). I borrow the phrase "days of gold" from Rohrbough, who borrows the phrase in turn from a popular song written two decades after the gold rush. Rohrbough, *Days of Gold*, 288.

105. Catherine C. LeGrand, "Living in Macondo: Economy and Culture in a United Fruit Company Banana Enclave in Colombia," in *Close Encounters of Empire*, ed. Joseph, LeGrand, and Salvatore, 334—335. Other works that have contributed to a rethinking of enclave economies include Aviva Chomsky, *West Indian Workers and the United Fruit Company in Costa Rica, 1870–1940* (Baton Rouge: Louisiana State University Press, 1996); Darío Euraque, *Reinterpreting the Banana Republic: Region and State in Honduras, 1870–1972* (Chapel Hill: University of North Carolina Press, 1996); Putnam, *The Company*; John Soluri, *Banana Cultures: Agriculture, Consumption, and Environmental Change in Honduras and the United States* (Austin: University of Texas Press, 2005), and the contributions to Steve Striffler and Mark Moberg, eds., *Banana Wars: Power, Production, and History in the Americas* (Durham, N.C.: Duke University Press, 2003).

3. Sovereignty on the Isthmus

1. Figueroa Navarro, *Dominio y sociedad*, 261.
2. Justo Arosemena, *El Estado Federal de Panamá*.
3. See Figueroa Navarro, *Dominio y sociedad*, 243–244 and Lasso, "La crisis política." On the political thought of Arosemena, see among other works Fernando Aparicio, "Justo Arosemena y el Estado Federal de Panamá, 1855–1863," in *Historia General de Panamá*, ed. Castillero Calvo, Vol. 2, 193–216; Figueroa Navarro, *Dominio y sociedad*, 320–329; Peter A. Szok, *"La última gaviota": Liberalism and Nostalgia in Early Twentieth-Century Panamá* (Westport, Conn.: Greenwood Press, 2001), esp., "The 'Hanseatic' Republic: Panamá in the Nineteenth Century;" and the works by Ricaurte Soler, Argelia Tello, and others in "Homenaje a Justo Arosemena," a special issue of *Tareas* 92 (January–April 1996).
4. Castillero Calvo, "El Movimiento Anseatista de 1826"; Figueroa Navarro, *Dominio y sociedad*, 243–244; Lasso, "La crisis política."
5. On the "Liberal Revolution" in Colombia, see Bushnell, *The Making of Modern Colombia*, esp., "The Nineteenth-Century Liberal Revolution (1849–1885)" and Frank Safford and Marco Palacios, *Colombia: Fragmented Land, Divided Society* (New York: Oxford University Press, 2002), chap. 10, "The Liberal Era, 1845–1876."
6. On the politics of bargaining and popular republicanism in Cauca and more broadly in Colombia in the 1850s, see James E. Sanders, *Contentious Republicans*, 18–23. On Liberals and Conservatives, see Frank Safford, "Social Aspects of Politics in Nineteenth-Century Spanish America: New Granada, 1825–1850," *Journal of Social History* 5 (Spring 1972): 344–370.
7. Figueroa Navarro, *Dominio y sociedad*, 342–44, and Helen Delpar, *Red against Blue: The Liberal Party in Colombia Politics, 1863–1899* (University: University of Alabama Press, 1981), 16–21. On a similar relationship between people of African descent and the Liberal party in Cauca in the same era, see Sanders, *Contentious Republicans*, 58–66. On Azuero and Veraguas, see Armando Muñoz Pinzón, *Un estudio de historia social panameña* (Panama City: Editorial Universitaria de

Panamá, 1980), and Armando Muñoz Pinzón, "El conflicto azureño de 1854," in *Historia general de Panamá*, ed. Castillero, vol. 2.

8. *El Panameño*, 4 January 1852; Roberto de la Guardia, *Los negros del Istmo de Panamá* (Panama City: Ediciones INAC, 1977), 161–163.

9. *El Vijilante*, 31 October 1852.

10. *El Vijilante*, 31 October 1852 and 14 November 1852.

11. On the concept of caste war or race war in Nueva Granada and Gran Colombia more generally in the early nineteenth century, see Helg, *Liberty & Equality*, 39, 42, and especially Lasso, "Race War and Nation in Caribbean Gran Colombia." On tensions between elites and the political mobilization of people of color in Cartagena, see Múnera, *El fracaso de la nación*, 194–215. On the "Caste War of Yucatán," see Nelson Reed, *The Caste War of Yucatán* (Stanford: Stanford University Press, 1964) and Terry Rugeley, *Yucatán's Maya Peasantry and the Origins of the Caste War* (Austin: University of Texas Press, 1996).

12. *El Vijilante*, 31 October 1852.

13. Ibid.

14. Ibid.

15. Ibid.

16. *Panama Star*, 4 October 1850 and 18 October 1850.

17. Quoted in Espinar, *Resumen histórico*, 2.

18. Espinar, *Resumen histórico*, 3–18, passim.

19. *El Día*, 3 July 1850. Also see Alfredo Castillero Calvo, "Un antecedente de la 'Tajada de Sandía,' " *Lotería* 6, 69 (August 1961): 20–23.

20. *El Día*, 3 July 1850.

21. Mosquera to Pedro Alcántara Herrán, 25 May 1850, Archivo General de la Nación (Colombia), Fondo Academia Colombiana de Historia, Colección Pedro Alcántara Herrán (hereafter AGN, ACH, PAH), microfilm roll 32 (original in caja 75, carpeta 216), 373–374.

22. "Situación actual de Panamá," *El Día* (Bogotá), 3 July 1850.

23. Mosquera to Herrán, 25 May 1850, AGN, ACH, PAH, microfilm roll 32 (original in caja 75, carpeta 216), 373–374.

24. Omar Jaén Suárez, *La población del Istmo de Panamá: Estudio de Geohistoria*, 3rd ed. (Madrid: Ediciones de Cultura Hispánica, 1998), 274–275.

25. Forster, "Field Notes," 12 March 1849, 15 March 1849.

26. Seacole, *Wonderful Adventures*, 44–45.

27. Ibid., 50–51.

28. Ibid., 72.

29. Lapp, *Blacks in Gold Rush California*, 43–44. Lapp also mentions a "colored man" named "Mr. Lyons" who established himself as a hotel-keeper in Panama. Lapp states that many slaves were brought by masters from the southern United States via Panama to California. Although he suggests that "robber bands on the isthmus went into the business of kidnapping slaves to resell in South America," I have found no contemporary evidence of such sales. On Joe Prince, see Tomes, *Panama in 1855*, 91, and *Panama Star and Herald*, 21 July 1855.

30. James Williams, *Life and Adventures of James Williams, A Fugitive Slave, with a Full Description of the Underground Railroad* (San Francisco: Women's Union Print, 1873), 27.

31. John L. Brown, William S. Safford, A. B. Miller, William Miller, and I. D. Farwell to President José Hilario López, 20 March 1850, Archivo del Ministerio de Relaciones Exteriores (hereafter AMRE), Colombia, Correspondence from the U.S. Legation in New Granada.

32. Ibid.

33. Armando Mártinez Garnica, "La acción de los liberals panameños en la determinación de las políticas del Estado de la Nueva Granada, 1848–1855," in *Colombia y Panamá*, ed. Bonilla and Montañez, 75–80.

34. Figueroa Navarro, *Dominio y sociedad*, 342–344.

35. Ibid.

36. See José de Obaldía, "Contestación del ex-gobernador," in *El Panameño*, 1 September 1850. For more on race and the language of republicanism in early-nineteenth-century Colombia, see Lasso, "Race War and Nation in Caribbean Gran Colombia." For an example from the late 1850s of the deployment of the term "el pueblo" as a synonym for the Arrabal, see *El Elector*, 27 May 1858.

37. Mariano Arosemena to Herrán, 19 December 1855, AGN, ACH, PAH, caja 62, carpeta 186, 121.

38. On the life and career of Justo Arosemena, see Fernando Aparicio, "Justo Arosemena," as well as Argelia Tello, "Estudio introductorio," in Justo Arosemena, *Escritos de Justo Arosemena: Estudio introductorio y antología*, ed. Argelia Tello Burgos (Panama City: Editorial Universitaria, 1985), xi–lxxii. Also see Octavio Méndez Pereira, *Justo Arosemena* (1919; Panama City: Editorial Universitaria, 1970) and José Dolores Moscote and Enrique Juan Arce, *La vida ejemplar de Justo Arosemena* (Panama City: Imprenta Nacional, 1956).

39. Arosemena, *El Estado Federal*, 45.

40. Arosemena, *El Estado Federal*, 76–79.

41. Justo Arosemena, "¡¡¡Alerta Istmeños!!!," 17 November 1850, in *Escritos de Justo Arosemena*, ed. Tello, 78.

42. Arosemena, *El Estado Federal*, 75–77.

43. Ibid., 70–87, passim.

44. Ibid., 60.

45. Ibid., 78–83.

46. Ibid., 39, 68.

47. Ibid., 36–37, 71–72.

48. Ibid., 9–10.

49. Ibid., 74.

50. Ibid., 14–15. On the concept of Westphalian sovereignty, see Stephen D. Krasner, *Sovereignty: Organized Hypocrisy* (Princeton: Princeton University Press, 1999), 3–4.

51. Aparicio, "Justo Arosemena," 209–210.

52. Muñóz Pinzón, "El conflicto," 178.

53. *Daily Panama Star and Herald*, 21 April 1855 and 15 May 1855. The quotation from *El Panameño* appears in the issue of 15 May 1855.

54. Affidavit of Arthur Mackenzie, 10 July 1856, USNA, DS, RG 59, M-139, roll 4.

55. Affidavit of Moses Brinkerhoff, 25 June 1856, USNA, DS, RG 59, M-139, roll 5.

56. Affidavit of Arthur Mackenzie, 10 July 1856.

57. Governor Salvador Camacho Roldán to Cabildo de Panamá, 10 May 1853, ACMP, tomo 11.

58. Petition of Peter Delfs, Eujenio Sapata, Rosalio Lopez, Joaquín Castillo, Miguel Abran, Marselino Golanilla, Carlos Cartas, Thomas Waterman, José García, 14 January 1855, ACMP, tomo 14.

59. See James Sanders's discussion of "popular liberalism" in Cauca in the mid-nineteenth century, including his consideration of the politics of boatmen in Cauca. Sanders, *Contentious Republicans*, 43–57.

60. José Victorino Soto, Commission Report on La Ciénaga, 13 April 1853, ACMP, tomo 11.

61. Saturnino Cano to Presidente del Cabildo de Panamá, 4 November 1852, ACMP, tomo 9.

62. Petition to Cabildo de Panamá, 22 October 1852, ACMP, tomo 9.

63. General Tomás Herrera to Presidente del Cabildo, 15 November 1852, ACMP, tomo 10.

64. Saturnino Cano to Cabildo de Panamá, 18 March 1852, ACMP, tomo 9.

65. Alcalde de Santa Ana to Antonio Planas, quoted in Antonio Planas to the President of the Cabildo of Panamá, 12 September 1852, ACMP, tomo 10.

66. Justo Arosemena to Cabildo de Panamá, 13 February 1853, ACMP, tomo 11.

67. Petition of Vecinos de la Ciénaga to Cabildo de Panamá, 16 February 1853, with addendum dated 18 February 1853, ACMP, tomo 11.

68. Totten to Gov. Manuel María Díaz, 22 August 1855, ACMP, tomo 14. The chief executive of the state of Panamá (*jefe superior del estado*), Justo Arosemena, granted La Ciénaga to the railroad company in two separate resolutions made on July 15 and August 9, 1855. According to the railroad company's contract with the national government of Nueva Granada, the company was entitled to public lands deemed necessary for the completion of the road. Arosemena agreed to transfer ownership of La Ciénaga to the company, deeming that La Ciénaga was necessary for the completion of the company's Pacific terminus.

69. Saturnino Cano to Cabildo de Panamá, 18 March 1852, ACMP, tomo 9.

70. Augusto Cristiano Fretz to Cabildo de Panamá, 11 January 1856, ACMP, tomo 15.

71. José María Aleman to Cabildo de Panamá, 30 April 1860, ACMP, tomo 17. See Totten to Mr. Joy, 26 February 1872, Totten Letters, vol. 2, USNA, RG 185.

72. Affidavit of Arthur Mackenzie, 10 July 1856, USNA, DS, RG 59, M-139, roll 5.

73. Mariano Arosemena to Herrán, 19 December 1855, AGN, ACH, PAH, caja 62, carpeta 186, 121.

74. Ibid.

75. Aparicio, "Justo Arosemena," 209–210.

76. Francisco de Fábrega to Herrán, 4 January 1856, ANP, PC, cajón 850, tomo 2166 [originally 2160], 60–61.

77. Castillero Calvo, "El oro de California."

78. Muñoz Pinzón, *Estudio de historia social.*

79. José Ignacio Borbúa to Secretario de Estado de Panamá, 14 January 1856, ANP, PC, cajón 839, tomo 1895.

80. Pedimento del Pueblo de Parita, 20 January 1856, ANP, PC, tomo 1895.

81. May, *Manifest Destiny's Underworld,* 40–42.

82. Burns, *Patriarch and Folk,* 160–237, passim, and Gobat, *Confronting the American Dream,* 29–41.

83. Kirsten Silva Gruesz, *Ambassadors of Culture: The Transamerican Origins of Latino Writing* (Princeton, N.J.: Princeton University Press, 2002), 168.

84. Burns, *Patriarch and Folk,* 209; Greenberg, *Manifest Manhood,* 150–151; May, *Manifest Destiny's Underground,* 111–112. Slavery was also re-established in the French colonial Caribbean after its first abolition in 1794. See Laurent Dubois, *A Colony of Citizens: Revolution and Slave Emancipation in the French Caribbean, 1787–1804* (Chapel Hill: University of North Carolina Press, 2004).

85. Francisco de Fábrega to Secretario de Estado del Despacho del Gobierno, 22 January 1856, ANP, PC, cajón 850, tomo 2166 [originally 2160], 65–67.

86. Francisco de Fábrega, Circular a los Señores Cónsules i Viceconsules estranejros en Panamá I Colón, 4 February 1856, ANP, PC, cajón 850, tomo 2166 [originally 2160], 72–73.

87. Francisco de Fábrega to Secretario de Estado del Despacho de Relaciones Esteriores, 7 March 1856, ANP, PC, Cajón 850, tomo 2166 (originally 2160), 78–79.

88. On debates surrounding women's suffrage in Vélez, see Bushnell, *The Making of Modern Colombia,* 108–109.

89. On the broader impact of the Panamanian experiment in federalism on Nueva Granada/Colombia as a whole as well as the national significance of other reforms undertaken in Panama in the early 1850s, including the establishment of free trade, trial by jury, and habeas corpus, see Martínez Garnica, "La acción," 37–91.

90. Appelbaum, *Muddied Waters,* chap. 3; Sanders, *Contentious Republicans,* 32–43.

91. Sucheng Chan, "A People of Exceptional Character: Ethnic Diversity, Nativism, and Racism in the California Gold Rush," in *Rooted in Barbarous Soil: People, Culture, and Community*

in Gold Rush California, ed. Kevin Starr and Richard J. Orsi (Berkeley: University of California Press, 2000); Johnson, *Domestic Life in the Diggings*; Rohrbough, *Days of Gold*, 216–229; Peter J. Blodgett, *Land of Golden Dreams: California in the Gold Rush Decade, 1848–1858* (San Marino, Calif.: Huntington Library, 1999), 100, 105–106. On Santa Barbara, see Louise Pubols, "Fathers of the Pueblo: Patriarchy and Power in Mexican California, 1800–1880," in *Continental Crossroads*, ed. Truett and Young, 67–93.

    92. *Panama Star and Herald*, 21 February 1856.

    93. *Panama Star and Herald*, 19 April 1856.

    94. Sanders, *Contentious Republicans*, 2, 18–57, passim.

4. "We Are Not in the United States Here"

    1. On the impact of the railroad on perceptions of space and time, see Cronon, *Nature's Metropolis*, 72–74, and Wolfgang Schivelbusch, *The Railway Journey: Trains and Travel in the Nineteenth Century* (Oxford: Blackwell, 1980).

    2. *Daily Alta California*, 20 March 1856.

    3. On Horace Bell and Anglo-American efforts to consolidate power through violence in Los Angeles and elsewhere in Southern California after 1848, see William Deverell, *Whitewashed Adobe: The Rise of Los Angeles and the Remaking of Its Mexican Past* (Berkeley: University of California Press, 2004), 13–14. On Joaquín Murrieta, see among other works Johnson, *Roaring Camp*, 25–53 passim; Streeby, *American Sensations*, 251–290, and Bruce Thornton, *Searching for Joaquín: Myth, Murieta, and History in California* (San Francisco: Encounter Books, 2003).

    4. Horace Bell, "Manifest Destiny as it appeared in Nicaragua in 1855, '56, '57," unpublished typescript, undated, Huntington Library, Horace Bell Collection, HM 39800, Box 3, 1. Also see Horace Bell, *Reminiscences of a Ranger; or, Early Times in Southern California* (Los Angeles: Yarnell, Caystile and Mathes, 1881), 350–369 passim. Thornton treats Bell's remembrances as unreliable and describes Bell as a "fabulist." Nevertheless, Bell's account of his experiences in Panama City on April 15, 1856, accords remarkably well with other accounts of the same event. See Thornton, *Searching*, 101.

    5. On the struggle over the Accessory Transit Company, see Folkman, *Nicaragua Route*, 77–78, Gobat, *Confronting the American Dream*, 30, and May, *Manifest Destiny's Underground*, 175–177.

    6. *Panama Star and Herald*, 8 April 1856, and May, *Manifest Destiny's Underground*, 234. On the *Cortes*'s delivery of recruits to Walker in October 1855, see William Walker, *The War in Nicaragua* (1860; Tucson: University of Arizona Press), 106.

    7. Bell, "Manifest Destiny." 3.

    8. On the first battle of Rivas, see Iván Molina Jiménez, *La Campaña Nacional (1856–1857): Una vision desde el siglo XXI* (Alajuela: Museo Histórico Cultural Jan Santamaría, 2000), 35–38.

    9. Bell, "Manifest Destiny," 3.

    10. On fears of filibusters in Panama City in early 1856, see May, *Manifest Destiny's Underworld: Filibustering in Antebellum America* (Chapel Hill: University of North Carolina Press, 2002), 234–235.

    11. "Hotel Aspinwall. Register, 1856–59," Bancroft Library BANC MSS 76/134 m.

    12. See, for example, the issue of the *Panama Star and Herald* that announced the arrival of the *Cortes*, which also detailed Walker's recent losses and his retrenchment in Rivas. *Panama Star and Herald*, 8 April 1856.

    13. On the increase in women and children after the initial gold rush immigration in 1848–1849, see Kemble, *Panama Route*, 149.

14. *Panama Star and Herald*, 19 April 1856.

15. Ibid.

16. Testimony of José Manuel Luna, *Gaceta del Estado*, 26 April 1856; Amos Corwine, "Report of Amos B. Corwine, United States Commissioner, respecting the Occurrences at Panamá on the 15 April 1856," USNA, DS, RG 59, M-139, roll 5.

17. On silversmiths during the colonial period, see Ángeles Ramos Baquero, "Platería y plateros durante la colonia," in *Historia General*, ed. Castillero Calvo, vol. 1, tomo 2.

18. List of results of election for the cabildo of parish of Santa Ana on December 8, 1851, ACMP, Tomo 8 (1851); "Padrón Electoral de la parroquia de Santa Ana," 21 August 1853, ACMP, Tomo 11 (1853). Of the 470 names listed on the electoral list of 1853, 313, or 67 percent, were declared to be capable of reading and writing. Since voting in 1853 was limited by property requirements, this electoral list represented a minority of adult men in a parish whose total population had probably grown to at least 4,000 by 1853.

19. In his account of his 1855 voyage to Panama, Robert Tomes noted that arriving passengers at the train station in Panama City were "followed by troops of native orange-women" as well as boatmen, whom he described as "naked ebony lads." Elsewhere in the same book, he described seeing "Jamaica negresses" and "natives" who offered fruit and other refreshments to passengers at the railroad station in Panama City. See Tomes, *Panama in 1855*, 95, 230.

20. Espinar, *Resumen histórico*, 5–6.

21. Declaration of José Manuel Luna, *Gaceta del Estado*, 26 April 1856.

22. Ibid. Luna's words were rendered in Spanish as follows: "Cuidado, que aquí no estamos en los Estados Unidos; págame mi real i estamos al corriente." The idiom "estar al corriente" may be translated variously as to be aware, up-to-date, or, in the context of an account or a transaction, to be paid up or even. The passenger's insult was translated in the *Gaceta del Estado* as "Bésame el culo."

23. Affidavit of Dennis Shannon, 30 April 1856, USNA, RG 59, M-139, roll 4.

24. Declaration of José Manuel Luna, *Gaceta del Estado*, 26 April 1856.

25. *Daily Alta California*, 2 May 1856.

26. Corwine, "Report."

27. Bell, *Reminiscences*, 360.

28. James Bowlin alluded to William Perry's statement in a reproachful letter to Lino de Pombo. See Bowlin to Pombo, 13 February 1857, reprinted in Nueva Granada, *Final controversia diplomática con relación a los sucesos de Panamá* (Bogotá: Imprenta del Estado, 1857), 28.

29. Lino de Pombo to Bowlin, 28 June 1856, reprinted in English translation in *Diplomatic Correspondence of the United States. Inter-American Affairs, 1831–1860*, ed. William R. Manning (Washington: Carnegie Endowment for International Peace, 1935), vol. 5, 734.

30. Bowlin to William L. Marcy, 20 February 1857, reprinted in *Diplomatic Correspondence*, ed. Manning, vol. 6, 844, 845.

31. *El Panameño*, 23 April 1856.

32. *El Centinela*, 27 August 1856.

33. Testimony of Miguel Habrahan, *Gaceta del Estado*, 26 April 1856.

34. Petition of Peter Delfs, Eujenio Sapata, Rosalio Lopez, Joaquín Castillo, Miguel Abran, Marselino Golanilla, Carlos Cartas, Thomas Waterman, José García, 14 January 1855, ACMP, tomo 14.

35. Affidavit of Ran Runnels, 24 April 1856, USNA, DS, RG 59, M-139, roll 4.

36. Declaration of Miguel Habrahan, *Gaceta del Estado*, 26 April 1856.

37. Ibid.; Corwine, "Report."

38. Declaration of Miguel Habrahan, *Gaceta del Estado*, 26 April 1856.

39. Corwine, "Report."

40. On the complexities of reading subaltern politics through official accounts, see Shahid Amin, *Event, Metaphor, Memory: Chauri Chaura, 1922–1992* (Berkeley: University of California Press, 1995) and Ranajit Guha, "The Prose of Counter-Insurgency," in *Selected Subaltern Studies*, ed. Ranajit Guha and Gayatri Chakravorty Spivak (Oxford: Oxford University Press, 1988).

41. Corwine, "Report."

42. Lino de Pombo and Florentino González to Bowlin and Isaac Morse, 23 February 1857, reprinted in *Final controversia*, 32–52.

43. *Panama Star and Herald*, 19 April 1856.

44. Ibid; Declaration of José María Borbúa, *Gaceta del Estado*, 26 April 1856.

45. Francisco de Fábrega, "Nota dando cuenta al Poder Ejecutivo de la República de los sucesos del 15 del corriente," 22 April 1856, in *Gaceta del Estado*, 26 April 1856; Declaration of José María Rodríguez, *Gaceta del Estado*, 26 April 1856.

46. Francisco de Fábrega, "Nota."

47. Corwine, "Report"; Ramón Gamboa, "Nota del Prefecto del Departamento de Panamá," *Gaceta del Estado*, 26 April 1856; Manuel María Garrido, "Nota del Jefe de la jendarmería," *Gaceta del Estado*, 26 April 1856.

48. Garrido, "Nota."

49. Thomas Ward to William Marcy, 18 April 1856, USNA, DS, RG 59, M-139, roll 4.

50. *Panama Star and Herald*, 19 April 1856; *Gaceta del Estado*, 26 April 1856.

51. "Report of Drs. E. LeBreton and I. Kratochwil in relation to the Dead and Wounded on the Night of April 15, 1856," 6 September 1856, USNA, DS, RG 59, M-139, roll 5.

52. Corwine, "Report."

53. Fábrega to Cavalcante d'Albuquerque, 3 May 1856, USNA, DS, RG 59, M-139, roll 5; Garrido, "Nota."

54. Affidavit of Arthur Mackenzie, 10 July 1856, USNA, DS, RG 59, M-139, roll 5.

55. Thomas Ward to William Marcy, 4 May 1856, USNA, DS, RG 59, M-139, roll 4.

56. Corwine, "Report."

57. Garrido, "Nota."

58. Declaration of Sebastián Díaz, *Gaceta del Estado*, 26 April 1856.

59. Declaration of T. B. Williams, *Gaceta del Estado*, 26 April 1856.

60. *El Panameño*, 23 April 1856.

61. Declaration of José María Rodríguez, *Gaceta del Estado*, 26 April 1856.

62. "Report of Drs. E. LeBreton and I. Kratochwil in relation to the Dead and Wounded on the Night of April 15, 1856," 6 September 1856, USNA, DS, RG 59, M-139, roll 5.

63. See Carrie Stevens Walter, "A Panama Riot," *Overland Monthly and Out West Magazine*, vol. 4, 24 (December 1884), 635–640, http://name.umdl.umich.edu/ahj1472.2-04.024 (16 May 2007). For this reference I am indebted to "The Panama Railroad," an excellent website dedicated to history and future of the Panama Railroad. See http://www.trainweb.org/panama/ (16 May 2007).

64. Thomas Ward to William Marcy, 18 April 1856, USNA, DS, RG 59, M-139, roll 4; Corwine, "Report"; affidavit of James William Johnson, April 25, 1856, USNA, DS, RG 59, M-139, roll 5.

65. Affidavit of Arthur Mackenzie, 10 July 1856, USNA, DS, RG 59, M-139, roll 5. See also the affidavit of Allen McLane, 8 July 1856, USNA, DS, RG 59, M-139, roll 5.

66. Affidavit of Frederick Ansoatigue, 11 July 1856, USNA, DS, RG 59, M-139, roll 5.

67. Affidavit of James Copeland, 10 July 1856, USNA, DS, RG 59, M-139, roll 5.

68. Affidavit of T. Bradford Williams, 15 July 1856, USNA, DS, RG 59, M-139, roll 5.

69. Lino de Pombo and González to Bowlin and Morse, 23 February 1857, reprinted in *Final controversia*, 32–52.

70. Bell, *Reminiscences*, 364–365.

71. Declaration of Alexander Henriquez, *Gaceta del Estado*, 26 April 1856.

72. *Panama Star and Herald*, 8 May 1856.

73. Fábrega to Cavalcanto d'Albuquerque, 3 May 1856, USNA, DS, RG 59, M-139, roll 5. The opinion that the violence of April 15 was caused by fears of a takeover by filibusters was also shared by the British chargé d'affaires in Nueva Granada, Philip Griffith. See May, *Manifest Destiny's Underworld*, 235.

74. Fábrega to Cavalcanto d'Albuquerque, 3 May 1856, USNA, DS, RG 59, M-139, roll 5.

75. *El Panameño*, 21 April 1856.

76. Bell, *Reminiscences*, 356.

77. Lino de Pombo and González to Bowlin and Morse, 23 February 1857, reprinted in *Final controversia*, 32–52.

78. Affidavit of Frederick Ansoatigue, 11 July 1856, USNA, DS, RG 59, M-139, roll 5.

79. Bell, *Reminiscences*, 365.

80. De Sabla to Ward, 18 April 1856, USNA, DS, RG 59, M-139, roll 4.

81. Affidavit of William Nelson, 18 April 1856, USNA, DS, RG 59, M-139, roll 4; *Panama Star and Herald*, 19 April 1856.

82. Apparently Allen, like Corwine, was convinced that the police had acted as one with the "mob." This assertion was contested by Fábrega. Affidavit of Edward Allen, 9 July 1856, USNA, DS, RG 59, M-139, roll 5.

83. Affidavit of José María Bravo, 18 April 1856, USNA, DS, RG 59, M-139, roll 4.

84. Declaration of Sebastián Díaz, *Gaceta del Estado*, 26 April 1856.

85. "Lista de los individuos que han sido capturados como sindicados de complicidad en los robos del 15 de abril," 6 May 1856, AMRE, Legación en Washington, 1857–58.

86. "Relación de las habitaciones que han sido allanadas por sospecharse que existieran en ellas efectos de los robados en la noche del 15 de abril," 6 May 1856, in "Documentos pa. La Concesión de Reclamos," AMRE, Legación en Washington, 1857–58.

87. Affidavit of T. B. Williams, 15 July 1856, USNA, DS, RG 59, M-139, roll 5.

88. *Weekly Panama Star and Herald*, 30 October 1854.

89. Affidavit of Ran Runnels, 24 April 1856, USNA, DS, RG 59, M-139, roll 4.

90. Ibid.

91. Ibid.

92. Corwine, "Report"; *Panama Star and Herald*, 19 April 1856; Affidavit of William Nelson, 11 June 1856, USNA, DS, RG 59, M-139, roll 5.

93. Fábrega, "Nota."

94. Affidavit of William Nelson, 18 April 1856, USNA, DS, RG 59, M-139, roll 4; on "el mulato Urriola," see Aristides Martínez Ortega, "La poesía panameña ordenada y comentada por Rodrigo Miró," forward to Rodrigo Miró, *Itinerario de la poesía en Panamá* (Panama City: Biblioteca de la Nacionalidad/Autoridad del Canal de Panamá, 1999), vol. 2, xv.

95. Testimony of Antonio Abad Monteser, 4 August 1856, ANP, PC, cajón 850, tomo 2166 [originally in tomo 2160], 252–253. See also the testimony of Martín Carransa, 5 August 1856, ANP, PC, cajón 850, tomo 2166 [originally in tomo 2160], 253–254.

96. Testimony of Pedro Ramos, 5 August 1856, ANP, PC, cajón 850, tomo 2166 [originally in tomo 2160], 254–255.

97. Testimony of José Isabel Maitín, 4 August 1856, ANP, PC, cajón 850, tomo 2166 [originally in tomo 2160], 250–252. On Maitín's activities as a Liberal deputy in September 1856, see *Panama Star and Herald*, 25 September 1856.

98. Testimony of Antonio Abad Monteser, 4 August 1856.

99. Ibid.

100. Testimony of Pedro Ramos, 5 August 1856.

101. Testimony of José Isabel Maitín, 4 August 1856.

102. Ramos Baquero, "Plateros."

103. List of results of election for the cabildo of parish of Santa Ana on December 8, 1851, ACMP, Tomo 8 (1851). Elections for cabildo elections before 1853 were not secret, and each voter voted for ten individuals in order of preference. Also listed on José Manuel Luna's ballot was the name of Manuel de los Ríos, who was possibly a silversmith as well. A "Manuel de los Ríos" worked as a silversmith in Panama City in the second half of the eighteenth century, and the craft was sometimes passed on from generation to generation. See Ramos Baquero, "Platería," 283.

104. See Margaret C. Jacob, *Living the Enlightenment: Freemasonry and Politics in Eighteenth Century Europe* (Oxford: Oxford University Press, 1991), 9–11, 23–24, 73–74.

105. Antonio Rafael de la Cova, "Filibusters and Freemasons: The Sworn Obligation," *Journal of the Early Republic* 17, no. 1 (Spring 1997): 95–120.

106. Fábrega, "Nota."

107. Alfredo Castillero Calvo identified the connection between May 1850 and April 1856 in Castillero Calvo, "Un antecedente de la 'Tajada de Sandía," *Lotería* 6, 69 (August 1961): 20–23.

108. Corwine, "Report."

109. *Panama Star and Herald*, 19 April 1856.

110. See the announcement of Manuel María Díaz's candidacy for state governor in *Panama Star and Herald*, 13 May 1856.

111. Tomes, *Panama in 1855*, 180–181.

112. Tomes, *Panama in 1855*, 144.

113. Peter Wood and Karen C. C. Dalton write that although visual images of African Americans with watermelon predate Reconstruction, the racist association of watermelon with grotesque portrayals of African Americans did not become a commonplace in the United States until the 1880s. See Wood and Dalton, *Winslow Homer's Images of Blacks: The Civil War and Reconstruction Years* (Austin: University of Texas Press, 1988), 122 n. 192.

5. U.S. Empire and the Boundaries of Latin America

1. Martin W. Lewis and Kären Wigen, *The Myth of Continents: A Critique of Metageography* (Berkeley: University of California Press, 1997), 181. I have previously explored the relationship between events in Panama in 1856 and the emergence of "Latin America" as a geopolitical entity in Aims McGuinness, "Searching for 'Latin America': Race and Sovereignty in the Americas in the 1850s," in *Race and Nation in Modern Latin America*, ed. Nancy P. Appelbaum, Anne S. Macpherson, and Karin Alejandra Rosemblatt (Chapel Hill: University of North Carolina Press, 2003), 87–107. I am particularly grateful to Nancy Appelbaum for her help in developing ideas expressed both in that essay and in his chapter.

2. John L. Phelan, "Pan-Latinism, French Intervention in Mexico (1861–1867), and the Genesis of the Idea of Latin America," in *Conciencia y autenticidad históricas*, ed. Juan A. Ortega y Medina (Mexico City: Universidad Nacional Autónoma de México, 1968), 279–298.

3. Arturo Ardao, *Génesis de la idea y el nombre de América Latina* (Caracas: Centro de Estudios Latinoamericanos Rómulo Gallegos, 1980), 82–86. See also Ardao, *América Latina y la latinidad* (Mexico City: Universidad Nacional Autónoma de México, 1993).

4. Miguel Rojas Mix, "Bilbao y el hallazgo de América latina: Unión continental, socialista y libertaria," *Cahiers du Monde Hispanique et Luso-Brasilien-Caravelle* 46 (1986), 35–47, and Rojas Mix, *Los cien nombres de América Latina: Eso que descubrió Colón* (San José: Editorial Universitaria de Costa Rica, 1991), 343–344.

5. Paul Estrade, "Del invento de 'América Latina' en París por latinoamericanos (1856–1889)," in *París y el mundo ibérico e iberoamericano*, ed. Jacques Maurice and Marie-Claire

Zimmerman (Paris: Université Paris X-Nanterre, 1998), 179–188, and Mónica Quijada, "Sobre el orígen y difusión del nombre 'América Latina' (o una variación heterodoxa en torno al tema de la construcción social de la verdad)," *Revista de Indias* 58 (1998), no. 214 (Sept.–Dec. 1998), 595–616. Also see David Bushnell and Neill Macaulay, *The Emergence of Latin America in the Nineteenth Century* (Oxford: Oxford University Press, 1988), 3; Walter D. Mignolo, *The Idea of Latin America* (Maldon: Blackwell Publishing, 2005), 77–81; and Vicente Romero, "Du nominal 'latin' pour l'Autre Amérique. Notes sur la naissance et le sens du nom 'Amérique latine' autour des annés 1850," *Histoire et sociétés de l'Amérique latine* 7, no. 1 (premier semestre 1998): 57–86.

6. For a panoramic vision of the hemisphere in the early 1850s, see James Dunkerley, *Americana: The Americas in the World, around 1850* (London: Verso, 2000). For a concise overview of U.S.-related conflicts in the Americas in the 1850s, see Gustave A. Nuermberger, "The Continental Treaties of 1856: An American Union 'Exclusive of the United States,' " *Hispanic American Historical Review* 20, no. 1 (Feb. 1940): 32–55. On Walker's activities in 1856, see May, *Manifest Destiny's Underworld*, 39–40, 193–211; On the "Water Witch" incident in Paraguay, see José B. Fernández and Jennifer M. Zimnoch, "Paraguay and Uruguay: On the Periphery II," in *United States–Latin American Relations, 1850–1903: Establishing a Relationship*, ed. Thomas M. Leonard (Tuscaloosa: University of Alabama Press, 1999), 228–233, and John H. Schroeder, *Shaping a Maritime Empire: The Commercial and Diplomatic Role of the American Navy, 1829–1861* (Westport: Greenwood Press, 1985), 115–116. On U.S. relations with Chile in the early 1850s, see William F. Sater, "Chile: Clash of Global Visions II," in *United States–Latin American Relations*, ed. Leonard, 170–172. On tensions surrounding the control of guano islands, see Christina Duffy Burnett, "The Edges of Empire and the Limits of Sovereignty: American Guano Islands," *American Quarterly* 57, no. 3 (September 2005): 779–803.

7. See Nuermberger, "The Continental Treaties of 1856," Germán Cavelier, *La política internacional de Colombia* (Bogotá: Editorial Iqueima), vol. 1, 183–190, and Thomas M. Leonard, "Introduction," in *United States–Latin America Relations*, ed. Leonard, 3.

8. Corwine, "Report."

9. Ibid.

10. *Daily Alta California*, 5 May 1856.

11. *Frank Leslie's Illustrated Newspaper*, 17 May 1856.

12. *Daily Alta California*, 8 May 1856.

13. Charles P. Duane, *Against the Vigilantes: The Recollections of Dutch Charley Duane*, ed. John Boessenecker (Norman: University of Oklahoma Press, 1999), 144. Duane himself was arrested and sent into exile by the vigilantes. His exile included a brief visit to Panama later in 1856.

14. Hoadley to J. C. Dobbin, 30 April 1856, USNA, Panama Railroad Company Letterbooks, box 5, vol. 10, 275.

15. Hoadley to Totten, 2 August 1856, USNA, RG 185, Panama Railroad Company Letterbooks, box 2, vol. 3, 94–96.

16. "Propositions handed by Messrs. Morse and Bowlin . . . of the Government of the United-States, to the Secretary of Foreign Affairs, on the 4th of February, 1857," in *Final controversia*, 2–18. See Conniff, *Panama and the United States*, 39; Helen Delpar, "Colombia: Troubled Friendship," in *United States–Latin American Relations, 1850–1903*, ed. Leonard, 67; and Stephen J. Randall, *Colombia and the United States: Hegemony and Interdependence* (Athens: University of Georgia Press, 1992), 40–42

17. Naylor, *Penny*, 181.

18. Bradford Perkins, *The Creation of a Republican Empire, 1776–1865*, vol. 1 of *The Cambridge History of American Foreign Relations*, ed. Warren I. Cohen (Cambridge: Cambridge University Press, 1993), 202–203; and John H. Schroeder, *Matthew Calbraith Perry: Antebellum Sailor and Diplomat* (Annapolis: Naval Institute Press, 2001), 233.

19. Delpar, "Colombia," 67, and Germán Cavelier, *La política internacional de Colombia* (Bogotá: Editorial Iqueima), vol. 1, 114.

20. See Safford and Palacios, *Colombia*, 217–221.

21. Justo Arosemena, "La cuestión americana i su importancia," *El Neogranadino*, 15 and 29 July 1856. Reprinted in Arosemena, *Escritos*, ed. Tello, 247–263.

22. Arosemena, "Cuestión americana," 248.

23. Ibid., 247.

24. Arosemena, "Cuestión americana," 250–257, *passim*.

25. Ibid., 257.

26. Ibid., 249.

27. Ibid., 249–250.

28. Ibid., 250–251, 259–260.

29. On ideas of Anglo-Saxon superiority in the 1850s, see Horsman, *Race and Manifest Destiny*, 229–248, and Matthew Jacobson, *Whiteness of a Different Color: European Immigrants and the Alchemy of Race* (Cambridge, Mass.: Harvard University Press, 1998), 205–213. On U.S. perceptions of elites in the Spanish-speaking Americas, see Pike, *United States and Latin America*, 195—196, and Streeby, *American Sensations*, 121–124.

30. Phelan, "Pan-Latinism," 281–282. On Saint Simonianism and Torres Caicedo's career in Europe, see Paul N. Edison, "Latinizing America: The French Scientific Study of México, 1830–1930" (Ph.D. diss., Columbia University, 1999).

31. Justo Arosemena, "Discurso pronunciado por el doctor Justo Arosemena, en julio de 1856," in Octavio Méndez Pereira, *Justo Arosemena* (1919; Panama City: Editorial Universitaria, 1970), 208–210. On aspirations to reconstitute a united Colombia that might include places in the Americas beyond those that originally formed "Gran Colombia," see Safford and Palacios, *Colombia*, 218.

32. See Ardao, *Génesis*, 31–61; Quijada, 605–607; and Romero, "Du nominal 'Latin,'" 66, 77–81.

33. José María Torres Caicedo, "Las dos Américas," originally published in *El Correo de Ultramar* (Paris), 15 February 1857, reprinted in Ardao, *Génesis*, 175–185.

34. Ardao, *Génesis*, 82–84.

35. Arosemena, "Cuestión americana," 261–262.

36. Ibid., 250, 259–261.

37. Ibid., 249–250, 262–263.

38. Arosemena, *Estado Federal*, 24.

39. Ibid., 260; *Estado Federal*, 75.

40. Theodorus Bailey to Fábrega, 23 April 1856, ANP, Hojas Sueltas.

41. Bailey to Fábrega, 25 April 1856, ANP, Hojas Sueltas.

42. Bailey to J. C. Dobbin, 2 May 1856, USNA, Record Group 45 (hereafter RG 45), Microfilm Series 147 (hereafter M-147), Letters received by the Secretary of the Navy from Commanders, 1804–1886 (hereafter Commanders' Letters), roll 50.

43. Fábrega to Ward, 28 April 1856, USNA, DS, RG 59, M-139, roll 4.

44. *Panama Star and Herald*, 17 May 1856.

45. On Democratic Societies, see Sanders, *Contentious Republicans*, 66–69; David Sowell, *The Early Colombian Labor Movement: Artisans and Politics in Bogotá, 1832–1919* (Philadelphia: Temple University Press, 1992), 46–52; and Margarita Pacheco, *La fiesta liberal en Cali* (Cali, Colombia: Universidad del Valle, 1992). Sowell notes that some artisan participants from Bogotá who took part in the so-called Melo revolt of 1854 were exiled to Panama. Although the possibility of a linkage between artisans from Bogotá and popular Liberals in the Arrabal is intriguing, I have been able to find no evidence of such a linkage. See Sowell, *Early Colombian Labor Movement*, 74–75.

46. See "Averiguación sumaria sobre la venida a esta Ciudad del reo Isabel Batista, alias, Chabelo, i compañeros suyos," 27 March 1856, ANP, Hojas Sueltas.

47. Ward to Fábrega, 15 May 1856, USNA, DS, RG 59, M-139, roll 4.

48. Fábrega to Ward, 15 May 1856, USNA, DS, RG 59, M-139, roll 4.

49. Fábrega to Ward, 30 May 1856, USNA, DS, RG 59, M-139, roll 4.

50. Fábrega to Ward, 15 May 1856, USNA, DS, RG 59, M-139, roll 4.

51. *Panama Star and Herald*, 17 May 1856.

52. *Panama Star and Herald*, 27 May 1856.

53. Fábrega to Ward, 24 May 1856, USNA, DS, RG 59, M-139, roll 5.

54. *Panama Star and Herald*, 3 June 1856; *El Panameño*, 28 May 1856.

55. Fábrega to Ward, May 21, 1856, USNA, DS, RG 59, M-139, roll 4.

56. Ward to Fábrega, May 22, 1856, USNA, DS, RG 59, M-139, roll 4. Also see *Panama Star and Herald*, 22 May 1856.

57. May, *Manifest Destiny's Underworld*, 177.

58. *Panama Star and Herald*, 27 May 1856. On the San Francisco meeting, see *Panama Star and Herald*, 5 June 1856.

59. Bailey to J.C. Dobbin, 2 June 1856, Commanders' Letters, USNA, RG 45, M–147, roll 50. Also see *Panama Star and Herald*, 27 May 1856.

60. *El Panameño*, 17 May 1856.

61. Francisco de Fábrega to Secretario de Estado del despacho de Relaciones Esteriores, 21 June 1856, ANP, PC, cajón 850, tomo 2166 [originally in tomo 2160], 136–137.

62. *El Centinela*, 27 August 1856.

63. *Panama Star and Herald*, 23 August 1856.

64. See Mariano Arosemena to Justo Arosemena, 29 October 1856, reprinted in Mariano Arosemena, *Historia y nacionalidad: Estudio preliminary*, ed. Argelia Tello (Panama City: Editorial Universitaria Panamá, 1979), 170–173, and Mariano Arosemena to Justo Arosemena, 18 November 1856, reprinted in Arosemena, *Historia y nacionalidad*, ed. Tello, 177–178.

65. See Simón Maldonado, "Asuntos políticos de Panamá," unpublished manuscript, undated, Bancroft Library, Hubert Howe Bancroft Collection, 14. The date of the writing of this brief account is unclear, but it was evidently written before 1890, as it is cited in Hubert Howe Bancroft, *History of Central America* (San Francisco: The History Company, 1890), vol. 3, 526–527.

66. William Mervine to Dobbin, 2 September 1856, USNA, Letters Received by the Secretary of the Navy from Commanding Officers of Squadrons (hereafter Squadron Letters), RG 45, Microfilm Series 89 (hereafter M-89), roll 38; Mervine to Fábrega, 10 September 1856, Squadron Letters, USNA, RG 45, M-89, roll 38.

67. De Sabla to Marcy, 18 September 1856, USNA, DS, RG 59, M-139, roll 5.

68. *Panama Star and Herald*, 2 September 1856.

69. *Panama Star and Herald*, 6 September 1856; Méndez Pereira, *Justo Arosemena*, 212.

70. *Panama Star and Herald*, 11 September 1856; *Panama Star and Herald*, 18 September 1856.

71. *Panama Star and Herald*, 11 September 1856; *Panama Star and Herald*, 18 September 1856.

72. Quoted in Hoadley to Amos Corwine, 17 September 1856, USNA, DS, RG 59, M-139, roll 5.

73. Manuel Hurtado, Pedro de Obarrio y Pérez, and others to Deputies of the Legislative Assembly, 10 September 1856, ANP, PC, cajón 866, tomo 2482, 131.

74. Mervine to Dobbin, 18 September 1856, Squadron Letters, USNA, RG 45, M-89, roll 38.

75. Ibid.

76. Letter of "J.D.A. de R.," 15 September 1856, reprinted in *Panama Star and Herald*, 30 October 1856. The same letter was reprinted in Spanish in the Conservative newspaper *El - Centinela* on 2 November 1856. Also see *Panama Star and Herald*, 18 September 1856.

77. Mervine to Dobbin, 18 September 1856, Squadron Letters, USNA, RG 45, M-89, roll 38; *Panama Star and Herald*, 16 September 1856, 18 September 1856.

78. Ibid.

79. De Sabla to Marcy, 18 September 1856, USNA, DS, RG 59, M-139, roll 5.

80. Mervine to Dobbin, 18 September 1856, Squadron Letters, USNA, RG 45, M-89, roll 38.

81. "Acta de la Asembla Legislativa," 18 September 1856, ANP, PC, cajón 866, tomo 2482, 137–144.

82. José Fábrega Barrera to Francisco de Fábrega, 18 September 1856, ANP, PC, cajón 866, tomo 2482, 127.

83. *Panama Star and Herald*, 20 September 1856.

84. De Sabla to Marcy, 2 October 1856, USNA, DS, RG 59, M-139, roll 5.

85. *Panama Star and Herald*, 20 September 1856.

86. *Panama Star and Herald*, 27 September 1856.

87. De Sabla to Marcy, 2 October 1856, USNA, DS, RG 59, M-139, roll 5.

88. Mervine to Dobbin, 3 October 1856, Squadron Letters, USNA, RG 45, M-89, roll 38.

89. De Sabla to Marcy, 2 October 1856, USNA, DS, RG 59, M-139, roll 5.

90. Mervine to Dobbin, 3 October 1856, Squadron Letters, USNA, RG 45, M-89, roll 38.

91. *Panama Star and Herald*, 25 September 1856.

92. Ibid.

93. Ibid.

94. "Acta de la session secreta celebrada por la Asamblea Legislativa del Estado de Panamá," 30 September 1856, ANP, Hojas Sueltas.

95. Bartolomé Calvo to Diputados [of the Asamblea Legislativa], 1 September 1857, ANP, PC, cajón 850, tomo 2157.

96. De Sabla to Marcy, 2 October 1856, USNA, DS, RG 59, M-139, roll 5. See also Juan B. Sosa and Enrique J. Arce, *Compendio de historia de Panamá* (1911; Panama City, n.d.), 222–224; Parks, *Colombia and the United States*, 219–261; and Conniff, *Panama and the United States*, 38–39.

97. *El Panameño*, 26 October 1856.

98. *El Elector*, 31 July 1858. For comparisons with Cuban struggles for independence in the late nineteenth century, see Ada Ferrer, *Insurgent Cuba: Race, Nation, and Revolution, 1868–1898* (Chapel Hill: University of Carolina Press, 1999), 64–65 and 86–76; Rebecca J. Scott, *Degrees of Freedom: Louisiana and Cuba after Slavery* (Cambridge: Harvard University Press, 2005), 139.

99. *El Elector*, 31 July 1858.

100. Mervine to Fábrega, 10 September 1856, Squadron Letters, USNA, RG 45, M-89, roll 38; Corwine, "Report."

101. De Sabla to Marcy, 2 October 1856, USNA, DS, RG 59, M-139, roll 5.

102. William Nelson quoted in Hoadley to Marcy, 29 September 1856, USNA, Panama Railroad Company Letterbooks, box 5, vol. 11, 168–170.

103. Ibid.

104. Hoadley to Amos Corwine, 17 September 1856, USNA, DS, RG 59, M-139, roll 5.

105. José Marcelino Hurtado to Pedro Alcántara Herrán, 3 July 1858, AGN, ACH, PAH, Serie "Correspondencia Asuntos Personales y Militares Proyecto de Empréstito," microfilm roll 9 (original in caja 17, carpeta 72), 90–91.

106. José Marcelino Hurtado to Pedro Alcántara Herrán, 3 July 1858, AGN, ACH, PAH, Serie "Correspondencia Asuntos Personales y Militares Proyecto de Empréstito," microfilm roll 9 (original in caja 17, carpeta 72), 90–91.

107. José Marcelino Hurtado to Herrán, 18 April 1859, AGN, ACH, PAH, Serie "Corre-spondencia Asuntos Personales y Militares Proyecto de Empréstito," microfilm roll 9 (original in caja 17, carpeta 72), 78–80.

108. Florentino González to Herrán, 10 April 1858, AGN, ACH, PAH, Serie "Correspon-dencia Asuntos Personales y Militares Proyecto de Empréstito," microfilm roll 9 (original in caja 17, carpeta 72), 71–73.

109. Herrán to Mariano Ospina Rodríguez, 15 April 1859, Libro de Manuscritos no. 189, Biblioteca Nacional de Colombia. On Ospina's exploration of the possibilities of annexation, see Frank Safford, "Politics, Ideology, and Society in Post-independence Spanish America," in *The Cambridge History of Latin America*, ed. Leslie Bethell (Cambridge: Cambridge University Press, 1984), vol. 3, 413.

110. Mervine to Dobbin, 18 March 1857, Squadron Letters, USNA, RG 45, M-89, roll 38.

111. Mervine to Dobbin, 2 April 1857, Squadron Letters, USNA, RG 45, M-89, roll 38.

112. *El Elector*, 22 August 1858.

113. See Michael A. Morrison, *Slavery and the American West: The Eclipse of Manifest Destiny and the Coming of the Civil War* (Chapel Hill: University of North Carolina Press, 1997).

114. Manuel María Díaz to Anselmo Pineda, Biblioteca Nacional de Colombia, Fondo Pineda, "Cartas de los amigos del Coronel Pineda," 22 September 1856, 228.

115. Mariano Arosemena to Justo Arosemena, 18 November 1856, reprinted in Arosemena, *Historia y nacionalidad*, ed. Tello, 177–178.

116. Mariano Arosemena to Justo Arosemena, 4 November 1856, reprinted in Arosemena, *Historia y nacionalidad*, ed. Tello, 174–176.

117. Justo Arosemena to Salvador Camacho Roldán, 6 December 1858, AGN, ACH, Colec-ción Salvador Camacho Roldán, microfilm roll 1 (original in caja 1, carpeta 6), 28. Similar opin-ions were voiced by the French consul in Panama City in 1859. See Figueroa Navarro, *Dominio y sociedad*, 343.

Conclusions: Conversations in the Museum of History

1. For a classic statement of this position, see Patricia Nelson Limerick, *Legacy of Conquest: The Unbroken Past of the American West* (New York: Norton, 1987).

2. Walter LaFeber, *The New Empire: An Interpretation of American Expansion, 1860–1898* (1963; Ithaca: Cornell University Press, 1998).

3. See, for example, Laura Briggs, *Reproducing Empire: Race, Sex, Science, and U.S. Imperialism in Puerto Rico* (Berkeley: University of California Press, 2002); Paul A. Kramer, *The Blood of Gov-ernment: Race, Empire, the United States, and the Philippines* (Chapel Hill: University of North Car-olina Press, 2006); Mary A. Renda, *Taking Haiti: Military Occupation and the Culture of U.S. Imperialism, 1915–1940* (Chapel Hill: University of North Carolina Press, 2001); and Ann Laura Stoler, ed., *Haunted by Empire: Geographies of Intimacy in North American History* (Durham, N.C.: Duke University Press, 2006).

4. See, for example, Greenberg, *Manifest Manhood* and Streeby, *American Sensations*.

5. Pubols, "Fathers of the Pueblo."

6. See Lester D. Langley and Thomas Schoonover, *The Banana Men: American Mercenaries and Entrepreneurs in Central America, 1880–1930* (Lexington: University of Kentucky Press, 1995); Thomas Schoonover, "The Confederates in Central America: Coming to Grips with the World System," in Schoonover, *The United States in Central America, 1860–1911* (Durham, N.C.: Duke University Press, 1991), and John Soluri, "Banana Cultures: Linking the Production and Consumption of Export Bananas, 1800–1900," in *Banana Wars*, ed. Moberg and Strifler, 48–79.

7. May, *Manifest Destiny's Underworld*, 207.

8. David Hoadley to William Nelson, 19 January 1857, Panama Railroad Company Letterbooks, USNA, RG 185, vol. 3, 356–358.

9. Ibid.

10. See Pantaleón García B., "Actividades productivas y comerciales en Panamá: 1869–1889," in *Historia General de Panamá*, ed. Castillero Calvo, vol. 2, 160–175, and Alfredo Castillero Calvo and Michael Conniff, "Proyectos para la construcción de un canal por Panamá, siglos XVI–XIX," in *Historia General de Panamá*, ed. Castillero Calvo, vol. 2, 292–309.

11. Conniff, *Panama and the United States*, 34.

12. Delpar, "Colombia," 67.

13. Thomas Schoonover, *The United States in Central America*, 100. Also see Everardo Bósquez de León, "Tensiones Diplomáticas y Tratados del Canal, 1845–1903," in Castillero Calvo, ed., *Historia General*, 2, 95–120.

14. Michael Doyle provides an abstract definition of informal empire as "a . . . pattern of control exercised indirectly, by bribes and manipulation of dependent collaborating elites, over the legally independent peripheral regime's domestic and external politics," in contrast to formal empire, which "signifies rule by annexation and government by colonial governors supported by metropolitan troops and local collaborators." See Michael W. Doyle, *Empires* (Ithaca: Cornell University Press), 135. On transport technology and informal empire in the nineteenth century, see Clarence B. Davis and Kenneth E. Wilburn Jr., eds., *Railway Imperialism* (Westport, Conn.: Greenwood Press, 1991), Daniel R. Headrick, *The Tentacles of Progress: Technology Transfer in the Age of Imperialism* (New York: Oxford University Press, 1988), and Michael Adas, *Dominance by Design: Technological Imperatives and America's Civilizing Mission* (Cambridge: Harvard University Press, 2006). On the role of the navy in U.S. informal empire in the mid-nineteenth century, see Schroeder, *Shaping a Maritime Empire*.

15. See Michael Conniff, *Black Labor on a White Canal: Panama, 1903–1981* (Pittsburgh: University of Pittsburgh Press, 1985); John Lindsay-Poland, *Emperors in the Jungle: The Secret History of the United States in Panama* (Durham, N.C.: Duke University Press, 2003); John Major, *Prize Possession: The United States Government and the Panama Canal, 1903–1979* (Cambridge: Cambridge University Press, 1993); as well as David McCullough's classic popular account, *The Path between the Seas: The Creation of the Panama Canal, 1870–1914* (New York: Simon and Schuster, 1977).

16. On U.S. empire in Panama in the early twentieth century, see Michael Conniff, "Panamá durante la época de construcción del Canal norteamericano," in *Historia General*, ed. Castillero Calvo, 24–33, and John Lindsay-Poland, *Emperors in the Jungle: The Hidden History of the U.S. in Panama* (Durham, N.C.: Duke University Press, 2003), 21–42, and the forthcoming study of labor and U.S. empire in the context of the canal's building by Julia Greene.

17. See Conniff, *Panama and the United States*, 76; Lindsay-Poland, *Emperors*, 40.

18. See Quijada, "Sobre el orígen," 609–610, and Mignolo, *The Idea of Latin America*, 89–91.

19. On the transnational dimensions of Spanish-language print culture in the nineteenth century, see Gruesz, *Ambassadors*.

20. On the complexities of the comparative study of race and nation in Latin America, see Nancy P. Appelbaum, Anne S. Macpherson, and Karin Alejandra Rosemblatt, "Racial Nations," in *Race and Nation*, eds. Appelbaum, Macpherson, and Rosemblatt, 1–31.

21. See Figueroa Navarro, *Dominio y sociedad*, 377–344, and Aparicio, "Federalismo y inestibilidad: Panamá bajo la Constitución de Río Negro," in *Historia General*, ed. Castillero Calvo, vol. 2, 217–235.

22. See Aparicio, "Justo Arosemena," and Ricaurte Soler, *Pensamiento Panameño y Concepción de la Nacionalidad durante el siglo XIX* (1954; Panama City: Imprenta Nacional, 1971).

23. See Fernando Aparicio, "Represión y explotación en Panamá durante la Regeneración," in *Historia General*, ed. Castillero Calvo, 236–255, and Celestino Andrés Araúz and Patricia

Pizzurno Gelós, *El Panamá Colombiano, 1821–1903* (Panama City: Primer Banco de Ahorros y Diario "La Prensa de Panamá," 1989), 279–297.

24. Fernando Aparicio, " 'Alcanzamos por fin la victoria': Tensiones y contradicciones del 3 de Noviembre de 1903," in *Historia General*, ed. Castillero Calvo, 372–392.

25. For an early twentieth-century discussion of "La California" as an event spanning the late 1840s and early 1850s, see Juan B. Sosa and Enrique J. Arce, *Compendio de Historia de Panamá* (1911; Panama City: Editorial Universitaria, 2003), 181–182.

26. On the reinterpretation of Arosemena's works in the twentieth century, see Szok, *La última Gaviota*, 28, n. 64. As Szok points out, a key figure in the interpretation of Arosemena as an anti-imperialist and ardent Panamanian nationalist was Ricaurte Soler. See, for example, Ricaurte Soler, *Pensamiento Panameño*. The Tajada de Sandía is portrayed as an unfortunate incident rather than a source of pride in the most successful textbook of Panamanian history for students in the second half of the twentieth century, Ernesto J. Castillero R.'s *Historia de Panamá* (1948; Panama City: N.P., 1989), 128–129. On the reinterpretation of the Tajada de Sandía as a source of pride and the point of origin for popular anti-imperialism in Panama in the context of tensions over the Panama Canal in the late twentieth century, see Alan McPherson, *Yankee No! Anti-Americanism in U.S.–Latin American Relations* (Cambridge: Harvard University Press, 2003), 203, n. 7. As with the reinterpretation of the work of Arosemena, a key figure of the transformation of the Tajada de Sandía into a source of pride and popular anti-imperialism was Ricaurte Soler. See, for example, Ricarte Soler, *Panamá en el Mundo Americano* (Panama City: Ediciones de la Revista Tareas, 1985), 51.

27. *Panama Star and Herald*, 17 May 1856.

Coda: With Dust in our Eyes

1. The U.S. invasion of Panama remains an intensely controversial event in Panama today. For a comprehensive overview, see the contributions by Thomas Pearcy, Carlos Guevara Mann, Carlos Bolívar Pedreshi, Reymundo Gurdián Guerra, and Salvador Sánchez González to *Historia General de Panamá*, ed. Castillero Calvo, vol. 3, tomo 2. For an incisive analysis that places the Noriega regime in the longer history of militarism in Panama, see Carlos Guevara Mann, *Panamanian Militarism: A Historical Interpretation* (Athens, Ohio: Ohio University Press, 1996), 158–169.

2. Independent Commission of Inquiry on the U.S. Invasion of Panama, *The U.S. Invasion of Panama: The Truth behind Operation 'Just Cause'* (Boston: South End Press, 1991), 40–45. On the history and destruction of El Chorrillo, see Alfredo Figueroa Navarro et al., *El Chorrillo: Situación y alternativas* (Panama City: IDEN, 1990).

3. See Michel Rolph Trouillot, *Silencing the Past: Power and the Production of History* (Boston: Beacon Press, 1995), 49.

Bibliography

Archives and Other Repositories

Colombia

Archivo General de la Nación (AGN)
Archivo del Ministerio de Relaciones Exteriores (AMRE)
Biblioteca Nacional

Panama

Archivo Nacional de Panamá (ANP)
Archivo del Consejo Municipal de Panamá (ACMP)

United States

Bancroft Library, University of California, Berkeley
Bentley Library, University of Michigan
California Historical Society
Georgetown University Library, Special Collections
Huntington Library
United States National Archives (USNA)

Newspapers

El Centinela (Panama City)
Daily Alta California (San Francisco)
El Día (Bogotá)
El Elector (Panama City)
Frank Leslie's Illustrated Newspaper (New York City)
Gaceta del Estado (Panama City)
New York Daily Times (New York City)
Panama Herald (Panama City)
El Neogranadino (Bogotá)
Panama Star (Panama City)
El Panameño (Panama City)
El Revisor de la Política y Literatura Americana (New York City)
Panama Star and Herald (Panama City)
El Vijilante (Panama City)

Printed Primary Sources

Arosemena, Justo. *Escritos de Justo Arosemena: Estudio introductorio y antología*. Ed. Argelia Tello. Panama City: Editorial Universitaria, 1985.

——. *El Estado Federal de Panamá*. 1855. Panama City: Editorial Universitaria de Panamá, 1982.

Arosemena, Mariano. *Historia y nacionalidad*. Ed. Argelia Tello. Panama City: Editorial Universitaria, 1979.

Bell, Horace. *On the Old West Coast: Being Further Reminiscences of a Ranger*. Ed. Lanier Bartlett. 1930. New York: Arno Press, 1976.

——. *Reminiscences of a Ranger; or, Early Times in Southern California*. Los Angeles: Yarnell, Caystile and Mathes, Printers, 1881.

Bidwell, Charles Toll. *The Isthmus of Panamá*. London: Chapman and Hall, 1865.

Bolívar, Simón. *Selected Writings of Bolívar*. Ed. Harold A. Bierck Jr. New York: Banco de Venezuela, 1951.

Brooks, Sarah Merriam. *Across the Isthmus to California in '52*. San Francisco: C. A. Murdock and Co., 1894.

Davis, Stephen Chapin. *California Gold Rush Merchant*. Ed. Benjamin B. Richards. Westport, Conn.: Greenwood Press, 1974.

Duane, Charles P. *Against the Vigilantes: The Recollections of Dutch Charley Duane*. Ed. John Boessenecker. Norman: University of Oklahoma Press, 1999.

Espinar, José Domingo. *Resumen histórico que hace el General José Domingo Espinar, de los acontecimientos políticos ocurridos en Panamá en el año 1830, apellidados ahora Revolución de Castas, por el Gobernador Señor José de Obaldía*. Panama City: Imprenta de José Angel Santos, 1851.

Johnson, Theodore T. *Sights in the Gold Region, and Scenes by the Way.* New York: Baker and Scribner, 1849.

Liddell, John A. "Upon the Medical Topography and Diseases of the Isthmus of Panama." *New York Journal of Medicine* 8 (1852): 242–259.

Manning, William R., ed. *Diplomatic Correspondence of the United States. Inter-American Affairs, 1831–1860.* Washington: Carnegie Endowment for International Peace, 1935.

Marryat, Frank. *Mountains and Molehills, or Recollections of a Burnt Journal.* New York: Harper and Brothers, 1855.

Megquier, Mary Jane. *Apron Full of Gold: The Letters of Mary Jane Megquier from San Francisco, 1849–1856.* Ed. Polly Welts Kaufman. Albuquerque: University of New Mexico Press, 1994.

Nueva Granada. *Final controversia diplomática con relación a los sucesos de Panamá del día 15 de abril de 1856.* Bogotá: Imprenta del Estado, 1857.

Orton, A. R. *"The Derienni"; or, Land Pirates of the Isthmus.* New Orleans, 1853.

Otis, Fessenden Nott. *Isthmus of Panama: History of the Panama Railroad and of the Pacific Mail Steamship Company.* New York: Harper and Brothers, 1867.

Seacole, Mary. *Wonderful Adventures of Mrs. Seacole in Many Lands.* 1857. New York: Oxford University Press, 1988.

Stephens, John Lloyd. *Incidents of Travel in Central America, Chiapas, and Yucatan.* New York: Harper and Brothers, 1841.

Taylor, Bayard. *El Dorado.* New York: G. P. Putnam, 1850.

Tomes, Robert. *Panama in 1855.* New York: Harper and Brothers, 1855.

Tyson, James L. *Diary of a Physician in California.* New York: D. Appleton, 1850.

Walter, Carrie Stevens. "A Panama Riot." *Overland Monthly and Out West Magazine* 4, no. 24 (December 1884): 635–640. http://name.umdl.umich.edu/ ahj1472.2-04.024 (16 May 2007).

Williams, James. *Life and Adventures of James Williams, A Fugitive Slave, with a Full Description of the Underground Railroad.* San Francisco: Women's Union Print, 1873.

Secondary Sources

Adas, Michael. *Dominance by Design: Technological Imperatives and America's Civilizing Mission.* Cambridge: Harvard University Press, 2006.

Amin, Shahid. *Event, Metaphor, Memory: Chauri Chaura, 1922–1992.* Berkeley: University of California Press, 1995.

Andrews, George Reid. *Afro-Latin America, 1800–2000.* Oxford: Oxford University Press, 2004.

Appelbaum, Nancy P. *Muddied Waters: Race, Region, and Local History in Colombia, 1846–1948.* Durham, N.C.: Duke University Press, 2003.

——. "Whitening the Region: Caucano Mediation and 'Antioqueño Colonization' in Nineteenth-Century Colombia." *Hispanic American Historical Review* 79, no. 4 (1999): 631–667.

Appelbaum, Nancy P., Anne S. Macpherson, and Karin Alejandra Rosemblatt, eds. *Race and Nation in Modern Latin America*. Chapel Hill: University of North Carolina Press, 2003.

Araúz, Celestino Andrés. *La independencia de Panamá en 1821: Antecedentes, balance y proyecciones*. Panama City: Academia Panameña de la Historia, 1980.

——. *Panamá y sus relaciones internacionales: Estudio introductorio, notas y antología*. 2 vols. Panama City: Editorial Universitaria, 1994.

Araúz, Celestino Andrés, and Patricia Pizzurno Gelós. *El Panamá colombiano (1821–1903)*. Panama City: Primer Banco de Ahorros y Diario La Prensa de Panamá, 1993.

Ardao, Arturo. *América Latina y la latinidad*. Mexico City: Universidad Nacional Autónoma de México, 1993.

——. *Génesis de la idea y el nombre de América Latina*. Caracas: Centro de Estudios Latinoamericanos Rómulo Gallegos, 1980.

Balf, Todd. *The Darkest Jungle: The True Story of the Darien Expedition and America's Ill-Fated Race to Connect the Seas*. New York: Crown Publishers, 2003.

Bancroft, Hubert Howe. *California Inter Pocula*. San Francisco: The History Company Publishers, 1888.

——. *History of Central America*. Vol. 3. San Francisco, 1887.

Bayly, C. A., Sven Beckert, Matthew Connelly, Isabel Hofmeyr, Wendy Kozol, and Patricia Seed. "AHR Conversation: On Transnational History." *American Historical Review* 111, no. 5 (2006): 1440–1464.

Bender, Thomas. *La Pietra Report*. Bloomington, Ind.: Organization of American Historians, 2000.

——. *A Nation among Nations: America's Place in World History*. New York: Hill and Wang, 2006.

——, ed. *Rethinking American History in a Global Age*. Berkeley: University of California Press, 2002.

Bergquist, Charles. *Labor and the Course of American Democracy: U.S. History in Latin American Perspective*. London: Verso, 1996.

Bethel, A. C. W. "The Golden Skein: California's Gold-Rush Transportation Network." In *A Golden State: Mining and Economic Development in Gold Rush California*, ed. James J. Rawls and Richard J. Orsi. Special issue, *California History* 77 (Winter 1998/99): 250–275.

Blodgett, Peter J. *Land of Golden Dreams: California in the Gold Rush Decade, 1848–1858*. San Marino, Calif.: Huntington Library, 1999.

Bonilla, Heraclio, and Gustavo Montañez, eds. *Colombia y Panamá: La metamorfosis de la nación en el siglo XX*. Bogotá: Red de Estudios de Espacio y Territorio et al., 2004.

Briggs, Laura. *Reproducing Empire: Race, Sex, Science, and U.S. Imperialism in Puerto Rico*. Berkeley: University of California Press, 2002.

Burns, E. Bradford. *Patriarch and Folk: The Emergence of Nicaragua, 1798–1858*. Cambridge, Mass.: Harvard University Press, 1991.

Bushnell, David. *The Making of Modern Colombia: A Nation in Spite of Itself*. Berkeley: University of California Press, 1993.

Bushnell, David, and Neill Macaulay. *The Emergence of Latin America in the Nineteenth Century*. Oxford: Oxford University Press, 1988.

Castillero Calvo, Alfredo. "Un antecedente de la 'Tajada de Sandía.' " *Lotería* 6 (August 1961): 20–23.

———. *Conquista, evangelización y resistencia*. Panama City: Impresora de la Nación, 1995.

———. "El Movimiento Anseatista de 1826: La primera tentative autonomista de los istmeños después de la anexión a Colombia." *Tareas* 1, no. 4 (1960): 12–56.

———. *Los negros y mulatos libres en la historia social panameña*. Panama City, 1973.

———. "El oro de California en la vida panameña." In *Relaciones entre Panamá y los Estados Unidos*, 117–128. Panama City: Biblioteca Nuevo Panamá and Ministerio de Educación, 1973.

———. *La ruta transístmica y las comunicaciones marítimas hispanas siglos XVI a XIX*. Panama City: Ediciones Nari, 1984.

———. *La vivienda colonial en Panamá: Arquitectura, urbanismo y sociedad; Historia de un sueño*. Panama City: Biblioteca Cultural Shell, 1994.

———, ed. *Historia General de Panamá*. 4 vols. Panama City: Comisión Nacional del Centenario, 2004.

Castillero Reyes, Ernesto J. *Historia de Panamá*. 1945. Panama City, 1989.

———. *La isla que se transformó en ciudad: Historia de un siglo de la ciudad de Colón*. Panama City, 1962.

———. "Ran Runnels en la ruta de 'El Dorado.' " *Lotería* 23 (October 1957): 88–97.

Chen Daley, Mercedes. "The Watermelon Riot: Cultural Encounters in Panama City, April 15, 1856." *Hispanic American Historical Review* 70 (February 1990): 85–108.

Chomsky, Aviva. *West Indian Workers and the United Fruit Company in Costa Rica, 1870–1940*. Baton Route: Louisiana State University Press, 1996.

Coates, Anthony G., ed. *Central America: A Natural and Cultural History*. New Haven: Yale University Press, 1997.

Conniff, Michael. *Black Labor on a White Canal: Panama, 1903–1981*. Pittsburgh: University of Pittsburgh Press, 1985.

———. *Panama and the United States: The Forced Alliance*. 2nd ed. Athens: University of Georgia Press, 2001.

Cronon, William. *Nature's Metropolis: Chicago and the Great West*. New York: Norton, 1991.

de la Cova, Antonio Rafael. "Filibusters and Freemasons: The Sworn Obligation." *Journal of the Early Republic*, 17, no. 1 (Spring 1997): 95–120

Delgado, James P. *To California by Sea: A Maritime History of the California Gold Rush*. Columbia: University of South Carolina Press, 1990.

Delpar, Helen. *Red against Blue: The Liberal Party in Colombia Politics, 1863–1899*. University: University of Alabama Press, 1981.

Deverell, William. *Whitewashed Adobe: The Rise of Los Angeles and the Remaking of Its Mexican Past*. Berkeley: University of California Press, 2004.

Doyle, Michael W. *Empires*. Ithaca: Cornell University Press, 1986.

Dubois, Laurent. *A Colony of Citizens: Revolution and Slave Emancipation in the French Caribbean, 1787–1804*. Chapel Hill: University of North Carolina Press, 2004.

Duffy Burnett, Christina. "The Edges of Empire and the Limits of Sovereignty: American Guano Islands." *American Quarterly* 57, no. 3 (September 2005): 779–803.

Dunkerley, James. *Americana: The Americas in the World, around 1850*. London: Verso, 2000.

Egan, Ferol. *The El Dorado Trail: The Story of the Gold Rush Routes across Mexico*. New York: McGraw-Hill, 1970.

Estrade, Paul. "Del invento de 'América Latina' en París por latinoamericanos (1856–1889)." In *París y el mundo ibérico e iberoamericano*, comp. Jacques Maurice and Marie-Claire Zimmerman, 179–188. Paris: Université Paris X-Nanterre, 1998.

Ethington, Philip J. *The Public City: The Political Construction of Urban Life in San Francisco, 1850–1900*. Cambridge: Cambridge University Press, 1994.

Euraque, Darío. *Reinterpreting the Banana Republic: Region and State in Honduras, 1870–1972*. Chapel Hill: University of North Carolina Press, 1996.

Ferrer, Ada. *Insurgent Cuba: Race, Nation, and Revolution, 1868–1898*. Chapel Hill: University of North Carolina Press, 1999.

Figueroa Navarro, Alfredo. *Dominio y sociedad en el Panamá colombiano*. Panama City: Editorial Universitaria, 1982.

———. "Seis aproximaciones a la historia social y demográfica de Panamá (siglos XVIII y XIX)." *Humanidades* 3, no. 2 (April 1994): 131–152.

Figueroa Navarro, Alfredo, et al. *El Chorrillo: Situación y alternativas*. Panama City: IDEN, 1990.

Folkman, David I., Jr. *The Nicaragua Route*. Salt Lake City: University of Utah Press, 1972.

Gallup-Díaz, Ignacio. *The Door of the Seas and Key to the Universe: Indian Politics and Imperial Rivalry in the Darién, 1640–1750* New York: Columbia University Press, 2004.

Gobat, Michel. *Confronting the American Dream: Nicaragua under U.S. Imperial Rule*. Durham, N.C.: Duke University Press, 2005.

Goodman, David. *Gold-Seeking: Victoria and California in the 1850s*. Stanford: Stanford University Press, 1994.

Grandin, Greg. *The Blood of Guatemala: A History of Race and Nation*. Durham, N.C.: Duke University Press, 2000.

Greenberg, Amy S. *Manifest Manhood and the Antebellum American Empire*. Cambridge: Cambridge University Press, 2005.

Gruesz, Kirsten Silva. *Ambassadors of Culture: The Transamerican Origins of Latino Writing*. Princeton, N.J.: Princeton University Press, 2002.

Guevara Mann, Carlos. *Panamanian Militarism: A Historical Interpretation*. Athens, Ohio: Ohio University Press, 1996.

Guha, Ranajit, and Gayatri Chakravorty Spivak, eds. *Selected Subaltern Studies*. Oxford: Oxford University Press, 1988.

Hansen, Thomas Blom and Finn Stepputat, eds. *Sovereign Bodies: Citizens, Migrants, and States in the Postcolonial World*. Princeton: Princeton University Press, 2005.

Headrick, Daniel R. *The Tentacles of Progress: Technology Transfer in the Age of Imperialism*. New York: Oxford University Press, 1988.

Helg, Aline. *Liberty and Equality in Caribbean Colombia, 1770–1835*. Chapel Hill: University of North Carolina Press, 2004.

Herrera C., Miguel Angel. *Bongos, bogas, vapores y marinos: Historia de los 'marineros' del río San Juan, 1849–1855*. Managua: Centro Nicaragüense de Escritores, 1999.

Hietala, Thomas. *Manifest Design: Anxious Aggrandizement in Late Jacksonian America*. Ithaca: Cornell University Press, 1985.

Holt, Thomas C. *The Problem of Freedom: Race, Labor, and Politics in Jamaica and Britain, 1832–1938*. Baltimore: Johns Hopkins University Press, 1992.

Horsman, Reginald. *Race and Manifest Destiny*. Cambridge, Mass.: Harvard University Press, 1981.

Howe, James. *A People Who Would Not Kneel: Panama, the United States, and the San Blas Kuna*. Washington, D.C.: Smithsonian Institution Press, 1998.

Hurtado, Albert L. *Intimate Frontiers: Sex, Gender, and Culture in Old California*. Albuquerque: University of New Mexico Press, 1999.

Independent Commission of Inquiry on the U.S. Invasion of Panama. *The U.S. Invasion of Panama: The Truth behind Operation 'Just Cause.'* Boston: South End Press, 1991.

Jacob, Margaret C. *Living the Enlightenment: Freemasonry and Politics in Eighteenth Century Europe*. Oxford: Oxford University Press, 1991.

Jacobson, Matthew. *Whiteness of a Different Color: European Immigrants and the Alchemy of Race*. Cambridge, Mass.: Harvard University Press, 1998.

Jaén Suárez, Omar. *La población del Istmo de Panamá: Estudio de geohistoria*. 3rd ed. Madrid: Ediciones de Cultura Hispánica, 1998.

James, C. L. R. *The Black Jacobins: Toussaint L'Ouverture and the San Domingo Revolution*. 1938. New York: Vintage, 1963.

Johnson, Susan Lee. *Roaring Camp: The Social World of the California Gold Rush*. New York: Norton, 2000.

Joseph, Gilbert M., Catherine C. Legrand, and Ricardo D. Salvatore, eds. *Close Encounters of Empire: Writing the Cultural History of U.S.–Latin American Relations*. Durham, N.C.: Duke University Press, 1998.

Kaplan, Amy and Donald E. Pease, eds. *Cultures of United States Imperialism*. Durham, N.C.: Duke University Press, 1993.

Kemble, John Haskell. *The Panama Route, 1848–1869*. 1943. Columbia: University of South Carolina Press, 1990.

Kramer, Paul A. *The Blood of Government: Race, Empire, the United States, and the Philippines*. Chapel Hill: University of North Carolina Press, 2006.

Krasner, Stephen D. *Sovereignty: Organized Hypocrisy*. Princeton: Princeton University Press, 1999.

LaFeber, Walter. *The New Empire: An Interpretation of American Expansion, 1860–1898*. 1963. Ithaca: Cornell University Press, 1998.

Langley, Lester D., and Thomas Schoonover. *The Banana Men: American Mercenaries and Entrepreneurs in Central America, 1880–1930.* Lexington: University of Kentucky Press, 1995.

Lapp, Rudolph. *Blacks in Gold Rush California.* New Haven, Conn.: Yale University Press, 1977.

Larson, Brooke. *Trials of Nation Making: Liberalism, Race, and Ethnicity in the Andes, 1810–1910.* Cambridge: Cambridge University Press, 2004.

Lasso, Marixa. "Race War and Nation in Caribbean Gran Colombia, Cartagena, 1810–1832." *American Historical Review* 111, no. 2 (2006): 336–361.

Leonard, Thomas M., ed. *United States–Latin American Relations, 1850–1903: Establishing a Relationship.* Tuscaloosa, Ala.: University of Alabama Press, 1999.

Lewis, Martin W., and Kären Wigen. *The Myth of Continents: A Critique of Metageography.* Berkeley: University of California Press, 1997.

Limerick, Patricia Nelson. *Legacy of Conquest: The Unbroken Past of the American West.* New York: Norton, 1987.

Lindsay-Poland, John. *Emperors in the Jungle: The Secret History of the United States in Panama.* Durham, N.C.: Duke University Press, 2003.

Look Lai, Walton. *Indentured Labor, Caribbean Sugar: Chinese and Indian Migrants to the British West Indies, 1838–1918.* Baltimore: Johns Hopkins University Press, 1993.

Lott, Eric. *Love and Theft: Blackface Minstrelsy and the American Working Class.* Oxford: Oxford University Press, 1993.

Mack, Gerstle. *The Land Divided: A History of the Panama Canal and Other Isthmian Canal Projects.* New York: Knopf, 1944.

Mallon, Florencia E. *Peasant and Nation: The Making of Postcolonial Mexico and Peru.* Berkeley: University of California Press, 1995.

Major, John. *Prize Possession: The United States Government and the Panama Canal, 1903–1979.* Cambridge: Cambridge University Press, 1993.

May, Robert E. *Manifest Destiny's Underworld: Filibustering in Antebellum America.* Chapel Hill: University of North Carolina Press, 2002.

McCullough, David. *The Path between the Seas: The Creation of the Panama Canal, 1870–1914.* New York: Simon and Schuster, 1977.

McGuinness, Aims. "Aquellos tiempos de California: El Ferrocarril de Panamá y la transformación de la zona de tránsito durante la Fiebre del Oro." In *Historia General de Panamá*, ed. Alfredo Castillero Calvo, 141–149. Panama City: Comisión Nacional del Centenario, 2004.

——. "Defendiendo el Istmo: Las luchas contra los filibusters en la Ciudad de Panamá en 1856." *Mesoamérica* 24, no. 45 (2003): 66–84.

——. "In the Path of Empire: Land, Labor, and Liberty in Panama during the California Gold Rush." Ph.D. diss., University of Michigan, 2001.

——. "Looking for 'Latin America': Race and Sovereignty in the Americas in the 1850s." In *Race and Nation in Modern Latin America*, ed. Nancy Appelbaum, Anne S. Macpherson, and Karin Alejandra Rosemblatt, 87–107. Chapel Hill: University of North Carolina Press, 2003.

——. "Raza, patriotismo e intervención estadounidense en Panamá, 1848–1860." In *Historia y memoria: Sociedad, cultura y vida cotidiana en Cuba, 1878–1917*, ed. José Amador, 243–263. Havana: Centro de Investigación y Desarrollo de la Cultura Cubana Juan Marinello; Ann Arbor: Latin American and Caribbean Studies Program of the University of Michigan, 2003.

McPherson, Alan. *Yankee No! Anti-Americanism in U.S.-Latin American Relations*. Cambridge: Harvard University Press, 2003.

Miró, Rodrigo. *Itinerario de la poesía en Panamá*. Panama City: Biblioteca de la Nacionalidad/Autoridad del Canal de Panamá, 1999.

Méndez Pereira, Octavio. *Justo Arosemena*. 1919. Panama City: Editorial Universitaria, 1970.

Mignolo, Walter. *The Darker Side of the Renaissance: Literacy, Territoriality, and Colonization*. Ann Arbor: University of Michigan Press, 1995.

——. *The Idea of Latin America*. Malden, Mass.: Blackwell, 2005.

Monaghan, Jay. *Chile, Peru, and the California Gold Rush of 1849*. Berkeley: University of California Press, 1973.

Moscote, José Dolores, and Enrique Juan Arce. *La vida ejemplar de Justo Arosemena*. Panama City: Imprenta Nacional, 1956.

Moscote, José Dolores, Octavio Méndez Pereira, Ricaurte Soler, Argelia Tello Burgos, Nils Castro, Humberto Ricord, and Miguel Candanedo. Special issue devoted to Justo Arosemena. *Tareas* 92 (January–April 1996).

Múnera, Alfonso. *El fracaso de la nación: Región, clase y raza en el Caribe colombiano (1717–1810)*. Bogotá: Banco de la República, 1998.

Muñoz Pinzón, Armando. *Un estudio de historia social panameña*. Panama City: Editorial Universitaria de Panamá, 1980.

Naylor, Robert A. *Penny Ante Imperialism: The Mosquito Shore and the Bay of Honduras, 1600–1914*. Cranbury, N.J.: Associated University Presses, 1989.

Nuermberger, Gustave A. "The Continental Treaties of 1856: An American Union 'Exclusive of the United States.'" *Hispanic American Historical Review* 20, no. 1 (Feb. 1940): 32–55.

Owens, Kenneth N., ed. *Riches for All: The California Gold Rush and the World*. Lincoln: University of Nebraska Press, 2002.

Pacheco, Margarita. *La fiesta liberal en Cali*. Cali, Colombia: Universidad del Valle, 1992.

Parks, E. Taylor. *Colombia and the United States, 1765–1934*. Durham: Duke University Press, 1935.

Patiño, Jorge E. "El acuerdo istmeño-norteamericano de 1851." *Revista Lotería* 336–337 (March/April 1984): 50–57.

Paul, Rodman K. *California Gold: The Beginning of Mining in the Far West*. Cambridge, Mass.: Harvard University Press, 1947.

Pearcy, Thomas L. *We Answer Only to God: Politics and the Military in Panama, 1903–1947*. Albuquerque: University of New Mexico Press, 1998.

Perkins, Bradford. *The Creation of a Republican Empire, 1776–1865*. Cambridge History of American Foreign Relations, vol. 1. Cambridge: Cambridge University Press, 1993.

Phelan, John L. "Pan-Latinism, French Intervention in Mexico (1861–1867), and the Genesis of the Idea of Latin America." In *Conciencia y autenticidad históricas*, ed. Juan A. Ortega y Medina, 279–298. Mexico City: Universidad Nacional Autónoma de México, 1968.

Pike, Frederick. *The United States and Latin America.* Austin: University of Texas Press, 1992.

Putnam, Lara. *The Company They Kept: Migrants and the Politics of Gender in Caribbean Costa Rica, 1870–1960.* Chapel Hill: University of North Carolina Press, 2002.

Quijada, Mónica. "Sobre el orígen y difusión del nombre 'América Latina' (o una variación heterodoxa en torno al tema de la construcción social de la verdad)." *Revista de Indias* 58 no. 214 (1998): 595–615.

Randall, Stephen J. *Colombia and the United Status: Hegemony and Interdependence.* Athens: University of Georgia Press, 1992.

Reed, Nelson. *The Caste War of Yucatán.* Stanford: Stanford University Press, 1964.

Renda, Mary A. *Taking Haiti: Military Occupation and the Culture of U.S. Imperialism, 1915–1940.* Chapel Hill: University of North Carolina Press, 2001.

Riley, Glenda. "Women on the Panama Trail to California, 1849–1869." *Pacific Historical Review* 55, no. 4 (1986): 531–548.

Roberts, Brian. *American Alchemy: The California Gold Rush and Middle-Class Culture.* Chapel Hill: University of North Carolina Press, 2000.

Rohrbough, Malcolm J. *Days of Gold: The California Gold Rush and the American Nation.* Berkeley: University of California Press, 1997.

Rojas Mix, Miguel. "Bilbao y el hallazgo de América latina: Unión continental, socialista y libertaria . . ." *Cahiers du Monde Hispanique et Luso-Brasilien-Caravelle* 46 (1986): 35–47.

———. *Los cien nombres de América Latina: Eso que descubrió Colón.* San José: Editorial Universitaria de Costa Rica, 1991.

Romero, Vicente. "Du nominal 'latin' pour l'Autre Amérique. Notes sur la naissance et le sens du nom 'Amérique latine' autour des annés 1850." *Histoire et sociétés de l'Amérique latine* 7, no. 1 (premier semestre 1998): 57–86.

Rugeley, Terry. *Yucatán's Maya Peasantry and the Origins of the Caste War.* Austin: University of Texas Press, 1996.

Safford, Frank. "Politics, Ideology, and Society in Post-independence Spanish America." In *The Cambridge History of Latin America*, ed. Leslie Bethell, 347–421. Cambridge: Cambridge University Press, 1984.

———. "Social Aspects of Politics in Nineteenth-Century Spanish America: New Granada, 1825–1850." *Journal of Social History* 5 (Spring 1972): 344–370.

Safford, Frank, and Marco Palacios. *Colombia: Fragmented Land, Divided Society.* Oxford: Oxford University Press, 2002.

Sanders, James E. *Contentious Republicans: Popular Politics, Race, and Class in Nineteenth-Century Colombia.* Durham, N.C.: Duke University Press, 2004.

Schivelbusch, Wolfgang. *The Railway Journey: Trains and Travel in the Nineteenth Century.* Oxford: Blackwell, 1980.

Schoonover, Thomas. *The United States in Central America, 1860–1911: Episodes of Social Imperialism and Imperial Rivalry in the World System*. Durham, N.C.: Duke University Press, 1991.

Schott, Joseph L. *Rails across Panama: The Story of the Building of the Panama Railroad, 1849–1855*. Indianapolis: Bobbs-Merrill, 1967.

Schroeder, John H. *Matthew Calbraith Perry: Antebellum Sailor and Diplomat*. Annapolis: Naval Institute Press, 2001.

——. *Shaping a Maritime Empire: The Commercial and Diplomatic Role of the American Navy, 1829–1861*. Westport, Conn.: Greenwood Press, 1985.

Scott, Rebecca J. *Degrees of Freedom: Louisiana and Cuba after Slavery*. Cambridge, Mass.: Harvard University Press, 2005.

Soler, Ricaurte. *Panamá en el Mundo Americano*. Panama City: Ediciones de la Revista Tareas, 1985.

——. *Pensamiento panameño y concepción de la nacionalidad durante el siglo XIX*. 2nd ed. Panama City: Librería Cultural Panameña, 1971.

——, ed. *Panamá y Nuestra América*. Mexico City: Universidad Nacional Autónoma de México and Biblioteca del Estudiante Universitario, 1981.

Soler, Ricaurte, et al. "Homenaje a Justo Arosemena." Special issue of *Tareas* 92 (January–April 1996).

Soluri, John. *Banana Cultures: Agriculture, Consumption, and Environmental Change in Honduras and the United States*. Austin: University of Texas Press, 2005.

Sosa, Juan B., and Enrique J. Arce. *Compendio de historia de Panamá*. 1911. Panama City: Editorial Universitaria, 2003.

Sowell, David. *The Early Colombian Labor Movement: Artisans and Politics in Bogotá, 1832–1919*. Philadelphia: Temple University Press, 1992.

Starr, Kevin, and Richard J. Orsi, eds. *Rooted in Barbarous Soil: People, Culture, and Community in Gold Rush California*. Berkeley: University of California Press, 2000.

Stoler, Laura Ann, ed. *Haunted by Empire: Geographies of Intimacy in North American History*. Durham, N.C.: Duke University Press, 2006.

Stoler, Laura Ann and Frederick Cooper, eds. *Tensions of Empire: Colonial Cultures in a Bourgeois World*. Berkeley: University of California Press, 1997.

Streeby, Shelley. *American Sensations: Class, Race, and Production of Popular Culture*. Berkeley: University of California Press, 2002.

Striffler, Steve, and Mark Moberg, eds. *Banana Wars: Power, Production and History in the Americas*. Durham, N.C.: Duke University Press, 2003.

Susto, Juan A. "La personalidad de Ran Runnels." *Lotería* 23 (October 1957): 97—99.

Szok, Peter A. *"La última gaviota": Liberalism and Nostalgia in Early Twentieth-Century Panamá*. Westport, Conn.: Greenwood Press, 2001.

Thelen, David, et al. "The Nation and Beyond." Special issue of the *Journal of American History* 86, no. 3 (December 1999).

Thornton, Bruce. *Searching for Joaquín: Myth, Murieta, and History in California*. San Francisco: Encounter Books, 2003.

Thurner, Mark. *From Two Republics to One Divided: Contradictions of Postcolonial Nation-making in Andean Peru.* Durham, N.C.: Duke University Press, 1997.

Trouillot, Michel Rolph. *Silencing the Past: Power and the Production of History.* Boston: Beacon Press, 1995.

Truett, Samuel, and Elliott Young, eds. *Continental Crossroads: Remapping U.S.-Mexico Borderlands History.* Durham, N.C.: Duke University Press, 2004.

Unruh, John D. *The Plains Across: The Overland Emigrants and the Trans-Mississipi West, 1840–1860.* 1979. 1st unabridged paperback edition. Urbana: University of Illinois Press, 1993.

Von Hagen, Victor. *Maya Explorer: John Lloyd Stephens and the Lost Cities of Central America and Yucatán.* Norman: University of Oklahoma Press, 1947.

Ward, Christopher. *Imperial Panama: Commerce and Conflict in Isthmian America, 1550–1800.* Albuquerque: University of New Mexico Press, 1999.

Wood, Peter, and Karen C. C. Dalton. *Winslow Homer's Images of Blacks: The Civil War and Reconstruction Years.* Austin: University of Texas Press, 1988.

Young, Alfred F. *The Shoemaker and the Tea Party: Memory and the American Revolution.* Boston: Beacon Press, 1999.

Index

Abad Monteser, Antonio, 144–46
Abrams, William Penn, 37
Abran, Miguel, 130
Accessory Transit Co., 125
Agnew, James, 38
Alemán, José María, 109–10
Allen, Edward, 141
American Hotel (Panama City), 26, 39
Amigos del Órden, 165–67, 169, 172–74
Ansoatigue, Frederick, 45, 138, 140
Archivo de Hojas Sueltas, 15, 200–201
Ardao, Arturo, 153
Argentina, 154
Arosemena, Justo, 11, 12, 109, 111, 167
    "American Question" of, 159–63, 181–82, 190
    economic views of, 38, 78–79
    Estado Federal de Panamá of, 85, 97–101, 163
    on enfranchisement, 45–46
    on free trade, 85, 97–98
    on Panamanian independence, 99–101
    racial views of, 116, 160–64, 181–83, 193
Arosemena, Mariano, 85, 89, 96, 109–11, 169
    exile of, 174, 182
    Mervine on, 170–71
    racial views of, 182
    Tajada de Sandía and, 139
Arosemena de Rice, Josefa Dolores, 170
Arrabal, 25, 37, 122
    Amigos del Órden of, 165–67, 169, 172–74
    conflict of May 18, 1850, and, 90–92, 114–17, 146–48
    ejidos of, 105–10
    Liberal Party and, 87, 96–97, 167–75, 194
    map of, 25
    Playa Prieta and, 102–4
    See also Ciénaga
Aspinwall, William Henry, 31, 55, 58–59, 68
Aspinwall (city), 82, 160
    Colón versus, 73–74, 82, 160
    governance of, 10–11, 74, 82, 158, 189
    map of, 8
Australia, 13, 16
Azuero province, 99, 102
    Liberal Party in, 87, 165
    map of, 24
    rebellion in, 112–17, 121

Bailey, Theodorus, 164, 167, 200
Balboa, Vasco Núñez de, 17
bandits, 75–77, 124
Bell, Horace, 76, 124–26, 129, 138, 140, 147
Bender, Thomas, 14
Bidlack-Mallarino Treaty (1846), 29–30, 98, 155, 177, 190
Bilbao, Francisco, 153, 163
boatmen, 33–34, 36
    Nahl's painting of, 44, 45
    negotiations with, 47–50, 56, 103
    railroad competition with, 10, 55–61, 68, 79–81, 138–39
    taxation of, 97–98, 104–5, 131
Bocas del Toro, 23, 24, 113, 114
Bolívar, Simón, 19, 20, 161–62
Bolivia, 154
Borland, John, 63
Bravo, José María, 141
Brazil, 154, 161
Briceño, Eladio, 87–88
Brinkerhoff, Moses, 103
Brooks, Sarah, 48, 50
Buchanan, James, 160, 188
Bush, George H. W., 202

California, 30, 81–82, 118–19, 185–87
    discovery of gold in, 4, 31–32, 185
    discrimination in, 34–35, 119, 187
    immigrants to, 6–7, 12, 16
    Mexico and, 16, 32, 113, 114, 119, 187
    slavery in, 119
    vigilantism in, 77, 119, 124, 154, 156
Calvo, Bartolomé, 102, 167–74, 180, 182, 188, 191–92
Camacho Roldán, Salvador, 104–5
Canada, 13, 30, 69
Cano, Saturnino, 108
Cape Horn, 7, 16, 18, 32, 126, 161
Cartagena, 59–62, 66, 72, 110, 141, 172, 174
castas, 22, 46, 87
    Espinar on, 25–29, 89–90
    race and, 11–12, 22, 44, 88–90
    See also caste war
caste war, rumors of, 88–92, 95–96, 102, 164–70, 174–76, 183
Castillero Calvo, Alfredo, 14
Cavalli, Carlos, 141
Chagres (city), 8, 57, 58, 63, 67–68
"Chagres Fever," 47
Chagres River, 8, 18, 36, 55–61, 64–69, 77, 83

Chevalier, Michel, 153, 162
Chile, 33–35, 154, 192
    immigrants to California from, 16, 32, 119, 124, 154
China
    immigrants to California from, 12, 16, 119
    immigrants to Panama from, 10, 70–71, 141
Chiriquí province, 24, 38, 70, 99
cholera, 36, 47
Ciénaga, La, 102–11, 120–22
    maps of, 104, 107
    Tajada de Sandía and, 1–2, 103, 126–51
    See also Arrabal
Clayton-Bulwer Treaty, 68
Colombia, 19, 85, 90, 189–90
    Constitution of, 194
    Panamanian independence from, 11, 20–22, 84–86, 89–90, 99–102, 189–91, 195
    See also Nueva Granada
Colón (Panama), 58, 59
    Aspinwall versus, 73–74, 82, 160
    governance of, 10–11, 74, 82, 158, 189
    map of, 8
    vigilantism in, 74–77
communication, definition of, 9
Compromise of 1850 (U.S.), 119
conflict
    of May 18, 1850, 90–92, 115–17, 146–48
    of October 1851, 57
    of April 15, 1856. *See* Tajada de Sandía
Conservative Party
    election of 1848 and, 86–87
    election of 1856 and, 167–75
    enclaves of, 87, 112
    Nicaraguan, 113–14
    Tajada de Sandía and, 143, 148
Constitution of 1863, 194
Constitution of 1853, 71–73, 86, 95, 99
continental treaty (1856), 154
convicts, 59, 94, 112
Copeland, James, 138
Correoso, Buenaventura, 95, 194
Corwine, Amos, 132, 135–36, 146–47, 155, 173, 176
Corwine, David, 132, 142
Costa Rica, 114, 152, 154–55
Cuba, 71

Darién province, 18, 24, 75–76, 99
Davis, Stephen Chapin, 57

Democratic Societies, 165
de Sabla, Theodore, 134, 141, 171, 174, 176
Díaz, Lucas Víctor, 127
Díaz, Manuel María, 116, 142–45, 148, 167, 173
Díaz, Sebastián, 136, 141
Dignity Battalions, 201
Douman, William, 141
Dred Scott decision, 150
Duane, Charles, 156
Dubois, Octave, 135
Dysentery, 65

Ecuador, 19, 20, 154
ejidos, 105–10
empire
    Spanish, 16–20, 41, 81, 162–63
    U.S., 11–13, 37–40, 75, 152–55, 182–193
enclave, economic, 82
enfranchisement. *See* suffrage
Espinar, José Domingo, 20–22, 79, 128
    on *castas,* 25–29, 89–90
    Obaldía and, 90, 95–96
    on *el pueblo,* 44, 89–90, 163–64
    1830 revolt and, 25
Estrade, Paul, 153

Fábrega, Francisco de, 101, 114, 175
    Azuero rebellion and, 112–17
    Tajada de Sandía and, 134, 135, 139, 143–45, 148
    tax policies of, 111–12, 168
    threat of U.S. occupation and, 164–68, 172, 173, 178, 182, 200
Feuillet, Tomás Martín, 79
fevers, 36, 61, 65–66
    See also health
Figueroa Navarro, Alfredo, 14, 84–85
filibusters, 11–12, 50, 77, 154
    Arosemena on, 159–60
    decline of, 155, 188–89
    in Mexico, 113, 114, 139
    in Nicaragua, 11, 113–14, 117, 124–26, 139, 156
    rumors of, 113–14, 132, 144–47, 166–67, 187
    slavery and, 114, 179, 186
    Tajada de Sandía and, 124–26, 132, 136, 139–40, 144–47
Flint, Edward, 76–77
Flores, Juan José, 113

Forster, John H., 40, 42, 48, 49, 92
France, 16, 39, 75–76, 189, 191
Freemasonry, 145–46
free trade, 85, 97–98, 158, 159
Fretz, August, 109–10

Gadsden Purchase, 154
gender, 186
    characterizations of Latin race and, 161
    concepts of honor and, 49–50, 135–37, 175–76
    women's suffrage and, 188
    women's work and, 36–37, 128
gente de color, 22–23, 25, 44, 52, 96, 112, 119
    See also race
globalization, 159
gold mining techniques, 81–82
González, Florentino, 132, 179
Goytía, José María, 171, 172, 174
Goytía, Pedro, 101–2, 112–13, 117, 165, 166, 171–74, 196
Gran Colombia, 19–22
    See also Nueva Granada
Grant, Ulysses S., 67
Great Britain, 39, 68, 75–76, 162, 177
Guadalupe-Hidalgo, Treaty of (1848), 158
Guatemala, 152, 154–55
guerra de castas. See caste war, rumors of

Habrahan, Miguel, 1, 129–32, 136, 141, 196
Haiti, 88, 90, 172–73
Hance, William B., 43, 93
Hanseatic League, 85–86, 97, 99
Hawaii, 12, 16, 32
health, 47, 61–62, 64–66
    Chinese workers and, 71
    folk medicine and, 36
Hendry, Peter, 76
Henriquez, Alexander, 138
Hernández, Manuel, 168
Herrán, Pedro A., 111, 154, 179
Herrera, Tomás, 87, 108
Hoadley, David, 70–72, 169
    Isthmus Guard and, 75–77
    U.S. involvement in Panama and, 158, 177
    on Walker, 188–89
Howland and Aspinwall Co., 55
Hughes, G. W., 57–58
Hurtado, José Marcelino, 177–78
Hurtado i Hermanos, 58, 68, 69

imperialism. *See* empire
Incidente de la Tajada de Sandía. *See* Tajada
de Sandía
Incident of the Slice of Watermelon. *See*
Tajada de Sandía
"Incident on the Chagres River" (painting),
44, 45
indentured workers, 59, 70–71
Indian workers, from Asia, 70
indigenous peoples, 18, 23, 61
Arosemena on, 163–64
conflicts with, 76, 186, 187
enfranchisement of, 119
race and, 22–23, 46
Irish workers, 10, 62, 63, 70
Isthmus Guard, 75–77, 82, 119, 142–43, 160,
187
See also vigilantism

Jamaica, 10, 35, 71, 144
boatmen from, 56, 57
Bolívar and, 19, 20
railroad workers from, 62, 64, 70, 110, 138
women entrepreneurs from, 36
Japan, trade with, 158, 160
Jim Crow laws, 150, 186
Jiménes, Pedro, 144
Johnson, Theodore, 42, 46, 48, 51
Joy and Co., 69

Kanagawa, Treaty of (1854), 158
Kemble, John Haskell, 6
King, I., 72
King, James, 156
Kinney, Henry, 113, 114
Kuna people, 23

LaFeber, Walter, 186
Lamennais, Félicité de, 162
Latin America, concept of, 12, 153, 160–64,
192–193, 204
Law, George, 31
LeGrand, Catherine, 82
lengua azul, 144
See also race
León, José María de, 106
Lewis, Martin, 153
Liberal Party
election of 1848 and, 86–87
election of 1856 and, 167–75
enclaves of, 87, 95–96, 112

Nicaraguan, 113–14
race and, 95–96, 116
Tajada de Sandía and, 143, 148
women's suffrage and, 118
Liddell, John A., 65–66
López, José Hilario, 86
Luna, José Manuel, 1–2, 107, 127–31, 141,
145–51, 171, 187, 195–99
Luna, Pío, 79

MacGregor, Gregor, 19
Mackenzie, Arthur, 103, 110, 135, 137–38
Madison, James, 100
Maitín, José Isabel, 145, 171
Manifest Destiny, 12, 125–26, 154, 160,
186
Manzanillo Island, 8, 61, 62, 64–65
map(s)
of California routes, 30
of Central America, 60
of Federal State of Panama, 24
of Nicaragua Route, 60
of Nueva Granada, 21
of Panama City, 26, 27, 104, 107
of Panama Route, 8, 60
Marks, Robert, 135, 140
maroons, 22
Marryat, Frank, 45, 46
Martí, José, 193, 195
Mason, Richard, 31–32
"Massacre at Panama" (image), 157
McAllister's store, 107, 133, 137
McAndrews, J.W., 150
McMurphy, James, 39–40
Megquier, Mary Jane, 36–37, 49
Mendoza, Carlos, 191–92
Mendoza, Juan, 95
Mervine, William, 168, 170–72, 176, 181
mestizos, 22
See also race
Mexico, 35, 152
California and, 16, 32, 113, 114, 119, 187
filibusters in, 113, 114, 139
transit across, 7, 29, 32, 92, 157
U.S. war with, 11, 29, 31, 37, 39, 154, 185
minstrelsy, blackface, 38–39, 51, 150
Morgan, Charles, 125
Morgan, Henry, 18, 25
Morrison & Co., 71
Mosquera, Tomás Cipriano de, 59, 68, 91
conflict of May 18, 1850, and, 117, 148

map of Nueva Grenada by, 21
state governor's election and, 167
Mosquitia, 29, 30
mulatos, 22, 93, 144, 164
   See also race
mule transportation, 18, 33–34, 36, 69
   negotiations with, 47–50
   railroad competition with, 55, 58–59, 68,
      69, 79–81, 138–39
   sketch of, 45
   taxation of, 97–98
Murrieta, Joaquín, 124

Nahl, Charles Christian, 44, 45, 83
Neira, Gabriel, 76
Nelson, William, 141, 143, 169, 177, 180, 189,
   192
New Granada. *See* Nueva Granada
Nicaragua, 152, 158
   filibusters in, 11, 113–14, 117, 124–26, 139,
      156, 189
   slavery in, 114, 181
   transit across, 7, 60, 68–69, 75, 78, 92, 125,
      156
Noriega, Manuel, 201
Nueva Granada, 97–98, 118–19, 152
   Bidlack-Mallarino Treaty with, 29–30, 98,
      155, 177, 190
   civil war of, 101–2
   Constitution of, 71–73, 86, 95, 99
   Democratic Societies of, 165
   immigrants to Panama from other regions
      of, 35
   justice system of, 94–95
   map of, 21
   railroad subsidy to, 81
   slavery in, 59, 84, 86–88
   Spanish independence and, 19–20
   Tajada de Sandía and, 132–33
   See also Colombia

Obaldía, José de, 89–91
   conflict of May 18, 1850, and, 117
   Espinar and, 90, 95–96
   housing ordinance of, 106
Obarrio i Pérez, Pedro, 136, 146
Olier, Eduardo, 141
Oliver, Jack, 107, 129–30, 132, 184, 197–99
Operation Just Cause (1989), 2, 202
Oregon, 29
Ospina Rodríguez, Mariano, 179

O'Sullivan, John L., 160
Otis, Fessenden Nott, 67, 70, 71
Owen, John, 141
Owens, Kenneth N., 13

Pacific Mail Steamship Co., 6–7, 33–35,
   56–59, 68–69
   Isthmus Guard and, 76–77
   railroad and, 78, 103
   U.S. contract with, 31
Palenque, 24
Panama, 5–6, 33–34, 97, 118–19, 184
   Congress of, 161
   Federal State of, 14, 24, 25, 84–86, 99–102,
      111–12, 118, 163
   independence of, 11, 19–22, 84–86, 89–90,
      99–102, 189–91, 195
   population of, 22–25
   slavery in, 23–25, 59, 181
   Spanish empire and, 16–20, 41, 81, 162–63
   U.S. empire and, 11–13, 38–40, 75, 182–93
   U.S. interventions in, 2, 164–68, 170–81,
      189–90, 201–2
   zona de tránsito across, 8, 9, 60, 75, 82, 99
Panama Canal, 75–76, 189–91, 195
Panama City, 25–29, 37, 58, 64, 74, 99, 102,
   158, 194
   maps of, 26, 27, 104, 107
   railroad terminal in, 69, 102–4, 107,
      109–10, 120–21
   See also Arrabal
"Panama Fever," 47, 65–66
Panama Railroad Co., 10, 54–83, 142, 187–91
   first passengers of, 66–68, 77–78
   formation of, 31, 54
   mule transportation and, 55, 68, 69, 138–39
   opposition to, 63, 137–39, 141–42, 156–58
   river transportation and, 10, 55–57, 68,
      79–81, 138–39
   taxation of, 98
   terminal of, 69, 102–4, 107, 109–10,
      120–21
   ticket prices of, 77–78, 123
   wages of, 58, 62, 73, 98
   workers for, 54–64, 69–73, 75, 110
Paraguay, 154
Paterson, William, 18
Peirce, Peter, 63
Perry, Matthew, 158, 160
Perry, William, 129
Peru, 32, 34, 35, 154, 155

Phelan, John L., 153
Pierce, Franklin, 157–58, 158, 160
pirates, 18, 25
    See also filibusters
Planas, Antonio, 106
Playa de San José, 106
Playa Prieta, 83, 102–5
    maps of, 104, 107
    railroad terminal at, 69, 102–3, 107,
        109–10, 120–21
Polk, James, 32
Pombo, Lino de, 130, 132
Pony Express, 6
Portobelo, 18, 19, 24, 58
Prados, Lucas, 135
Prescott, William H., 38–39
Prince, Joe, 93
prisoners, 59, 94, 112
Progressivism, 186
prostitution, 36
pueblo, el, 96, 108, 176
    Azuero rebellion and, 112–13
    Espinar on, 25–29, 44, 89–90, 163–64
    Tajada de Sandía and, 136, 139–40, 160
    Torres Caicedo on, 161–62

Quijada, Mónica, 153

race, 42–46, 87–88, 175–80
    Arosemena's views of, 116, 160–64,
        181–83, 193
    castas and, 11–12, 22, 44, 88–90
    census and, 22
    concepts of honor and, 49–52, 135–37
    gente de color and, 22–23, 25, 44, 52, 96,
        112, 119
    indigenous people and, 22–23, 46
    Jim Crow laws and, 150
    Latin, 160–64, 193
    mulatos and, 22, 93, 144, 164
    political power and, 92–96, 102, 116
    slavery and, 22–23, 62, 102
    suffrage and, 119–20
    U.S. empire and, 191–192
railroad, second transcontinental (across
        United States), 6, 195
    See also Panama Railroad Co.
Ramos, Pedro, 144
Ramos Baquero, Ángeles, 145
Rangers, 124
religious practices, 40, 86

revolutions of 1848, 86–87
river boatmen. *See* boatmen
Roberts, Brian, 40–41
Rodó, José Enrique, 193
Rodríguez, José María, 136–37
Rojas Mix, Miguel, 153
Royal Mail Steamship Co., 58–59
Runnels, Ran, 69, 148
    Isthmus Guard and, 75, 76, 141–43, 160, 187
    racial views of, 192

Sabla, Theodore de, 134, 141, 171, 174, 176
San Felipe, Parish of, 25, 26, 37, 87, 106
    conflict of May 18, 1850, and, 90–92,
        114–17
    ruins of, 41–42
San Juan del Norte, 158
San Juan del Sur, 125
San Lorenzo, fortress of, 41, 57
Santa Ana, Parish of. *See* Arrabal
Scott, Dred, 150
Seacole, Mary, 36, 50–52, 92–94
Shakespeare, William, 98
Shannon, Dennis, 129
slavery, 18, 131, 181, 185
    abolition of, 11, 59, 84, 87–88, 198
    in California, 119
    filibusters and, 114, 179, 186
    in Nicaragua, 114, 181
    in Panama, 23–25, 59, 181
    Panamanian opposition to, 45–46, 51–52
    race and, 22–23, 62, 102
    in United States, 75, 119, 150, 152,
        179–81
Smith, Persifor, 34–35, 52, 187
sovereignty, 9–11, 71–73, 82, 190
    future of, 193–95
    justice system and, 94–95
    taxation and, 98
    U.S. Canal Zone and, 191
    "Westphalian," 100
    See also Bidlack-Mallarino Treaty
Spain
    empire of, 16–20, 41, 81, 162–63
    U.S. war of 1898 against, 185
    wars of independence from, 19–20
Stephens, John L., 31, 55, 68, 73–74
Stokes, Joseph, 135, 140, 147
Story, Minor, 69–70
suffrage, 11, 71–72, 84–89, 119–20
    Arosemena on, 45–46

Conservative views of, 89
of indigenous people, 119
Liberal views of, 181, 185
women's, 118, 187
syphilis, 66

Taboga Island, 36, 149
Tajada de Sandía, Incidente de la, 1–2, 11–14,
103, 127–51, 195–99
casualties of, 134–35
image of, 157
investigation by Nueva Granada of,
132–33
Panamanian nationalism and, 195–99
reparations from, 190
U.S. accounts of, 131–35, 147, 155–59
U.S. intervention after, 164–68
taxation, 97–98, 104–5, 111, 131, 168, 194
Taylor, Bayard, 47, 51
Tehuantepec, Isthmus of, 29, 92, 157
telegraph, across the United States, 6
Texas, 75
Tocqueville, Alexis de, 99, 101
Tomes, Robert, 43, 44, 79–80, 102, 149–50
Torres Caicedo, José María, 153, 161–63, 193
Totten, George, 31, 58–77, 157
transit zone. *See* zona de tránsito
treaty ports, 158
Trujillo, Juan Bautista, 76
Tyson, James, 47

United Fruit Co., 82, 188, 189
United States
empire of, 11–13, 37–40, 75, 152–55, 182–93
Japanese trade and, 158, 160
Jim Crow laws of, 150, 186
Manifest Destiny doctrine of, 12, 125–26,
154, 160, 186
Mexican War of, 11, 29, 31, 37, 39, 154, 185
slavery in, 75, 119, 150, 152, 179–81
war against Spain (1898) of, 185
United States Mail Steamship Co., 6–7, 33,
68, 78
government contract with, 31
Isthmus Guard and, 77
United States Topographical Corps, 57–58
Unruh, John, 6
Urriola, Dolores, 143–44
Urrutia Añino, José María, 76

Vanderbilt, Cornelius, 68–69, 124–25
Venezuela, 19, 20, 154, 155
Veraguas province, 70, 99, 115
Conservative Party in, 87, 112, 165
gold mining in, 36
map of, 24
Vernon, Edward, 18
vigilantism
in California, 77, 119, 124, 154, 156
in Colón, 74–77
See also Isthmus Guard

wages, 56, 58, 62, 73, 98
Walker, William, 154–56, 167, 188–89
Arosemena on, 159–60
Hoadley on, 188–89
in Mexico, 113
in Nicaragua, 11, 113–14, 117, 124–26, 156,
189
Torres Caicedo on, 162
Walter, Carrie Stevens, 137
Ward, Thomas, 114, 141
Washington, George, 195
Watermelon Slice Incident. *See* Tajada de
Sandía
Wells Fargo Co.; 7, 142
"Westphalian sovereignty," 100
Wigen, Kären, 153
Williams, James, 93–94
Williams, T. B., 136, 138, 141–42
Winslow, Charles, 41, 56
workers, 54–64, 69–73
Chinese, 70–71
convict, 59
desertion by, 61–62, 64, 75
health of, 61–62, 64–66, 71
indentured, 59, 70–71
Irish, 63, 70
Jamaican, 56, 57, 62, 64, 70
"native," 59–61
politics of, 62–64, 71–73, 110
slavery and, 59
wages of, 56, 58, 62, 73, 98
women, 36–37

Zachrisson, Carlos, 76
zambo, 127, 168
See also race
zona de tránsito, 8, 9, 60, 75, 82, 99